Cambridge Imperial and Post-Colonial Studies Series

General Editors: **Meghan Vaughan**, King's College, Cambridge, UK, and **Richard Drayton**, Corpus Christi College, Cambridge, UK

This informative series covers the broad span of modern imperial history while also exploring the recent developments in former colonial states where residues of empire can still be found. The books provide in-depth examinations of empires as competing and complementary power structures, encouraging the reader to reconsider their understanding of international and world history during recent centuries.

Titles include:

Sunil S.Amrith
DECOLONIZING INTERNATIONAL HEALTH
India and Southeast Asia, 1930–65

Tony Ballantyne
ORIENTALISM AND RACE
Aryanism in the British Empire

Peter F. Bang and C. A. Bayly (*editors*)
TRIBUTARY EMPIRES IN GLOBAL HISTORY

James Beattie
EMPIRE AND ENVIRONMENTAL ANXIETY
Health, Science, Arts and Conservation in South Asia and Australasia, 1800–1920

Robert J. Blyth
THE EMPIRE OF THE RAJ
India, Eastern Africa and the Middle East, 1858–1947

Roy Bridges (*editor*)
IMPERIALISM, DECOLONIZATION AND AFRICA
Studies Presented to John Hargreaves

L. J. Butler
COPPER EMPIRE
Mining and the Colonial State in Northern Rhodesia, c.1930–64

Hilary M. Carey (*editor*)
EMPIRES OF RELIGION

Nandini Chatterjee
THE MAKING OF INDIAN SECULARISM
Empire, Law and Christianity, 1830–1960

Esme Cleall
MISSIONARY DISCOURSES OF DIFFERENCE
Negotiating Otherness in the British Empire, 1840–1900

T. J. Cribb (*editor*)
IMAGINED COMMONWEALTH
Cambridge Essays on Commonwealth and International Literature in English

Michael S. Dodson
ORIENTALISM, EMPIRE AND NATIONAL CULTURE
India, 1770–1880

Jost Dülffer and Marc Frey (*editors*)
ELITES AND DECOLONIZATION IN THE TWENTIETH CENTURY

Ulrike Hillemann
ASIAN EMPIRE AND BRITISH KNOWLEDGE
China and the Networks of British Imperial Expansion

B.D. Hopkins
THE MAKING OF MODERN AFGHANISTAN

Ronald Hyam
BRITAIN'S IMPERIAL CENTURY, 1815–1914
A Study of Empire and Expansion

Iftekhar Iqbal
THE BENGAL DELTA
Ecology, State and Social Change, 1840–1943

Brian Ireland
THE US MILITARY IN HAWAI'I
Colonialism, Memory and Resistance

Robin Jeffrey
POLITICS, WOMEN AND WELL-BEING
How Kerala Became 'a Model'

Gerold Krozewski
MONEY AND THE END OF EMPIRE
British International Economic Policy and the Colonies, 1947–58

Sloan Mahone and Megan Vaughan (*editors*)
PSYCHIATRY AND EMPIRE

Javed Majeed
AUTOBIOGRAPHY, TRAVEL AND POSTNATIONAL IDENTITY
Gandhi, Nehru and Iqbal

Francine McKenzie
REDEFINING THE BONDS OF COMMONWEALTH, 1939–1948
The Politics of Preference

Gabriel Paquette
ENLIGHTENMENT, GOVERNANCE, AND REFORM IN SPAIN AND ITS EMPIRE, 1759–1808

Sandhya L. Polu
INFECTIOUS DISEASE IN INDIA 1892–1940
Policy-making and the Perception of Risk

Ricardo Roque
HEADHUNTING AND COLONIALISM
Anthropology and the Circulation of Human Skulls in the Portuguese Empire, 1870–1930

Michael Silvestri
IRELAND AND INDIA
Nationalism, Empire and Memory

Aparna Vaidik
IMPERIAL ANDAMANS
Colonial Encounter and Island History

Kim A. Wagner (*editor*)
THUGGEE
Banditry and the British in Early Nineteenth-Century India

Jon E. Wilson
THE DOMINATION OF STRANGERS
Modern Governance in Eastern India, 1780–1835

Cambridge Imperial and Post-Colonial Studies Series
Series Standing Order ISBN 978–0–333–91908–8 (Hardback) 978–0–333–91909–5 (Paperback)
(*outside North America only*)

You can receive future titles in this series as they are published by placing a standing order. Please contact your bookseller or, in case of difficulty, write to us at the address below with your name and address, the title of the series and the ISBN quoted above.

Customer Services Department, Macmillan Distribution Ltd, Houndmills, Basingstoke, Hampshire RG21 6XS, England

Missionary Discourses of Difference

Negotiating Otherness in the British Empire, 1840–1900

Esme Cleall
Lecturer in the History of the British Empire, University of Sheffield, UK

palgrave
macmillan

First published 2012 by
PALGRAVE MACMILLAN

Palgrave Macmillan in the UK is an imprint of Macmillan Publishers Limited, registered in England, company number 785998, of Houndmills, Basingstoke, Hampshire RG21 6XS.

Palgrave Macmillan in the US is a division of St Martin's Press LLC, 175 Fifth Avenue, New York, NY 10010.

Palgrave Macmillan is the global academic imprint of the above companies and has companies and representatives throughout the world.

Palgrave® and Macmillan® are registered trademarks in the United States, the United Kingdom, Europe and other countries.

ISBN 978–0–230–29680–0

This book is printed on paper suitable for recycling and made from fully managed and sustained forest sources. Logging, pulping and manufacturing processes are expected to conform to the environmental regulations of the country of origin.

A catalogue record for this book is available from the British Library.

A catalog record for this book is available from the Library of Congress.

10 9 8 7 6 5 4 3 2 1
21 20 19 18 17 16 15 14 13 12

Printed and bound in Great Britain by
CPI Antony Rowe, Chippenham and Eastbourne

To Erin and Catherine

Contents

Illustrations

Acknowledgements

I would like to thank the Arts and Humanities Research Council for funding the thesis from which this book began; Catherine Hall for being a wonderful supervisor; Alan Lester and Megan Vaughan for their support and for their incisive comments; and Keith McClelland for his elucidating sessions on theory and advice. My thinking about race, gender and religion developed during a year spent working in the Anthropology Department at UCL (University College London): my thanks to UCL Graduate School for a Cross-Disciplinary Training Scholarship for funding this growth and to Allen Abramson and Charles Stewart for guiding me through their discipline. Zoë Laidlaw first made me interested in the history of the British Empire, and her supervision, both during my undergraduate and postgraduate days, was invaluable.

I have drawn many ideas and much support from the academic communities of which I have been lucky enough to have been a part over the last few years. The Postcolonial and Colonial Workshop that Rachel Bright, Emily Manktelow and I founded at the IHR (Institute of Historical Research) has been a useful intellectual forum: my thanks to all participants. The History of Feminism Collective provided inspiration and friendship: my thanks to Marc Calvini Lefebrve, Angela Grainger, Daniel Grey, Naomi Hetherington and Laura Schwartz. At UCL, I found a supportive postgraduate community – my thanks to everyone there, particularly to members of our reading groups.

I am grateful for the advice of many colleagues, friends and teachers; especial thanks to: Simone Borgstede, Rachel Bright, Andrew Cohen, Erin Cullen, Anna Davin, Daniel Grey, Anna Gust, Liz Harvey, Laura Ishiguro, Zoë Laidlaw, Marc Calvini Lefebrve, Emily Manktelow, Jonathon Saha and John Stevens for their careful reading and advice. Thanks also to Keith McClelland and David Cleall for their help with the referencing.

I am very aware that this book is not a product of intellectual labour alone but also of all the social reproduction that has gone into allowing me to write it and the 'emotional work' of sustaining me through a difficult time. I cannot thank everyone enough for their generosity and hospitality in feeding me, listening to me and caring for me. I have been touched by the kindness of many, of whom I can name only a few here. Simone's thoughtfulness and wisdom have been much needed and much appreciated. Rachel has kept encouraging me. Rene has kept me cheerful. Members of the Feminist Fightback collective have kept me engaged politically. I am grateful to my parents for many things, not least for letting me live and work in their home when writing. The book is dedicated to Catherine and to Erin. Catherine has been a source of inspiration, life and hope for me – I am so thankful for everything but most especially for helping me to understand. Erin has not only read numerous drafts of my work (from 'A' level coursework onwards!) but has kept me going mentally and physically at every stage. She is the best friend I can possibly imagine; no words can express the love I feel for her.

London, 2011

Note on Terminology

The categories of analysis I explore (race, gender, disability) are socially constructed. Enclosing such terms in inverted commas identifies them as problematic, unhinged from an essential meaning; however, I have chosen not to do so as their use would be so widespread as to reduce their meaning and become obstructive or distracting. I expect that the reader will not need them to be aware of the difficulties such terms pose.

Many of the terms which missionaries used to refer to the ethnic groups they encountered are now offensive (and in some cases were then). Where possible, I have replaced offensive racial terminology in my writing, thus using Xhosa rather than 'Caffre' or 'Kafir', and replacing 'Matabele' with 'Ndebele'. But many terms were too integral to missionary thinking in their offensive formulation to be sanitised in this way. What missionaries meant when they spoke of a 'heathen' world would be lost if I referred to 'non-Christian peoples'. Similarly, to replace 'Boer' with 'Afrikaner' would be to use an anachronistic term that overlooks the complex historiographical development of national identity in southern Africa. In these cases, I have retained the original vocabulary, and again, hope they will be read in this light.

India and southern Africa have different political and historiographical traditions in regard to the complex field of the politics of naming. In regard to places, I use the names used by missionaries themselves to avoid confusion with my primary sources and to denote their use as signifiers of power. Similarly, for the most part, I use the nineteenth-century missionary orthography.

Introduction: Difference and Discourse in the British Empire

When Richard Lovett came to write a history of the London Missionary Society (LMS) on its centenary in the 1890s, he prefaced his two-volume work with three quotations. The first was taken from the Book of Mark (Mark, iv, 30–32): 'How shall we liken the Kingdom of God?' 'Like a mustard seed', came the scriptural reply, from which, despite its small appearance, great branches could flourish.[1] It was the LMS itself, of course, that Lovett saw as the proverbial seed so potent that its branches stretched out from its roots in London across many continents. Over the course of the nineteenth century, these branches had matured into channels of communication through which people, information and images passed. Some had broken, or died, in stunted missionary activity, others had blossomed into burgeoning Christian communities, each, so the missionary imaginary would have it, growing organically from the metropolitan trunk. Established during the late eighteenth-century religious revival, the LMS was nourished with evangelical religiosity, each new shoot reaching upwards towards the 'Kingdom of God'.[2] Realising this Kingdom was not limited to theological conversion, but meant a widespread programme of cultural change. Dress, education, sexuality, the organisation of time and the demarcation of space were all sources of missionary concern. The second and third quotations Lovett chose were thus concerned with God's *earthly* kingdom and taken from speeches made at the LMS's inauguration:

> We are commanded 'to love our neighbour as ourselves'; and Christ has taught us that *every* man is our neighbour. But do we display this love while we allow gross darkness to cover the Pagan and Mahometan nations, and are at no pains to send them the glad tidings of salvation through the sufferings and death of the Son of God?[3]

> Let it be remembered that Britain, Christian Britain, was once an island of idolatrous barbarians; and such it had yet remained, unless some of God's dear people in distant countries had formed the benevolent plan of sending missionaries hither. Let us in return 'go and do likewise.'[4]

Elements of this world view, articulated in the 1790s, were still powerful orientating frameworks a century later. The differences between peoples were so great, it was suggested, that a British Christian might easily forget that '*every* man' was owed the Gospel, even those who were 'heathen' or 'Mahometan'. Britain had an imperative to enlighten them, not least through the debt it had incurred through its own (stadially advanced) proselytisation years before. Difference (and difference that also marked hierarchy) was taken for granted in missionary discourse, and it was difference that anchored Britain's place in the world and enabled it to bestow light on these 'dark' places. In private letters and journals, missionaries agonised over the peoples and cultures they encountered and recorded their horror and disorientation (as well as their excitement) at customs they could never have imagined 'back home'. Through their copious published writings, missionaries conveyed such horrors, hopes and anxieties to the imperial metropole producing a much-consumed strand of colonial discourse that allowed the British public to imagine Indians, Africans and other peoples of empire and the 'distant countries' they inhabited. These constructions were not, of course, all about otherness, but also about imagining the self, as the authors (and readers) of such literature sought to make sense of their own identities in colonial contexts. It is all these constructions I seek to examine.

In *Missionary Discourses of Difference*, I use the writings of missionaries working for the London Missionary Society (LMS) as a prism through which I can think about colonial discourse. I examine the construction of difference across colonial sites and analyse the images of empire projected back to Britain. My research draws on missionary writings from two large and very different areas of LMS enterprise, India and southern Africa, and focuses on three important themes in missionary writing: the family, sickness and violence.

This introduction is structured around my research questions and the frameworks through which I will discuss them throughout the book. Firstly I introduce the concept of 'discourses of difference', asking how difference was constituted in colonial thinking. I think about the kinds of difference that can be identified in missionary writing and consider the roles that 'race' and 'gender' played as markers of difference. Secondly, I explore the relationship between categories that might be described as 'colonisers' and 'colonised' to consider the utility of categories of 'self' and 'other' in missionary discourse. I think about the ways in which the relationship between 'colonisers' and 'colonised' was negotiated and probe the ambivalences that complicated and disturbed this categorisation. Thirdly, I consider the historical context of my subjects: what colonising projects shaped the construction of difference in the nineteenth century? I outline some of the ways in which missionaries operated in southern Africa and India, and in particular the extent to which discourses of difference were coherent and consistent, and the extent to which they were shaped by the specificities of particular colonial sites. Lastly, I look at issues of presentation and dissemination of images of difference in missionary writing: in what forms of writing were ideas about difference articulated? Here, I focus on the channels of communication through which the missionary message was spread.

Discourses of difference

Missionary thinking was orientated around the concept of difference – the practice of marking 'like' from 'unlike', a way of positioning things, people and concepts relationally. The missionary premise – the belief that 'Christian' and 'heathen' were absolute and adverse conditions, the denial of ambiguous ground between them and the unquestioning assumption that the former was desirable and the later abominable – is rooted in the logic of difference, whatever proclamations missionaries may also have made (often sincerely) about human universalism. Interrogating how difference operates discursively means drawing from and building on the critical colonial history and postcolonial theory of empire, to think about how difference is structured and how its constitution is specific to time and place.

Colonial cultures depended on a series of discursive oppositions constructed between 'the coloniser' (identified as 'self'), who was 'white', 'Christian' and 'civilised', and 'the colonised' (identified as 'other'), who was 'black', 'heathen' and 'savage'.[5] Frantz Fanon's work powerfully evoked the force with which colonialism was structured through the marking of difference and the inferiority it signified.[6] He argued that the violent encounter between coloniser and colonised constituted these categories of people as so unlike each other that they appeared to become 'two different species'.[7] Difference was inscribed at the heart of the colonial relationship and on the psyches it forged. Poststructuralist thinkers have elucidated the shifting and unstable nature of such oppositions. Jacques Derrida discussed a 'play of difference' (which he called *différance*), where meaning is always deferred, and the signifiers of difference are contingently placed within a fluid, relational system.[8] Relationships between concepts operate both oppositionally and through an ever-fragmenting fracturing of differentiation. Colonial discourses, as Homi Bhabha, amongst others, has explored, are ambivalent, slippery and unstable.[9]

Fluency of meaning should not be understood to reflect relations that are equal or unfettered. As Stuart Hall argues, relations of difference are usually inflected by power dynamics which privilege certain positions and attempt to 'fix' this privileged positioning.[10] In colonial discourse, difference from the position of the coloniser meant inferiority. Indigenous peoples of empire were constructed through their alleged otherness to (or perversion of) the 'western' self. Race, culture and language (amongst other markers) were used to codify deviation from a European 'norm'.[11] It was through difference that colonialism, a rule based on inequality, was justified, and imperialism, political and cultural, rationalised.

Partha Chatterjee has described how the 'rule of colonial difference', that is, how 'representing the "other" as inferior and radically different, and hence incorrigibly inferior', was part of the 'strategy for the deployment of the modern forms of disciplinary power'.[12] The colonial insistence on difference at the same time as on 'progress' demonstrates the insidious power of difference endlessly to remake itself. Indians, in Chatterjee's analysis, and by extension other peoples of empire, would never 'catch up'; the 'normalizing mission' was 'destined' never to be fulfilled because 'the premise of power was preserving the alienness of the ruling group'.[13] Missionary thinking was structured similarly. Indigenous converts were always marked as of 'weaker' faith than the 'civilised' peoples missionaries represented. As Chatterjee found, the lines around which otherness was constructed could shift with cunning mobility: 'difference can be marked by many signs, and varying with the context, one could displace another as the most practicable application of the rule.'[14] Chatterjee, like Fanon, claimed the most obvious signifier of colonial difference was race.

Many historians of missionaries have found their attitudes towards race frustratingly difficult to disentangle because the word 'race' often acts apparently interchangeably with those of 'nation, 'blood' or 'tribe'.[15] Yet, given that race is a socially constructed category, it is unsurprising that missionary articulations on the subject were unstable.

Indeed, these very slippages, suggestive as they are of the conceptual instability of race, are important subjects of investigation in their own right. The moments at which they occur reveal ruptures in the dominant discourses. The relationships between 'nation', 'race' and 'tribe' point to the overlapping and interlocking nature of these categories of difference.

What race denotes varies over time, place, context and discursive community.[16] Part of the power of race lies in its ability to be naturalised by numerous visible signifiers. Complexion, IQ, religion, language, behaviour and dress have, amongst other signs, been used to mark racial difference.[17] Such markers are sometimes thought of as divisible into 'biological' signifiers, based around 'physical' difference, and 'cultural' signifiers, linked to 'ethnicity'. I have followed Stuart Hall in treating 'culture' and 'biology', not as separate discourses but as two 'logics' or 'registers' of race that are 'always present', though 'in different combinations and grounded in different contexts and in relation to different subject populations'.[18] My analysis of the simultaneous production of difference amongst the diverse subject populations of the British Empire demonstrates that patterns of racialisation vary greatly, even within the missionary strand of British colonial discourse that I take as my example.

Over the course of the nineteenth century, a shift has been identified from the predominance of 'cultural' registers of 'race' to 'biological' ones. In the early nineteenth century, as in the eighteenth, cultural markers, such as clothing, had been powerful indicators of otherness.[19] Enlightenment thinking had posited a 'stadial theory' of race, whereby 'uncivilised' peoples would follow Europeans 'upwards' along a single route of 'progress'. Whilst these thinkers did not necessarily advocate proselytisation, their reasoning was broadly sympathetic to missionary work because they shared the premise that all had the potential to be 'civilised' and 'improved'. Gradually, however, skin colour, nose shape and hair type, for example, became more important to the codification of difference. Phrenologists hoped to prove that Europeans had bigger brains than other races (and that bigger brains meant greater intelligence). Commitment to monogenism (the belief that humans descended from common ancestors) waned, and polygenism (the belief that there were many creations, and therefore no one 'family of man') gained popularity as biblical criticism increased. Many interpreted the Cape Frontier Wars, the Indian Rebellion and the Morant Bay Uprising as the rejection of British civilising efforts by 'ungrateful' indigenous populations and despaired that the 'conversion of the heathen' was possible. These shifts have been widely read as a 'hardening' of racial attitudes because they occurred alongside, and as part of, an intensified intolerance of difference and quickening territorial colonialism.[20] They changed the cultural climate in which missionaries operated and contributed to the waning popularity of their work in later nineteenth-century Britain.

Historiographical questions have been raised about the extent to which missionary thinking about 'race' became alienated from the mainstream. Some missionaries were openly hostile to theorising that posited 'race' as 'species', and professionally antagonistic to anthropological thought, which was where they located and sought to contain these ideas.[21] When missionaries spoke about race directly, they tended to pay homage to the universality of mankind rather than to the lines of difference which undermined it, but these lines were always present. In 1840, the famous missionary to southern Africa, Robert Moffat, claimed he saw the recently 'enfranchised subjects in the West Indies' as 'part of [his] family' for 'wherever I look upon anyone connected with Africa, no matter how black his face, I regards [sic] him or her as my own son or daughter'.[22] Despite his evocation of the family of man, Moffat had noticed skin colour and, in denying its impact, invested it with meaning, not least in the subordinated position on the familial hierarchy in which he placed black people.

Racial thinking strayed beyond explicit theorising to permeate everyday conversations and observations. Racial structures within the missionary movement took the form of unspoken rules, unarticulated by missionaries themselves, but determining nonetheless who could marry whom, who was given what job, and the professional and social status accorded to each individual. In fact, it was particularly when they were freed from the self-consciousness of participation in a controversial debate explicitly about race that missionaries evoked a world structured through difference.

In the discussion above, I have been using 'race' to discuss constructions of 'otherness', and in the nineteenth century it was often evoked as such. But race is also a way of imagining the self. Blackness and brownness were given meaning through their implicit framing against (naturalised) whiteness. Catherine Hall has powerfully demonstrated that coloniser and colonised were 'mutually constituted' and that the identities of colonisers were at stake in processes of colonisation as well as those of the colonised.[23] She explored how Englishness was an identity formed in part through its positioning against understandings of enslaved men and women of African origin in the Caribbean. This study builds on her work by interrogating the interplay between self and other in missionary thinking and on other sites of empire.

Whilst race was central to the rule of difference, it always operated in negotiation with other relational markers, not least gender.[24] Of course gender has its own histories of construction and reconstruction as a 'tool of historical analysis' and is crucial to social, cultural and political power dynamics, identity formation and experience.[25] What it meant to be a coloniser or to be colonised was shaped by one's gender, and what it meant to be a woman, or a man, was shaped by one's colonial positioning. The lives of missionary men and missionary women were shaped differently by gender difference.[26] At the same time, gender was central to their colonial critique of indigenous societies.[27] That gender relations in India and southern Africa were not only 'disordered' but oppressive, cruel and misogynistic was a staple of 'Enlightened' colonial discourse. The idea that white men saved brown women from brown men, as Gayatri Spivak memorably put it, was so effective because it drew on these two forms of difference simultaneously.[28]

As Anna Johnston has explored, missionary discourse often traded in stock images of race and gender which were influential back in Britain as well as reflective of missionary thinking in the colonies.[29] Missionary propaganda presented missionary women as ideal wives and mothers, and 'heathen' women as deficient; English men as 'heroic', and indigenous men as 'unmanly'. This study builds on Johnston's work by exploring the ruptures that troubled these discourses and the tensions generated between these ideal types and the ambivalence of other kinds of experience.

Race (and gender) also intersected with further discourses. The languages of class and race inter-cut and one discourse of difference was often displaced onto the other.[30] As Susan Thorne has demonstrated, the 'heathen at home', othered through his or her class, could prove just as 'foreign' a missionary subject as the 'heathen overseas' and could be found in quarters that, like colonial spaces, appeared 'dark' and 'dangerous' to middle-class evangelical observers. The phrase 'the heathen at home' was used to underscore the depth of working-class degradation.[31]

Wellness, sickness and disability are also relational discourses. Whilst what it means to be 'disabled' is read off a variety of visible and medical markers, 'disability' has no inherent meaning. Like race and gender, disability is often naturalised as a state of being that deviates from an imagined norm. Both postcolonial and disability theorists have drawn attention to the intersections between race, colonialism and disability.[32] Postcolonial legacies of warfare and poverty in the Majority World have created disability. Some ethnic groups and some people with disabilities occupy similarly stigmatised positions socially and disadvantaged positions economically. There are also rhetorical slippages between the languages of the sociopolitical 'disablement' of the colonised and the 'colonising' subjugation of disabled people. Despite these links, historical exploration of the contribution made by discourses of disability to colonial constructions of difference has, as yet, been minimal.[33] This must change. Part 2, which interrogates the connections between a 'sick' body and a 'sick' soul in the missionary imaginary, is intended as a step in this direction.

The intersectionality of discourses of race, religion, gender, class and disability, their constant cross-cutting, interconnections and shared meanings is historical as well as conceptual.[34] Over the eighteenth and nineteenth centuries the *scientific* codification of the body, for example, was increasingly used to 'prove' difference. Pseudo-scientific medical diagrams developed as a powerful means of articulating and visualising sex, disability, race and class. Analogy and metaphorical slippage meant race, gender and class differences were spoken and imagined through each other.[35] They were relational constructs in a fluid web of meaning that always had to be rewoven.

Difference is made in multiple ways simultaneously. Difference can be negotiated through the institutional structures of the state, internalised in the psyches of individuals and of communities, performed in social relations, embodied in experiences, relived through memory, articulated through language and 'seen' on the body. The insidiousness of difference is that it is not only imagined and fluid but that it is also lived, and often appears resiliently fixed. However constructed, the experience of being made different, seen as different and seeing oneself as different from an imagined norm is very real. The work of the critical colonial historian is to try and unravel these threads, to disentangle some of the complex processes by which difference was created, maintained and naturalised.

Missionary Discourses of Difference is concerned with investigating the processes through which difference was made, remade, ruptured and re-encrusted in missionary writing. I explore missionary thinking as a Foucauldian discourse where individual statements about encounters with Indian 'Hindus' and African 'pagans', for example, worked together as an internally coherent 'regime of truth' where 'heathens' were cruel, 'savage' and 'other'. Following Bhabha, I take colonial discourses to be forked, ambivalent and endlessly subject to renegotiation. I think about what the ruptures, contradictions and ambiguities that characterise missionary discourse meant for the making of difference. I explore such constructions through the interplay between the (unstable and ever-fragmenting) categories of colonisers and colonised.

Colonisers and colonised

When Fanon evoked the 'colonial world', he described it as 'divided into compartments ... cut in two ... inhabited by two different species'; the 'colonial world', he wrote, 'is a Manichean world'.[36] Writing in the adversarial context of a war of decolonisation, Fanon's world was binary and his divisions stark. In the postcolonial absorption, critique and development of his thinking by a generation of poststructuralist scholars, his ideas have been nuanced. Modifications have taken two angles (though they have often been formulated by the same scholars): the first replaces '*the* colonial relationship' with a multiplicity of colonial relationships; the second reconsiders their 'Manichean' positioning.

Fanon was explicating '*the* colonial relationship', a model he extended beyond French rule in Algeria to the wider European colonisation of the 'Third World'. But colonial relationships took many forms. The British, French and Belgian empires were distinct. Colonial relationships also operated differently across imperial sites within the same empire. Difference was registered in ways particular to metropole or colony, to settler societies or dependencies, to colonies in Europe or those in 'the tropics'. Johnston has demonstrated that colonial evangelism was 'a broad-based, globalised project, but carried out in diverse ways in different colonies'.[37] I argue that her conclusion can also be reversed: diverse (local) experiences were also being filtered back into the (globalised) project itself.

Furthermore, if 'the colonial relationship' is made plural, and we acknowledge multiple colonisers and colonised, forging relationships in many contexts, we not only get a greater historicisation of these relationships but a different *theoretical* reading of the 'rule of difference'.[38] As Catherine Hall argued, 'different colonial projects give access to different meanings of empire', and even the British Empire was a battleground for ideological struggles between competing colonial visions.[39] Discriminating between colonisers is helpful in considering the status of missionaries as colonial actors. Some historians of missionaries have been reluctant to discuss missionaries as colonisers, maintaining that they were not welcomed by colonial governments and were outsiders who cannot be 'lumped in' with settlers, slavers and soldiers.[40] To do so would indeed be misleading. Yet, however unstable their ideological and administrative relationship with imperial officials, missionaries too had colonising tendencies. The expansionist missionary enterprise sought to defame and deny indigenous cultures, creeds and social orders and replace them with one that was not only Christian, but was also 'English'. Missionary discourses, like those of explorers, politicians and novelists, contributed to the colonial construction of difference. Whether supporting or critiquing imperial endeavour, 'The British Empire' was a concept with which missionaries were 'at home'. Making plural the coloniser circumnavigates some of these contradictions and allows for a better appreciation of both the fluctuating relationship between missionaries and other colonisers, and the inconsistent aspirations of the missionary movement itself.

The second critique of Fanon's 'colonial relationship' focused on the *nature* of relations between colonisers and colonised, within their historically and geographically specific situations, to argue that they were not always or necessarily Manichean but were ambivalent, fluid and overlapping. Cooper and Stoler demanded attention be given to the interconnecting worlds of colonised and coloniser both overseas and at home (colonial geographies, they argued, were falsely dislocated and better understood when placed in the 'same analytic field').[41] Stoler argued that the traditional historiographical division between 'colonizer' and 'colonized' risks reproducing the colonial fiction that Europeans in the colonies were racially and culturally a 'natural community' and that lines between the 'rulers' and the 'ruled' were thus 'self-evident and easily drawn'.[42]

Stoler has rigorously interrogated the ambiguities and permeations between colonisers and colonised.[43] She conceived many such slippages as occurring in 'intimate' spaces and argued that sexuality and procreation were particularly 'dense points of transfer'.[44] Servant–master relationships, concubinage, prostitution and children born of mixed-race relationships all transgressed supposed lines of delineation and subordination. Some have argued, however, that Stoler focuses too tightly on sexuality.[45] Religion, sibling relationships and platonic friendships have been offered as alternative 'critical arenas of intimacy'.[46] I too am keen to emphasise that there are many 'intimate spaces' and 'dense points of transfer' where ambiguous colonial relations occurred.

Missionary writing reveals many sites of intimacy, and I have chosen three to structure *Missionary Discourses of Difference*. The first part of the book explores families, households and sexuality, areas that have, as discussed above, been well established as 'intimate spaces'. The second part of the book explores sickness which, I argue, occasions increased intimacy between the sufferer and friends, families and colleagues around them. Sickness itself pervades the body, alters the way in which the body is felt and makes one aware of the body in new ways. Medical observation and treatment can transcend or penetrate the bodily boundary itself. Likewise, violence, the focus of the third part of the book, can also be read as a site of intimate encounter, not only when it involves close bodily contact but in the feelings of vulnerability, invasion and helplessness it can internalise. Ideas about family, sickness and violence were critical to missionary thinking in both India and southern Africa but were manifested in ways particular to each colonial site.

The relationships between colonisers and colonised, and the discourses of difference that marked them, were not coherent and consistent relationships but were always shaped by the specific geographical and temporal context. This project, then, uses material from both southern Africa and India to think about the divergent formation of difference. I focus on the LMS as one of the largest British missionary organisations and one which made a significant impact on British imperial culture. My period, c. 1840–1900, covers the second 'phase' of LMS missionary activity and a period associated with the 'hardening' of racial attitudes and accelerated colonial expansion.

Britain and its colonising projects

The missionary conception of Britain and her 'others' was rooted in wider colonial imaginings of Britain as occupying a 'higher' place of cultural and intellectual development, and of 'civilisation' emanating from her shores. The LMS developed in a period that saw the rethinking of the British Empire after the loss of the American colonies. In places they conceived as 'The Foreign Field' and 'Home', missionaries inhabited spaces that were inflected by European colonising projects, geopolitical shifts wrought by imperial expansion and violent colonial encounters. Besides their material implications, such projects shaped the ideological grids through which missionary thought filtered.

At different points during the nineteenth century, various colonising projects cooperated or conflicted with each other in ways dictated by both metropolitan and local trends. By 1840, when this study begins, many such projects were already in place. Humanitarianism, associated with evangelical belief, paternalistic imperialism and a universalistic conceptualisation of 'the family of man', had reached its zenith in the 1830s with the triumph of the Emancipationist campaign. But it remained influential, and closely, if in a complex way, connected with the missionary enterprise.[47] British settlers were making homes in Canada, Australia, the Cape Colony and New Zealand in ever-increasing numbers. Despite widespread conceptions of extra-European spaces as *terra nullius*, such settlers not only encountered non-European peoples, both indigenous and themselves migratory, but also other European settlers such as the French in Canada and Dutch in southern Africa.

Meanwhile, the colonial project as an imperial project was rapidly developing as the British Government increasingly intervened to defend, support and maintain its possessions around the world. Capitalist or 'company' colonialism was well underway, not least in India where the East India Company (EIC) controlled extensive territories.

By 1840, the missionary project was also in full swing.[48] Originally named '*The* Missionary Society', the LMS had catholic pretensions that lasted well beyond its transition into a decidedly nonconformist, and predominantly Congregationalist, organisation. The seed of the LMS germinated in 1795 during the Evangelical Revival and amidst a flurry of missionary society formation.[49] At home, it sprouted substantial support networks facilitated by the proliferation of Britain's churches and chapels in the first half of the nineteenth century.[50] Sunday schools, which attracted high numbers throughout the century, proved particularly fertile ground both in galvanising young fundraisers and providing a forum for the dissemination of missionary propaganda.[51] Emancipationism had helped to cement what Hall has called the 'Missionary Public', a 'site' for 'the constitution of Christian subjects', particularly amongst the middle, lower-middle and artisan classes: a public sphere dependent on collective and individual acts of commitment, and the consumption of missionary literature.[52]

Despite a period of optimism in the 1830s, as the LMS approached its half centenary in 1845, support was contracting, and its directorate reflected on their first 50 years with unease about the future.[53] In Britain, the LMS faced public criticism, a lack of recruits and financial problems – difficulties which would dog the organisation for the rest of the century. Overseas, work was frustratingly slow and missionaries were increasingly sceptical that converts would ever be 'civilised' enough to operate independently from European guidance. But despite this, missionary organisations continued to influence both the representations of colonial places circulating at home and the course colonialism took overseas.[54] Amidst these developments, the 1840s also saw a considerable growth of missionary enterprise, particularly in Africa and India, where the LMS saw a mass of 'unenlightened peoples' in dire need of Christianisation.

Southern Africa

Long after other spaces of empire had been subordinated to an imperial gaze, Africa signified a place of darkness, mystery and ignorance.[55] The darkness was, of course, symbolic, deepened rather than relieved by the 'light' thrown on it by European travellers.[56] As missionaries, colonists, traders and gold-seekers trickled into the interior the aura of 'adventure' and 'exploration' was maintained until late in the nineteenth century. The stories missionaries told of southern Africa were ones of discovery, adventure and movement. Although all missionaries travelled, in southern Africa mobility was paradigmatic, and missionaries often journeyed several steps ahead of the ever-changing colonial frontiers. Their travels, Livingstone's most notably, were emblazoned on LMS propaganda and into the consciousness of the missionary public.[57]

The first LMS missionaries to arrive at the Cape in the 1790s encountered a society not only internally complex but already enveloped in complicated colonial claims. British rule had replaced Dutch, and a colonial society, characterised by slave labour and the subordination of indigenous Khoi and San, developed in the fertile lands of the Western Cape. European incursions were also being made in the Eastern Cape, though expansion into these 'wild' terrains was proving harder, and wars over the contested frontiers repeatedly erupted.[58]

Early LMS workers in southern Africa tended to be of a working-class, artisanal background.[59] There was a high proportion of Scots and some Europeans.[60] During the early nineteenth century, LMS missionaries to southern Africa acquired a reputation for sexual improprieties (including with African women) and hostility to settlers.[61] In the 1830s, some campaigned against the effective enslavement of the KhoiKhoi and the post-emancipation vagrancy legislation.[62] Reflecting wider enthusiasm for humanitarianism in this period, LMS missionaries contributed to the Aborigines Select Committee's reports and mobilised networks of information and patronage to bring the violent abuses of indigenous people by Europeans to the attention of the metropole.[63]

In 1840, southern Africa was still geopolitically unstable, turbulent and violent, with ongoing frontier wars, expansionist European settlement and a fluctuating relationship with Britain. For the LMS, the 1840s were a period of major change. Ruptures to missionary humanitarianism, which splintered across the globe in the mid-nineteenth century, began to impact southern Africa in the 1840s.[64] As with the perceived 'failure' of emancipated men and women to be reconfigured into a 'civilised' workforce in the Caribbean, some argued that the KhoiKhoi seemed 'ungrateful' for their 'liberation'. These claims were intensified by a rebellion at Kat River (a hitherto successful missionary institution) which became emblematic of the collapse of missionary humanitarianism in the region.[65] These traumas, and frustration with the slow pace of Xhosa conversion, generated questions about the rationale, direction and conduct of the LMS in the Cape generally. After heated discussions, the society decided to withdraw resources from its long-established missions (with hope that they would become self-supporting) and redeploy them elsewhere in southern Africa.[66]

Reorientating itself northwards, the LMS joined several other colonial groups looking into the African interior in this period. During the 1830s, many Dutch-speaking settlers left the Cape in the much mythologised 'Great Trek' to 'freedom' from British rule.[67] The 'Voortrekkers' consolidated their power through mercenary alliances, regrouping under what became the Orange Free State and the Transvaal.[68] British settlers were also pushing northwards.[69] Each new step of colonial expansion, plunder and bloodshed was met with indigenous resistance, most notably from the Xhosa, Zulu, Pedi and Ndebele.[70] The LMS expansion, spurred on by Livingstone's 'discoveries' in the interior, clustered around two main fields: Bechuanaland and Ndebeleland.

The 'Bechuana Mission Field' denoted LMS work both in the territories that, in the 1880s, were to come within the British Protectorate of Bechuanaland and those much further south in Griqualand West. It encompassed many African peoples including the Kgatla, Tlokwa, Tlhaping, Kwena, Rrolong, Hurutshe, Ngwaketse and the Tswana.[71] Experiences with different polities varied. A king or chief's conversion was crucial, bestowing status on the new religion and hoping to encourage his people to follow. Khama III's conversion was particularly significant for the LMS. Khama became King of the Ngwato in 1875; during 50 years of rule, he provided a symbol of hope for African Christianity in LMS propaganda.[72]

The other LMS field in southern Africa was Ndebeleland, which, after an initial period of optimism on its establishment in the 1850s, became notorious as the LMS's most hopeless African enterprise. There was not a single convert until 1890.[73] Constant raiding between the Ndebele and neighbouring polities disrupted all work, and the Ndebele King, Mzilikazi, not only forbade his people to convert but often prohibited literacy teaching, and sometimes preaching. Little changed when Mzilikazi died, and he was succeeded by his son, Lobengula.

When the LMS first became acquainted with both Bechuanaland and Ndebeleland, their large territories were beyond the boundaries of formal imperial rule. Over the course of the nineteenth century, fortune seekers and gold-diggers started to enter the area, people characterised in missionary writing as gold-grabbing vigilantes, who were frequently violent and were actively seeking the 'lawlessness' of extra-colonial territories. But at the same time, the discovery of minerals and the widespread conviction that these territories would yield further riches ensnared both Bechuanaland and Ndebeleland in complicated power struggles and aggressive colonial and imperial politics.

Bechuanaland's diamond fields were coveted by the British southern African colonies; the two Boer Republics and different indigenous groups, particularly the Rrolong, the Ngwaketse and the Tlhaping. Over the second half of the nineteenth century, Bechuana territories were subject to a series of annexations, retractions and re-annexations. Several LMS missionaries became deeply entangled in these projects, particularly John Mackenzie who fervently believed that peace could only be brought to southern Africa through a system of 'Territorial Government' administered by the British.[74]

Meanwhile it was rumoured that a second rand of gold lay under the Ndebele plateau. As such, both the Transvaal and the British colonies in southern Africa coveted Ndebeleland, which, during the 1880s, became a focus of Boer–British rivalry. German and Portuguese interests were also competing for the region's land and wealth. Furthermore, a formidable entrepreneur-turned-politician, Cecil Rhodes, who had amassed a huge personal fortune through diamond prospecting, also had designs on Ndebeleland.[75] He used his financial influence to pursue an aggressively expansionist policy in southern Africa through his British South Africa Company (BSAC). In the context of the wider 'scramble for Africa', and through a series of very underhand treaties, the BSAC colonised Ndebeleland. LMS missionaries were profoundly implicated in these machinations. Bloody warfare and resistance followed in the 1890s.[76] Whilst the LMS had long prayed for Ndebele power to be crushed, when it finally was, they were caught up in the ensuing devastation, complicating the 'hopeful signs' of conversions that occurred in its wake.[77]

This book ends in the early stages of the (Second) South Africa ('Boer') War (1899–1901) and the violence it unleashed.[78] In its aftermath, borders were redrawn and the Union of South Africa was created in 1910. Over the nineteenth century, the political landscape of southern Africa changed significantly. For much of my period, LMS missionaries in southern Africa were working in liminal spaces of empire beyond formal colonial borders, but they were always inflected by colonising influences.

The geopolitical conditions of missionary work (and its success rate) differed substantially between its clusters in the Cape, Bechuanaland and Ndebeleland, although settlers, minerals, indigenous politics and colonial instability were common threads. Colonial and missionary discourse stereotyped southern African people according to essentialised but differentiated understandings of 'tribe' and 'race', from the 'fearless' Ndebele, Zulu and Xhosa to the 'peaceable' Khoi and 'Bechuana'. At the same time, these constructions were homogenised into an umbrella construction of 'The African'. This generalised grouping is most starkly realised when placed against other colonial constructions, such as those to 'The East'.

India

The stories missionaries told about their encounters in India differ profoundly from those told of southern Africa. This is unsurprising because India occupied a very different place in the imperial imagination. Whilst in the 1840s, Africa was still an 'unknown' continent, India was already familiar back home, albeit as somewhere 'exotic'. Furthermore, despite the recently concluded Punjabi Wars, the fact that India was a garrison state, and the major upheaval the subcontinent would face in the 1850s, British power in India, be it commercial or governmental, was perceived as pervasive, even by 1840. Indeed, in stark contrast to Africa, it was the conception of India as a 'wholly accessible' mission field, not least because of British influence, which recommended it for missionary work.

British engagement with India was certainly long-standing and, by the end of the eighteenth century, Indian cultures had become objects of 'Orientalist' scholarship.[79] Whilst British knowledge about India should not be overestimated, many missionaries, such as the Reverend Edward Storrow, deeply believed 'Englishmen ought to be better informed about India than any other heathen land.'[80] The idea that India could be 'known', even 'scientifically', was widespread and affected how missionaries engaged with the region. Whilst in Africa, missionaries such as Livingstone and Moffat often presented *themselves* discovering, recording and mapping 'new' lands, in India, missionaries acknowledged that they were operating within frameworks already established.

The East India Company (EIC) was one such formative framework, determining missionary deployment in India.[81] By the early nineteenth century, the EIC had extended a widespread influence across India, particularly at its ports. Missionaries considered the EIC an ambivalent force, potentially civilising but worryingly condoning of 'heathen' customs. Moreover, the EIC was cautious of proselytisation, fearing that the 'traditional' Indian cultures it constructed as highly conservative would not tolerate this form of western intervention.[82] It was not until 1813, when evangelical petitioning forced a change in the EIC's charter, that missionaries entered British India in significant numbers.[83] Thereon, and particularly after 1833, when licensing was removed altogether, work increased rapidly.

LMS missions were developed in Bengal (particularly around Calcutta), south India (in Madras and Mysore) and, separated from the latter by the Nilgiri Hills, Travancore (particularly around Nagercoil and Neyoor).[84] Along with a smaller mission in west India, these remained the centres of LMS activity throughout the century. Geography and linguistic diversity structured the organisation of labour. The south Indian sphere, for example, was split into Tamil, Telegu and Canarese missions. Although they encountered a multitude of cultures, languages and faiths, missionaries across India's divergent regions evoked notably similar concerns – the 'horrors' of caste, idolatry and 'degraded' womanhood. These issues did not only concern missionaries. During the early 1830s, the so-called reforming EIC governors, such as William Bentinck (Governor-General 1829–1835), presided over legislation prohibiting female infanticide and abolishing *sati* (widow-burning). Like missionaries, 'reforming Liberals', such as James Mill, abhorred 'despotism', 'priestcraft' and 'superstition', deeming them 'shackles' to be removed.[85]

By 1840, missionaries in India had already adopted the evangelising tactics they used throughout the century. They preached in public bazaars, visited private homes and produced tracts and scriptural translations. They attended and preached at Indian festivals, which they deplored as 'irrational' and 'revolting' rituals in lurid propaganda circulated back home.[86] Since the 1820s, constructing schools had been an important enterprise.[87] By the 1840s, missionary wives, particularly Mrs Porter in Madras and Mrs Rice in Bangalore, were establishing institutions for girls, and female education became an important area of work and writing.[88] Caste was a major concern, both for the 'enslaving' consequences it had on 'untouchables' and as a perceived obstacle to Christianisation amongst the higher castes. As in southern Africa, Indian missionaries felt the effects of the world-wide reorientation of missionary work in the mid-nineteenth century. The position of India within the British Empire, disappointment with the post-emancipation West Indies and new patterns of racialisation which tended to represent Indians (as 'Caucasians' or 'Aryans') as having more potential than 'Black' people contributed to a reorientation of missionary activity to the East.[89]

The Rebellion, which erupted in May 1857, dramatically influenced how missionaries experienced and imagined India. The subsequent siege at Lucknow and massacre of European women at Kanpur became iconic moments in the imperial imagination. Apparently spurred on by the attack on women and children, the British Army took horrible reprisals.[90] The Rebellion was a terrifying experience.[91] Although remarkably (the LMS argued providentially) no LMS missionaries died, in the course of the uprising five government chaplains, 15 ministers of the Gospel and more than ten missionaries of other societies were killed.[92]

In the Rebellion's wake, colonial rule was significantly reorganised.[93] The EIC's power was reduced and soon disappeared completely. Instead, the Government of India Act (1858) placed 'British India' under the crown, a relationship formalised in 1876, when Queen Victoria was named Empress.[94] The Princely states that had remained beyond direct EIC control in 1857 retained some independence and henceforth became known as the 'Native States'. LMS missions in India fell under both forms of rule.

In the aftermath of the Rebellion, the LMS had to negotiate shifting opinions both in India and back home, some of which held missionaries and their 'meddling' influence responsible for antagonising the 'traditional' Indian forces, upon which the Rebellion was blamed. In an attempt to quell Indian anxieties about westernisation, Victoria issued a proclamation ambiguously promising that 'subjects would not be favoured or disquieted by dint of faith or race, whether at law or relative to appointments.'[95] Vehemently rejecting suggestions that they should proceed more cautiously, the LMS decided to read the Proclamation as an encouragement to further work, and saw India's new imperial status as an additional imperative for evangelisation.[96] Claiming the Rebellion was a divinely ordained punishment for their failure to evangelise India on a mass scale hitherto, many missionaries in India demanded the LMS increase its numbers there.[97] In doing so, they emphasised the size of India's population, the degree of 'heathen degradation', the 'intelligence' of Indian people and the special responsibility Britain now owed the Raj.[98] This thinking was not new, but during the late 1850s, such claims became stronger and Britain's responsibility for its 'own *fellow subjects*' was repeatedly emphasised.[99]

The admission of single female missionaries into the LMS during the 1860s greatly influenced the course of its activity in India. Zenana missions developed, which, drawing on long-standing tropes of 'degraded' Indian women, aimed to 'penetrate' the 'secluded' quarters of the Hindu home and 'rescue' the women imprisoned therein. By 1895 there were 32 single female missionaries working in India, many of whom were engaged in zenana work.[100] Zenana visitation was also part of a wider tendency of the LMS to develop specialised 'agencies' in India. Medicine, industry and education were all developed as specialised forms of missionary activity around institutional structures.

Towards the close of my time frame, India was in the grip of one of the devastating famines that killed millions over the second half of the nineteenth century.[101] Between 1896 and 1902, it is estimated that between 6.1 and 19 million died.[102] The 1876–1879 famine had been similarly awful. Even the lull between these cataclysmic periods was haunted by localised famine. Often situated within relatively isolated rural communities and in close contact with the poorer members of society, missionaries could not escape the gruesome impact of famine as many other colonists seem to have done. The LMS saw itself as vital in distributing 'help to all classes and all creeds' at a time when it claimed 'no other provision has been made'.[103]

By the 1890s, the LMS reflected on a century that had brought some success, but had by no means achieved the hoped-for evangelisation of India. Compared to southern Africa, the three large Indian missions of South India, Travancore and Bengal varied less in terms of the structures of their work and their geopolitical circumstances. Some regional differences were noted, however, and the LMS believed it had enjoyed 'a much more cordial welcome among the devil-worshippers of Travancore than among the haughty Muhammadans of the north'.[104]

A differentiated mission field

India and Africa, then, were constituted very differently in the missionary imagination, and this affected both their representation by the LMS and the proselytising strategy they deployed in each site. India had notably more developed schools, churches and medical missions than southern Africa, proportionally, as well as more workers. In southern Africa, missionaries intervened in indigenous, colonial and international politics far more frequently than they did in Asia. These variations, illuminated here by comparative work, have often gone unnoticed. It seems that historiographical bias towards India had obscured the fact that the 'feminisation of missionary work', the development of medical missions and the alleged missionary love of institutionalisation are changes that, whilst often generally asserted, primarily occurred in 'the East'.[105] For example, when the LMS started to employ single women missionaries from the 1860s onwards, it did so unevenly, sending most to India and China and leaving other areas (including southern Africa) with few, if any, single women workers.[106]

Discrepancies in strategy point to the inability (or unwillingness) of the LMS to dictate a uniform policy from the metropole outwards. This is not to argue that circumstances 'in the field' outweighed those in the metropole: a more complicated process was at work. As critical colonial historians and postcolonial geographers have effectively demonstrated, people, power, information and ideas moved around the empire in complex ways.[107] In this case, pre-existing stereotypes, earlier missionary reports and wider colonial discourses shaped what missionaries expected of different mission fields. These expectations impacted the strategies deployed in different places. In turn, the tools of conversion deployed shaped particular indigenous responses to Christianisation (as, of course, did radically different indigenous cultures and local historical contexts). Often, inconsistencies in the reception of the missionary message were then explained by the racial potential of indigenous groups and a deterministic understanding of their cultures. These responses then fed back into the representations of indigenous people circulating in colonial and missionary discourse. Such processes point to the necessity of following missionaries and their discourses across the divergent sites that constituted their 'foreign field' to produce a differentiated picture of missionary work.

Spreading the missionary message

Far more than missionary men and women themselves, textual articulations of missionary discourse webbed the globe. The technologies of missionary literature production were a powerful way through which the diverse 'dark and distant lands' individual missionaries encountered were woven into a wider missionary imaginary.

Throughout the nineteenth century, the LMS, like other missionary societies, produced vast amounts of propaganda to promote their work, raise funds and recruit volunteers. Biographies and memoirs were important means of publicising missionary work and glorifying its employees. Exhibitions, lectures by missionaries on furlough, plays, children's recitals and Sunday school songs were also widely used and all involved representing the colonial 'other' to those at home.[108] The intertextuality between these sources is striking, with material often 'recycled' between publications.[109] As Susan Thorne has demonstrated, missionary writings were one of 'the myriad sites at which ordinary Britons encountered the colonies' at home and 'an effective conduit of information about the empire'.[110]

A particularly useful source for exploring missionary thinking are the LMS's leading journals: *The Missionary Magazine and Chronicle* (hereafter

Missionary Magazine) up to 1867 and the *Chronicle of the London Missionary Society* (hereafter *Chronicle*) thereon.[111] These magazines contained lengthy extracts of letters from missionaries overseas, notices, reports from the society's annual meetings, financial records, biographies, histories of individual missions and of the society, illustrations, maps and, towards the end of the century, photographs. Published monthly, the *Missionary Magazine* and *Chronicle* were the principal means the LMS used to communicate with its supporters and the medium through which its directors strove for the 'wider diffusion of Missionary intelligence' to the general public.[112] Although never as widely purchased as the LMS would have liked (circulation figures in 1887 were 37,000), at 1d, the price of the magazine was affordable to a reasonably large readership. The magazine was actively consumed by missionary supporters, churchgoers and Sunday school pupils. It was distributed at prayer meetings, contemplated privately, read aloud publicly, discussed at missionary meetings and generally claimed to be a source of inspiration. It was an important means of forging identity amongst the missionary public at home. As such, these monthly periodicals can be seen as an important medium through which ideas about difference and colonial sites were constructed and disseminated.

Importantly for my exploration of difference across colonial sites, missionary periodicals presented different articulations of missionary thinking alongside each other. Although, as Anna Johnston notes, editorial control could be 'obsessive' and contributions were often manipulated or 'corrected' prior to publication, missionary periodicals nevertheless incorporated a range of voices.[113] Whilst the editors controlled what was included and excluded, and until the 1880s the magazine was edited by the foreign secretary of the LMS and was thus very much the organ of its executive, the copious volume and speed of production meant that this filtering process was not always so scrupulous as has sometimes been assumed. Very often inconsistencies appear between accounts in fact as well as in tone, dappling the picture of work overseas and illuminating the instability and diversity of missionary discourse. On the other hand, this same volume and speed of production meant that reliance on set tropes, stereotypes and recycled material was strong and increased the tendency to reinforce dominant discourses.

In their propaganda, missionaries themselves only appeared in very stylised ways, in which their lives were sanitised and rendered heroic. In order to explore issues of the self, therefore, I have delved into the LMS's extensive official correspondence. LMS missionaries were required to maintain regular contact with employers through letters, annual reviews and other forms of documentation. To some extent, a public/private divide distinguishes correspondence from the published material discussed above. Personal squabbles and professional disagreements which riddle the correspondence were, for the most part, kept out of the public arena, as were the anxieties missionaries expressed privately about lack of success, apathy or crises of faith. In practice, however, there were many slippages between 'public' and 'private' writings. 'Private' letters were passed informally between families and friends, and letters to employers were a staple source of material for the *Chronicle*. I have therefore been able to move easily between different types of sources in my analysis.

Scope

This book aims to further understandings of how difference was formulated in colonial discourse by exploring constructions of 'self' and 'other' in missionary writings. It builds on the findings of Thorne, Hall and Johnston by investigating the heterogeneity of 'heathens' in missionary literature and the ambivalence of missionary identity. It contributes to wider projects of unpicking colonial identities, mapping the development of ideas about race and gender and exploring the relationship between colonisers and colonised.

The project is a multisite analysis using material from southern Africa and India to explore how these sites developed as distinct places in the missionary imagination and the consequences of this divergence for the fragmented formulation of difference. As geopolitical entities, India and southern Africa were important sites in the imperial imagination and very different ones. India was the 'jewel' of the British Empire. Southern Africa was a troublesome area liable to be volatile in terms of settler and indigenous populations alike. They were both areas of substantial LMS investment and enterprise. I prefer 'site' to 'colony' partly to allow for intra-regional variations and partly because I follow missionaries beyond the formal frontiers of British rule and into the liminal spaces of empire. I use the term 'colonial space' broadly to evoke areas experiencing indigenous disempowerment, the coming and consolidation of British influence and the perception of a space and its peoples as ripe for cultural and/or political colonisation.

At the heart of my analysis is attention to the slippages between 'global' and 'local' thinking in missionary discourse. In the various 'distant lands' in which they worked, missionaries recorded significant variations between places and peoples (between Hindus and Muslims, between Tswana and Xhosa). In the metropole these distinctions tended to be dissolved under broad regional labels: 'Africa' and 'the East'. Even the very divergent discursive constructions of India and southern Africa also operated alongside a more homogenised missionary imaginary which simply posited Britain as 'enlightened' and other regions as 'sunk in heathen darkness'. India and southern Africa were both imagined as parts of a 'heathen world' and geopolitical spaces within, or related to, expansionist imperial frameworks. Many tropes knitted representations of diverse and differentiated peoples into one of the 'degraded heathen'. Lack of education, the oppression of women, the violence of 'native' cultures, the 'ignorance' of their children, the 'cruelty' of their parents and their desperate 'need' for British intervention were claimed of widely diverse 'foreign fields'. I am concerned with analysing how attention to detail expanded and contracted, how places were sometimes differentiated and sometimes likened in missionary thinking, as colonial difference was formed, challenged and remade in missionary writing.

Working on the assumption that the registering of difference cannot be confined to explicit race and gender theorising, this book examines missionary thinking through three themes: 'Families and Households', 'Sickness' and 'Violence'. These themes have arisen from the sources – they were major missionary preoccupations and recur in both public and private writings and proved to be useful axes in understanding their ideas of difference. I explore each theme from two angles, looking firstly at the structuring of difference as essentialised and static and then at more ambivalent or ruptured treatments of these topics. This division tends to map itself over representations of the 'other' and the 'self' respectively, although, of course, the two are always in negotiation. By 'rupture', I mean the interruption of a discourse, discursive inconsistencies or contradictions, or points that appear to represent a break or transition in dominant ways of thinking. By 'encrustment' I mean the closure of ruptures. The word suggests the layering up of discourse and the (almost organic) messiness of these processes; ruptures are not simply 'forgotten' but become part of the archaeology of the discourse.

Part I examines the role of gendered domesticity in missionary thinking. Chapter 1 explores images of the family in missionary propaganda, illuminating the dichotomies drawn between the 'Christian Family', as represented by missionaries' own households, and 'heathen home life', characterised by cruelty. Chapter 2 examines ruptures posed to these constructions by experiences in the 'foreign field' and argues that conversion, domestic service and inter-cultural sexuality were areas of colonial intimacy demonstrative of a more ambiguous relationship between 'self' and 'other'.

Part II considers the embodiment of difference in missionary thinking. Chapter 3 discusses sickness and the representation of the 'other'. It explores how 'sickness' and 'heathenism' were linked through the metaphorical pathologisation of 'heathenism' and discusses the development of medical missions as a manifestation and extension of these linkages. Given the association between sickness and 'heathenism', Chapter 4 examines how missionaries dealt with their own experiences of becoming ill overseas.

Part III explores violence, a theme little associated with missionaries yet ever-present in their fields of work. In Chapter 5, I argue that violence operated as a racialising mechanism in missionary thinking: from *sati* to cannibalism, missionaries used accounts of violence to demonstrate that 'heathenism' was cruel, violent and different. I argue that aligning violence with otherness allowed missionaries emotively to justify colonial intervention and associate British colonialism with the mitigation of violence rather than its perpetration. In Chapter 6, I juxtapose this with a consideration of how missionaries reflected on *colonial* violence committed by Europeans. In doing so, I interrogate a larger 'self' within which missionaries sometimes operated and the slippery identifications with 'white', 'British' or 'English' identities as they solidified, melted and reformed in missionary thought.

My argument is that writings about families, sickness and violence all demonstrate that, while principally articulating itself in terms of spirituality, difference was also understood by missionaries through the body. Each theme was manifested differently in India and southern Africa, suggesting that colonial discourse was significantly differentiated by spatial and temporal specificities. Each theme demonstrates a complex interplay between 'self' and 'other' in missionary thinking.

Part I

Families and Households: Difference and Domesticity

Overview

The family and domesticity were important discourses in missionary writing. Marriage had the potential to legitimise sexual relations about which missionaries were anxious. Kinship and genealogy provided some means of categorising and organising the peoples and cultures missionaries encountered. Gender relations, considered a measure of 'civilisation', were often framed through familial relationships. Domesticity was central to evangelical ideology and fundamental to both the doctrine missionaries sought to impart and the standards they were determined to 'uphold' when posted abroad. The very concepts of 'family' and 'domesticity', understood in supremely ethnocentric terms, were held by missionaries as formations that could and should be universal in application.

Many ties link the intersecting discourses of gender, sexuality and race. As Sander Gilman argued, by the eighteenth century, black men and women had become iconic of 'deviant sexuality'.[1] Transgressive sexualities, from sex work to promiscuity, polygamy and homosexuality were frequently racialised. At the same time, attitudes towards race were often sexualised, at least from the early modern period.[2] Erotic images of 'exotic' others pepper European travel writing, art and literature and 'the Orient' was thought to offer kinds of sexual experience impossible in the West.[3] Whilst these intersections are always present, they are correlated in forms specific to time and place. Over the nineteenth century fears of miscegenation grew, leading attitudes towards cross-cultural relationships to become increasingly prohibitive. At any specific moment in this period, images of Polynesian sexual availability coexisted alongside very different pictures of the Middle Eastern harem, depicted as secluded, yet also highly sexualised. Erotic images of African and Indian women differed markedly, yet both drew on tropes of disordered sexuality.[4] So did coexistent images of Bengali men as effeminate and African men as sexually aggressive.[5] Associations between race and sexuality structured colonial discourses over the coming centuries and primed missionaries to respond to indigenous families and households with concern.

Enlightenment thinking suggested that the social position occupied by women was a core indicator of the level of civilisation a given culture had reached.[6] In an influential treatise on Indian history, the EIC administrator and historian James Mill argued that '[a]mong rude people, the women are generally degraded; among civilized people they are exalted.'[7] At the apex of civilisation were European women, gendered by emergent evangelical discourses. At the bottom of the hierarchy lurked many 'degraded' women ranging from those in southern Africa where 'the women are reckoned unworthy to eat with the men', to those in India where Hindu women occupied a position than which a 'state of dependence more strict and humiliating ... cannot easily be conceived.'[8] Such imagery also characterised nineteenth-century missionary writings. Missionaries claimed that '[t]he condition of women in all heathen countries is one of mental no less than moral debasement, the one naturally tending to the other', a sentiment reiterated endlessly to weave together encounters in India, Africa and other sites of missionary activity, into a single narrative of female heathen degradation.[9]

In missionary and other reforming colonial discourses, what this 'degradation' entailed oscillated between women's oppression and women's disorder. In India, the discourse of women's oppression became a key justification for colonial intervention. In the early nineteenth century, *sati* was increasingly used to imagine Indian women's victimised state.[10] Over the following decades, concerns about Hindu women's oppression were reconfigured around various other tropes, from the child bride to the zenana woman. Elsewhere, women conceived as 'unrestrained' by patriarchal structures proved equally challenging to colonial expectation, and were denigrated as 'uncivilised' and potentially subversive.[11] Whilst colonial discourse often operated through oppositional formations – there were 'proper' ways of constructing a family and 'disordered' ones – the 'other' was always fragmented and contained within it oppositions of its own.

Concurrent with ideas of self and other, then, was a graded discourse of progress. Mill continued, 'The history of uncultivated nations uniformly represents the women as in a state of abject slavery, from which they slowly emerge, as civilisation advances.'[12] Missionaries were interested in speeding up this change, and in raising the 'condition of women' in the family and in society more widely. Ensuring that masculinity was 'correctly' performed was equally crucial to this project.

Throughout the nineteenth century missionaries criticised indigenous men for being 'idle' and 'indolent'. Indian and African men were both accused of failing to provide for their wives and children, roles that missionaries considered crucial to 'civilised' masculinity.[13] As Catherine Hall argued, 'forms of companionate marriage', and ' "proper" relations between men and women', were central to realising the condition of women deemed constitutive of civilisation.[14] The effects of this were both linked to and compounded by a developing bourgeois ideology of home, family and the domestic.

During the Evangelical Revival, religiosity was gendered through an ideological division of home and work, and women and men, into 'separate spheres'.[15] The domestic was increasingly construed as a religious site residing within a feminine sphere of influence. Women, constructed as morally 'pure', and beacons of religiosity, were vested with responsibility for their family's spiritual well-being as well as for its domestic upkeep, a task newly imbued with moral status. Families and households were central to reaffirming missionaries' sense of religious and social self when overseas, but, as such, they were inevitably also sites of potential insecurity. The 'foreign field' was feared to harbour forces of corruption and contamination which, through the family, could corrode the very identities of missionaries. Over the course of the nineteenth century, missionaries, like other colonial thinkers, increasingly feared 'degeneration' overseas as one such threat. But family and household structures were also a way of resisting change or corruption overseas. Further anxieties, therefore, were generated from the 1860s by the employment of single women missionaries who operated outside the family structure.

Part I uses families and households to explore the intersections between gender, sexuality and race as they developed as discourses of difference. Chapter 1 examines the essentialised ways in which missionaries wrote about family 'types' both idealised and demonised. Chapter 2 explores the ambiguous intersections between these 'types' in the 'foreign field'. My understanding of what constitutes 'family' is broad. Following Davidoff et al., I use 'blood, contract and intimacy' as markers around which the concept of the family can be hung.[16] I see the family as a fluid space where people can come and go and where belonging and membership are insecure.

1
Representing Homes: Gender and Sexuality in Missionary Writing

The language of family in missionary discourse

Missionary projects were theologically and rhetorically embedded in concepts of kinship: the language of family and universal brotherhood permeated their writing. The habitual addressing of fellow missionaries as 'sisters' and 'brethren' reinforced the identification of colleagues in familial terms and the conceptualisation of the LMS itself as a missionary 'family'. At least rhetorically, this was extended to both the missionary-supporting public in Britain and to the peoples missionaries encountered overseas. The LMS believed the Gospel of Christ was 'calculated to put an end to the strifes and contentions which distract the human family' and to 're-unite' it 'in the bonds of a holy and happy brotherhood.'[1] But what did this language mean for their construction of difference? And to what extent was difference mixed with contrary ideas about cross-cultural sameness and human universality?

One use of such language was to suggest to those at 'home' that they had familial connections with unknown 'heathen' kin overseas and thus evoke a means of identifying with those who otherwise seemed remote. Female missionaries were particularly adept at deploying familial terminology to create bonds of sympathy and especially effectively so between India and England. Confident that English women were 'sheltered', 'chivalrously cared for' and 'shared the blessings of education, culture, freedom, and above all, of love in happy English home[s]', female missionaries appealed to English women to take pity on their 'less fortunate' 'sisters abroad' still suffering under 'the yoke of oppression'.[2] Missionaries were not alone in deploying such language. By the late nineteenth century, depictions of Britain's 'Indian sisters' were widespread in the metropolitan press. Many reforming groups depicted Indian women as 'degraded sisters' and 'needy daughters' dependent on British help.[3] The missionary and reforming use of familial language in Britain implied a common belonging, an implication that wider debates over the unity of humanity were calling into question. But of course, the language of family did not necessarily mean sameness. Families harbour their own very unequal power dynamics and evangelical families were demarcated by age, gender and marital status amongst other markers of difference. Missionaries tended to posit indigenous people as their younger brothers and sisters (occasionally as their children), not as equals. Furthermore, whilst such language was immortalised in the early nineteenth-century Abolitionists' slogan 'Am I not a man and a brother?', in the later nineteenth century, white missionaries far more commonly evoked sisterly ties with Indian women than with Africans. Kinship, it seems, only extended so far down the racial hierarchy.

The language of kinship could also be used slightly differently – to claim not only that indigenous people were related *to* British people but that kinship relations were culturally transferable. Missionaries suggested, for example, that British mothers would identify with Indian or African women as *fellow* mothers. 'She is dark-skinned, she is a heathen, she is frightfully oppressed – but she is a mother!' Will Bentall, a medical missionary in Neyoor, wrote of an Indian woman, continuing more generally that 'the cries of the down-trodden and cruelly-treated mothers rise, only to be heard by our loving Father.'[4] It was the woman's racial, religious and social differences that seem to have struck Bentall first, but then, in marking her motherhood, he pulled back from this encompassing otherness, salvaging her through reference to a condition imagined to have a universal meaning (and finally, through referencing a paternalistic God, connected her with a wider human family). Such understandings were an important counterpoint to emergent polygenistic discourses in the nineteenth century which stated that there was nothing familial between Africans and Indians. But at the same time, it was this conviction of the universality of relational family roles as timeless, spaceless and without cultural inflection that made missionaries so unable to allow for the cultural constructedness of such positions. 'Motherhood' could never 'only' mean the biological production of a child by a female parent but entailed nurturing the child 'appropriately' and fidelity to the child's biological father. Universalising discourses neutralised the specificity of this construction. Whilst missionaries may have claimed 'a mother is a mother all the world over', that mother was not imagined to be nine years old, sexually promiscuous or someone who harmed her children. This differed from emergent ethnographical thinking which, though often disapproving of or exoticising of alternative family formations, did, to some degree, recognise them. In missionary discourse, indigenous families could never be represented as coherent social entities, because 'mothers', 'fathers' and 'daughters' were understood through evangelical English formations.

Missionaries found deviations from their understandings of familial roles profoundly shocking and tellingly labelled them 'unnatural.' Coexisting with sympathetic portrayals of men and women as parents, and children as sons and daughters, were the most damning portrayals of indigenous people: that their very families themselves were perverted. Both African and Indian missionaries reported chilling incidents of intra-familial 'cruelty' as examples of 'heathen' otherness, and told multiple stories to illustrate such claims, ranging from Hindu children drowning their fathers in the Ganges, to the 'unnatural cruelty of a heathen son to his parents' in Africa.[5]

The duality of imagining all individuals through kinship positions, and denying validating familial discourses to actual domestic arrangements, created a dislocating effect essential to missionary thinking. On the one hand, it allowed individuals to be abstracted from indigenous family arrangements, of which missionaries did not approve, whilst retaining the positive associations of those kinship roles. On the other hand, it allowed 'the family', elsewhere represented as so 'natural', so human and so praiseworthy, to be reconstituted as a problem. This insistence on difference alongside the ideological commitment to sameness was a tension typical in missionary thinking. One of the places in which this lesion is very obvious is in discourses about the Missionary Family, a supremely ethnocentric construction which, nevertheless, was conceptualised as a model to emulate.

Constructing an ideal: the Missionary Family in missionary literature

Referring to the LMS in southern Africa, Wardlaw Thomson, Foreign Secretary of the LMS, evoked an image of the Missionary Family common in missionary discourse:

> No one has done so much for their temporal well-being as the missionary and his family. In his house building, garden cultivation, domestic arrangements, and simple and cleanly habits of life; in the attachment of each member of the family to the others, and their

> purity of speech and honesty of conduct, the missionary family is undoubtedly the greatest civilizing agency in the country.[6]

In Thomson's depiction, missionary families embodied the ideology of the enterprise. 'Family' not only meant kin but its organisation into 'pure' and 'loving' relationships; 'home' meant a 'cultivated garden', 'cleanly habits' and a respectable household. Marriage formed an ideological shaft central to these constructions. Defining themselves against celibate Catholic missionaries, and exporting the community role of the English dissenting minister abroad, LMS missionaries usually travelled to their stations with their (often newly wedded) wives and saw themselves not only as missionaries but as patriarchs: fathers and heads of their households.[7] Such marriages were sentimentally represented in missionary literature as exemplars of compatible gender relations. Robert and Mary Moffat were emblematic of the missionary partnership. 'Born in the same year (1795), and married in 1819', one eulogy began, 'they spent together fifty years of wedded life, united by many ties, one in faith and sympathy, in object and effort, enduring, labouring and rejoicing together.'[8] Even after death they were imagined 'together learning more fully than ever before the meaning of the expression "the crown of life"'.[9] The missionary home formed another important element of this, and building a house and planting a garden were achievements proudly noted in missionary periodicals and accompanied by idyllic engravings that presented an overseas reconstitution of British Protestant Victorian family life.

As Thomson suggested, missionary families were intended to have a didactic function as an 'object lesson' which indigenous people, imagined to be imitative of Europeans, were hoped to emulate.[10] Idealised representations of the Missionary Family also performed an important role in literature intended for *British* consumption. Idyllic depictions were confirming of missionary identity, and their presentation re-enforced the 'proper' way of conducting a family perverted in representations of 'heathens'. The presentation of the 'other' was always contingent on a representation of the 'self'. In published missionary writing, the self-conscious construction of 'self' as a role model, contributed to the idealised representation of, not so much 'missionary families', but the 'Missionary Family' as a static point of reference. Despite the way in which missionaries naturalised Protestant British familial forms in their thinking, the Missionary Family was always marked.

This doublethink had several consequences for missionary thought. It meant that the missionary wife could be lauded in some writings as a 'brave hearted woman' who was her husband's ally 'in his conflict with barbarism and in his routine to elevate and bless'; at the same time her very real contribution to the well-running of the mission was obscured.[11] Thomson, for example, was not constructing a single male missionary but a married one, whose status in part depended on his home and family, yet he failed to mention who exactly it was who made 'his house' or conducted his 'domestic arrangements'.[12] As Reverend Stratham confessed when he considered missionary women: 'We too often forget them, even in our homes; we often take the head of the table, and all the honour.'[13]

However, particularly after the 1870s, when the radical potential in the employment of single women missionaries encouraged many of the society's members to turn to the hitherto unnoticed work of their wives, there was a certain celebration of their 'heroism'.[14] Unlike the heroisation of male missionaries, whose lives were recorded individually (albeit somewhat formulaically) in biographies and memoirs as personal stories of triumph, the celebration of 'the missionary wife' was usually generic. Usually nameless, it was simply stated of these women that her 'domestic life is a daily power for good, silently instructive as to women's rightful place in the family'.[15] Within the partnership, and even in those accounts which constructed their society as one 'wherein men and women work side by side, as *helpmeets* in the true sense of the word, at home and abroad', it was always assumed that women performed the supportive role their gender demanded.[16] Alternative genderings of the family were considered both threatening and degenerate.

To return to Thomson's remarks, the Missionary Family was intended to serve a didactic purpose overseas, by giving what a different missionary discussed as 'a practical illustration of the working of the Christian principle in home life'.[17] But its idealised representation in missionary periodicals was also intended for British audiences. It reproduced an image of domesticity with which the evangelical recipients of missionary literature in Britain would have been 'at home'.[18] As I will discuss in the following chapter, maintaining English domesticity in the transitory lives missionaries often led proved deeply problematic, but in their published writings, missionaries represented themselves as reproducing almost reified forms of Victorian domesticity overseas. The trans-imperial families missionaries did form were actually fairly common in the nineteenth-century British Empire, but they did not enter hegemonic representations of family life in which close proximity was always implicit.[19] Public depictions of missionary families were comfortable images that rarely raised anxieties about their racial status. Representations of missionary homes as 'untainted' and even unaltered by colonial experience re-confirmed missionaries as moral representatives of beliefs shared by supporters back home. In doing so, the idealised Missionary Family formed a powerful discursive foil to those 'other' families missionaries encountered, ensuring the difference represented by indigenous peoples always appeared at its most stark.

The family and heathenism

'There is no such thing as home-life in India, at least, not in our sense of the term – and what there is is mostly impure and dangerous', wrote Miss Barclay, a female missionary in Madras.[20] The claim that 'heathens have no home life' was a truism of missionary discourse. This is unsurprising given how much missionaries invested in the concept of 'Home'. The very words 'home' and 'family' were imbued with an emotional value that missionary discourse could not allow indigenous families to possess, partly because of their conviction that 'heathen' families were emotionally starved, but also because missionaries themselves could not emotionally (or sometimes physically) enter these 'other' homes and so were estranged from them.

Missionaries refused to accept alternative patterns of sexuality, household structure, or marriage as 'legitimate' or even *as* 'familial'; 'the family' was a validating discourse that could be denied. Missionaries often claimed that family was of no importance to 'heathens', reading the absence of *familiar* kinship patterns as the absence of family life altogether. The denial of alternative family arrangements was a powerful discursive mechanism that had several uses. One was that missionaries could present their task as *introducing* the concepts of 'family' and 'home' to those they encountered, rather than as reorganising those already in place. A second was that missionaries did not have to acknowledge the fragmentary consequences that conversion had on indigenous families, many of which were torn apart by the 'loss' of loved ones to an alien religion. A third consequence was that 'heathen' families were less commonly represented in missionary discourse than it initially appears. Whilst abstracted individuals defined through a familial position (for example, as a 'daughter', 'wife' or 'widow') were very common, discussions of indigenous *families* as collective entities were less so, and when they did appear, they often did so incoherently. The Indian zenana, for example, which as I will discuss below, appears very frequently in missionary literature, represented only part of a home, amputated from the masculine domestic sphere. At the same time as its existence was denied, denunciations of the 'heathen family' as a source of evil were common – it is this duality of claims that is represented by Barclay, quoted above.

As Patricia Grimshaw noted, 'missionaries knew better ways, it seemed, to do just about anything,' particularly in regard to family life and child rearing.[21] Implicit in these criticisms were both the missionary desire to *intervene* materially in indigenous families and their representation of British models as 'superior'. Missionaries commented negatively on non-Christian marital arrangements, critiquing wedding ceremonies, the conjugal division of labour, the age of marriage and polygamy. Dwellings lacked the material culture thought integral to domesticity. Tables (if indeed there were tables) were wanting in the accoutrements deemed necessary for a 'civilised' meal. Food that was eaten with hands, or uncooked, subverted the missionary sense of domestic order. The architectural structures of African homes were scorned, huts were considered primitive, the separation of men and women in communal living arrangements fragmented the nuclear family and wider kinship networks were not considered equivalent to the extended families missionaries valued 'at home'. Indigenous divisions between 'private' and 'public' space were considered particularly problematic, and failure to contain sexual relations within a private 'bedroom' turned the home from a sacred domain to a degraded sexualised space.[22] Dress (or undress) was used to similar effect, as missionaries read as sexual men and women's refusal to clothe themselves in a manner which conformed to British understandings of modesty.

Running alongside criticism of non-European family structures was a powerful discourse that 'the heathen' was 'without natural affection' and that non-Christian familial relationships were emotionally inadequate.[23] Missionaries in both Africa and India suggested that 'heathen' families lacked the love such relationships should 'naturally' involve. Numerous incidents were recounted as 'awful proofs both of parental and filial cruelty' amongst non-Christian peoples.[24] From discussions of caste, to bridewealth, to infanticide, 'heathen' parents were portrayed as devoid of maternal or paternal instincts. Examples of the 'unnatural cruelty' of 'heathen' children to their parents (such as the killing of aged relatives) were also common missionary tropes. These caricatures of cruelty were directly attributed to and used to demonstrate cultural failings by the weaving of specific incidents into homogenised understandings. In the missionary press, editorials did much of this discursive work. In the editorial comments preceding a collection of letters from southern Africa, for example, an account by missionary Joseph Read of a mother who had burned her child to death, was explicitly linked with one from John Philip, of the murder of a father by his son. The editor claimed that '[t]he character of the Fingoes [Mfengu] in their heathen state strikingly answers to the inspired portraiture of Paganism, in which it is exhibited as destitute of natural affection.'[25] 'Absent' or 'corrupted' families were clearly, in missionary thinking, in dire need of change. In published writings, missionaries used horrified, piteous and scornful tones to assert the difference of heathen familial arrangements to English ones.[26] But, whilst woven in a single fabric, representations of African and Indian families were othered from the English 'norm' in notably different ways.

The family in Africa: disorder, sexuality and domesticity

In southern Africa, the LMS encountered a complex array of family structures. In the Cape, missionaries operated within a post-emancipation society and were primarily concerned with issues of marriage and fidelity. Amongst the Ndebele, where adherence to age-regimens prevented marriage and reproductive sex until later life, enforced 'virginity' was a more unusual missionary concern. Whilst some missionaries argued that the Tswana were 'naturally domestic', other groups, such as the Khoi, were thought to lack domesticity entirely. While grappling with this diversity, however, missionaries also operated within a homogenising discursive framework through which an undifferentiated 'African' sexuality had already been identified as 'problematic' and 'African' family life defined as 'debased'. Highly sexualised images of African women, widespread since the eighteenth century, would have been familiar to the earliest LMS missionaries before they 'discovered' them for themselves. By the mid-nineteenth century, such images were extended to all black people and meant that public representations of African family life tended to obscure demographic diversity behind set tropes.

One trope, which exemplifies these homogenising processes, is that of polygamy. Not all southern African societies were polygamous, and even in those that were, it was not universally practised. But hints at polygamy reverberated throughout missionary representations of Africa unhinged from actual encounters with it, and it was often claimed that certain 'tribes' were polygamous well after the practice had become obsolete.[27] In missionary periodicals and memoirs, generalised impressions of polygamy were amplified by certain flamboyant examples, usually those of kings and chiefs. Mzilikazi, for example, the infamous

King of the Ndebele, was said to have 'some eighty children' and 'many more wives'.[28] The numerous letters in which missionaries recorded their encounters with Mzilikazi, the reproduction of this material in their memoirs and accounts of the king's virility even by those who never met him, demonstrate how powerfully Mzilikazi's 'harem' captured the missionary imagination.[29] The harem's representation was imbued with dubious sexuality. Even virginity was treated suspiciously and without the implication of virtuous purity evoked by the word in relation to English women. Moffat wrote of the King's daughters scornfully as 'plump and fat, at least thirty years of age, and ... doomed to perpetual virginity'.[30]

In missionary discourse, polygamy never just meant the marriage of one man to more than one woman; it meant a 'formidable barrier to the success of the gospel among barbarous nations' and the corrosion of every aspect of family life.[31] Polygamy carried suggestions of illicit sexuality, the degradation of womenkind and a fragmented domestic space. Most threateningly it signified the perversion of Christian marriage, reducing the position of 'wife' to that of 'concubine' or even 'slave'. 'Polygamy entailed many evils', Reverend Wookey claimed (discussing a period some 50 years earlier): 'Wives were purchased with cattle ... When a man tired of his wife, he purchased another, and another and another, often leaving the former ones to shift for themselves.'[32]

The connection between polygamy and slavery, which itself haunted representations of Africa and Africans throughout the century, was also linked to the amorphous phenomenon of bridewealth. As Reverend Birt described the process amongst the Xhosa, it formalised the link between money, sexuality and property and meant 'the daughters of Caffreland are looked upon by their nation as so much property.'[33] A Xhosa woman, he wrote, 'becomes a slave the day that she is made a wife. She works extremely hard, so as to bring on premature old age. She is in most instances then laid aside and another wife is taken.'[34] Missionaries saw this division of labour as a disordered state of gender relations where the 'weak' and 'fragile' bodies of women were abused, and men, through their lack of work, were emasculated. As such, 'both sexes need a reformation', Birt argued, and given that 'the females are the sufferers' it was, he wrote, 'obvious that the raising of the female character will greatly tend to ameliorate the condition of the whole'[35] Discourses about polygamy fed easily into the missionary worldview: that 'heathen' families oppressed women, economically, sexually and socially and that this was 'other' to (patriarchal) Protestant families. The plight of women in Africa (and as I will argue, in India) could be used both to demonstrate the 'degraded' state of indigenous civilisations and to justify missionary intervention.

This said, perhaps the gender relations missionaries found most frightening in Africa were not polygamy, which confirmed their worst expectations, but the rarer examples of politically and domestically matriarchal societies. In the 1850s, both Livingstone and Moffat commented on what they perceived as the 'reversal' of gender roles in the societies they encountered. Livingstone was disturbed that, amongst the BaLonda, 'the relative position of man and woman [were] reversed.'[36] Shocked, he discussed the BaLonda at length in a series of public meetings and published letters. The perceived 'reversal' of gender roles was in part political: women sat on 'the councils of the nation' and 'were often made chieftains.'[37] It was the domestic arrangements, however, that Livingstone found most disturbing: 'men had to check with "the lady superior" before accepting any kind of work' and 'the wife alone could divorce the husband'; if divorced, 'she took the children away with her.'[38] Livingstone was particularly horrified to find that women punished their husbands by withholding food.[39] Worse yet, he exclaimed, 'the ladies... will sometimes even dare to enforce their authority over their husbands with cuffs and blows.'[40] These 'indications of female supremacy' flouted all Livingstone's expectations of gender roles, a 'reversal' inscribed on the bodies of one wife and husband who he described, respectively, as 'a great masculine creature, and a withered scraggy old man'.[41]

Not only did such societies contradict the 'proper' gender roles, but they threatened to disrupt the general missionary understanding that heathen societies were misogynistic. The editorial comments surrounding Livingstone's contributions strove to close this rupture, clearly reasserting that 'As a rule it has been found that heathenism deprives woman of her rightful status in society, and dooms her to drudgery and degradation. It is so with the Caffres and other natives of the south with whom our traveller was familiar.'[42]

In part, missionaries held that the disordered gender relations they perceived as so problematic in Africa stemmed from the 'absence' of recognisable forms of domesticity. Architectural structures were too minimal to constitute 'homes' and their interiors were squalid. Physical 'dirtiness' was conceptually linked with moral 'impurity' and societal 'backwardness'. Whilst, as I discuss below, Indian domesticity was often attributed to oppressive yet complex civilisations, African living conditions, suggested to be 'primitive', were used as evidence that civilisation was lacking altogether.

For example, one long piece in the *Chronicle* entitled 'The Koranna', quoted extensively from the work of the Czech explorer and scientist, Dr. Emil Holub, alongside extracts from Reverend John Mackenzie's recently published *Ten Years North of the Orange River*, to claim that 'Koranna' (Kaonde) architecture was 'of the very lowest grade'.[43] Like Mackenzie, Holub used domestic structure as a visible marker of 'civilisation' through which he could map societies onto a closely graduated racial hierarchy. 'Of all South African races', he wrote, 'the Korannas bestow the least labour upon the structure, and the least care upon the internal arrangements of their dwellings.'[44] Their rapid construction which, Holub wrote, 'as their appearance suggests, is of the most primitive order', further evidenced both their lack of domesticity and of 'skill' and 'civilisation' more broadly, as did the 'squalid and comfortless' interior.[45] Such living standards were directly related to 'heathen' underdevelopment and embodied in the behaviour of their inhabitants, and the atmosphere of their homes where, '[i]n these dreariest of abodes a dull dumb silence usually prevails... all is stillness and stagnation'.[46] The tendency to see 'civilisation' (or lack of it) inscribed on both people and place is typical of the slippage between 'race' and 'culture' in missionary writing and those other discourses, like Holub's, they absorbed.

Descriptions of polygamy, the reversal of gender roles, and the lack of domesticity, essentialised African family life. They represented 'difference' both to naturalised assumptions about 'English' domesticity and the more marked example of the Missionary Family. These depictions both contributed to an oppositional colonial discourse and were formed alongside representations of other 'heathen' families, not least in India.

Indian families and discourses of the zenana

Whilst Africans were claimed to be devoid of family structures, Indians were claimed to be stifled by 'a family consisting of grandparents, parents, uncles and aunts, and cousins to the second or third degree' who left 'no room for any play of individuality'.[47] Missionaries in India never claimed that a domestic sphere did not exist or that it was anything other than patriarchal. Instead, the Indian home came to symbolise a corrosive element of Indian society and women's oppression within it.

From the LMS's earliest days in India, Indian women had been represented through their victimhood. In particular, the 'Hindoo woman' was a *cause célèbre* in nineteenth-century reformist writings.[48] These images were fluid, differentiated and sometimes conflicting. To take *sati* (widow-burning) as the most iconic example, Andrea Major has argued that eighteenth-century British attitudes towards *sati* were ambivalent: although many found it disturbing, women were nonetheless seen as having agency, *choosing* their *sati*, and some, particularly those of a Romantic inclination, interpreted it as an act of martyrdom.[49] Only by the early nineteenth century was the practice widely condemned, as women were reconfigured as passive victims, acting without volition. Even then, Major suggests, interpretations of *sati* occurred in conversation with each other. Images of Indian women were inflected by concurrent debates about British women in the metropole. The late nineteenth-century reconfiguration of the 'degraded' Hindu woman as the 'child bride' during the Age of Consent Controversy, for example, must be seen alongside metropolitan concerns about maternity and motherhood.[50] In missionary writing, the zenana, a secluded female area of some Indian homes, was used to domesticate many of the earlier missionary tropes of Indian womanhood. Most of these, like the *sati* widow, were already defined through a familial position, but through the zenana they were relocated and reconfigured through a discourse explicitly about the Indian 'home'.

Mrs Mullens, who is often attributed with pioneering the zenana movement within the LMS, made her first visit to a zenana in 1860, as part of a trend of 'zenana visitation' that was capturing the imagination of many missionaries in India.[51] With her colleague, Mrs Cowen, Mrs Mullens went on to establish four 'zenana schools' in Calcutta and the surrounding area. Within a year they had 77 pupils between them. They taught reading and sewing to high-caste Hindu women in the privacy of their own homes. Training and ideally converting these women was hoped to have significant consequences, as it was claimed that many such women, as wives and mothers, had 'gone forth who are diffusing blessings in their households'.[52]

From the mid-1860s, zenana work proliferated and became a central preoccupation of the missionary imagination. Encounters with the zenana evoked images of the Middle Eastern harem and its 'indulgent sexuality' already familiar to British readers of 'Orientalist' travel writing and proved an exotic and useful site of reform. Depictions of zenanas occurred in periodicals and were central themes of missionary poems, tableaux and recitals.[53] The zenana was a key exhibit in missionary exhibitions and formed a grandstand for depictions of Indian women more generally.[54] The zenana became *the* Indian home in missionary writing, acting metonymically for all of Indian family life. Other domestic spheres in India with which missionaries were acquainted tended to be marginalised in their writing. The *Chronicle* seldom recorded the phenomenon of visiting the Bytakhana or Baithakháná visitation (the male domestic space that formed the zenana's counterpart), preferring to depict work with men in public spheres and contain the representation of the domestic to discussions of women.[55] Similarly, whilst purdah (seclusion) and the keeping of a zenana only ever affected a minority of Indian women, it soon became a framework through which to organise thinking about *all* Indian families. Although many missionaries (particularly male ones who were denied access) urged readers to recall the limited extent of purdah practices, the 'penetration' of the zenana became idealised as a way of bringing the liberties enjoyed by British women to their oppressed sisters.[56]

Zenana visitation appealed to LMS concerns about caste as well as gender. Early LMS work in India, particularly in the south, had been most successful amongst low-caste men and women, *dalet* ('untouchable') communities, orphans and other social outcasts.[57] This was disappointing as missionaries had always prized 'high caste' and Muslim converts as particular trophies of success. These groups were considered hardest to convert because they were thought to have the most to lose by the social isolation that often followed conversion. Furthermore, despite their professed hatred for the caste system, many missionaries seem to have been awed by the 'delicate', 'fair' skins, wealth and 'genteel manners' they believed marked the higher castes, through a combination of their own class and race prejudices. But as with others attempting colonial reform, missionaries found accessing high-caste women difficult. Male missionaries were often prohibited from approaching women due to local constructions of female modesty, and high-caste attendance at missionary schools was low.[58] Zenana visitation by missionary women allowed some of these prohibitions to be circumnavigated.

In an interesting echo from other to self, zenana work also offered a way around restrictions of gender difference faced by female missionaries. Although it had been pioneered by two married women, the development of zenana work in the 1860s coincided with the entry of single women into LMS as missionaries. Newly employed single women were able to use their privileged access to the zenana to forge a specifically female missionary role in India. Zenana visitation circumvented the potential challenges the employment of women involved, returning British women moving outside their own homes, back into a domestic sphere that, despite its vilification in missionary discourse, had some resonance with evangelical understandings of 'separate spheres'.[59] Single female missionaries were thus able to forge a role for themselves in India in a way they could not in southern Africa or on other sites where indigenous gender divisions were less prohibitive to male missionary work.

Reverberations between 'self' and 'other' were abundant in the intimate context of the zenana. In contrast to the stock image of female victimhood which had circulated in the 1840s and 1850s, early zenana writings presented more nuanced depictions of Indian womanhood, and, whilst certainly patronising, also reflected cautious admiration of Indian women, particularly of their beauty and their 'eagerness'.[60] These missionaries depicted 'interesting women' who gave them insights into Indian culture as they 'freely' talked 'of their manners and customs', marriages and funerals.[61] Sewell, an early zenana worker, depicted zenanas as lively, busy places, where missionary work was constantly disturbed by the 'excitement and insubordination of the children' and 'incessant interruptions' from children 'constantly rushing into the room.'[62]

The relationships forged between missionaries and Indian women in this context could be more reflexive than other arenas of activity allowed and more conducive to exploring the bonds between Indian and British women than the differences that divided them. Housework, demarcated as 'women's work' in both Indian and British cultures, proved one area in which practices could be compared. Mrs Sewell, for example, suggested Indian women were nervous about the time she urged them to dedicate to reading-practice, asking 'what would become of the house if [they] were to sit and occupy ourselves with work of this kind?'[63] Sewell was glad to reply and did so '[g]iving to domestic duties their full importance, and advocating the most scrupulous attention to household affairs, children and servants', yet she 'contended that, by early rising, method, and diligence, two or three hours a day might be secured for mental improvement and fancy work.'[64] Identifications forged on gender lines were always tempered by those of cultural or racial difference. Anxious to underline the English commitment to domesticity, Sewell continued to inform the zenana women that 'if they supposed that European women considered themselves justified in spending their time over books, &c. to the neglect of their tables, wardrobes, children, and servants, they were most mistaken'; she believed 'no nation in the world had so much home comfort as Englishmen.'[65] Class was also noticed and defended. When the Indian women objected that English women had cooks and ayahs to help them, she took great pains to detail the additional burdens of English housekeeping. 'They soon looked aghast', Sewell wrote, 'and confessed that we too had household cares, and, though very different, not lighter than their own.'[66] Whilst missionary women may have worked outside their own homes, passages like this reconnected them with English domesticity. In doing so, they ensured that representations of home life in India were positioned relationally to domesticity 'back home'. Sewell was convinced of the supremacy of English domesticity, but did acknowledge that Indian women had, at least, some domestic understanding of their own.

Over the course of the century, connections between Indian women and missionary women became more uncommon and images of the zenana became bleaker. By the turn of the century, they were typically described as 'a dull prison-like place, with the windows so high up that no one can look out of them'. With the household chores of Indian women apparently forgotten, it was claimed, 'the women in these Zenanas have nothing to do all day long.'[67] As descriptions of 'seclusion' changed to those of 'imprisonment', the mobility that characterised portrayals of zenanas in the 1860s was replaced by stagnancy, and the overwhelming adjective in describing zenanas became that of 'darkness'.[68] The zenana was presented as an *unhealthy* space harbouring an 'almost incredible' 'amount of sickness and suffering'.[69] Such discourses were part of an explosion of late nineteenth-century critiques of the zenana by medical reformers, feminists and other humanitarian thinkers, about Indian women prohibited from being examined by white doctors and literally trapped inside the zenana.[70]

The increasing tendency to depict zenanas as inauspicious spaces was shadowed by a shift in the representation of their inhabitants. The subtlety of earlier descriptions was soon lost, and the zenana became a framework through which one could anchor and amplify longstanding set tropes of Indian womanhood, especially 'child-brides', 'widows' and 'degraded mothers'. These figures appear in a huge range of missionary discourse including diary accounts about ('actual') zenana visitations, sketches of pitiful, cowering figures, or as characters in fictional pieces.[71] In missionary plays, tableaux and recitals, children dressed in saris would recite rhymes which depicted zenanas as miserable places, located stock figures within them and specifically appealed to British women. A typical example ran thus:

> Hidden away in ZENANAS so drear,
> Living in ignorance, darkness and fear,
> Mothers and child-widows, daughters and wives,
> No ray of Christ's love to gladden their lives!
> Go to them sisters, for none can but you –
> Tell them of Jesus the Tender and True.[72]

The emotionally manipulative tone of these writings dictated British responses to Indian women: they were objects of pity, they were in a worse position than themselves and they were different. Even those located in the metropole could mobilise this discourse. 'Are you aware of the awful lives that those poor creatures live?' Reverend Burman, Rector of St George's Southwark, told attendees at the LMS's anniversary meeting in 1881: 'They are sometimes married as early as nine years of age, and if their boy husband dies on the next day they are condemned to perpetual widowhood.'[73] In widowhood, he deplored, they were 'condemned ... to miseries which it would be impossible to describe ... I verily believe that many of these poor girl-widows ... would rather have died, and have gone through the few minutes of agony of a fire, than have lived on through this most wretched and unhappy life.[74] It is both typical of such writings and significant that Burman found it 'impossible' to describe what he found; the impossibility of conveying the otherness of an Indian home is a key trope of such writings, always constitutive of difference. In this piece and others, the unfavourable comparison drawn between widowhood and death was used to keep images of *sati* alive late into the nineteenth century. Burman's depiction of an Indian 'girl' is one crying out for the sympathy of a British audience and shows a determined commitment to essentialism in discussing Indian women.

That representations of the zenana as a physical space became more severe at the same time as depictions of Indian women reconsolidated is unsurprising. Depictions of 'culture' and those of 'race' were always formed together and through each other. The slippage between people (albeit in essentialised roles) and space is a formulation where this constant imbrication of 'race' and 'culture' can be identified in missionary thinking. Whilst the stated causes of 'inadequacy' were apparently cultural, this was embodied in Indian women and in the process acquired racial undertones.

'Degraded' sexuality was one such discourse embodied in both the corrupted child-wives and extended into the very space of the zenana. Sexually charged language evoking 'dark', 'unpenetrated' spaces served to colour Indian households generally with suggestions of 'perverse' sexuality. Even for unmarried girls, the sexuality of the Indian home was presented as a constant threat: Miss Barclay claimed that Indian homes were saturated with 'filthy language' and 'indecent practices'.[75] Discourses of sexuality could therefore have the effect of webbing together household, society, culture, religion, body, nation and morality.

Age was another embodied discourse of difference which cut across those of race and culture shaping family power dynamics and their representation. Many critiques of the zenana evoke a sense that Indian families were perverted, through suggestions that their generational and age structures were disordered. As debates developed in Britain and India about the age of consent, missionaries increasingly represented the 'child bride' as a site of concern, embodying all kinds of missionary concerns from sexuality to misogyny.[76] Indian mothers, even those in middle age, were infantilised and alleged to have 'terribly little idea' of the 'right way' to bring up their children.[77] Miss Barclay (not a mother herself) suggested that their failings were due to the 'fact' that 'Mothers in the East are children, and remain so mentally for life. Their talk is childish, and consists of gossip about jewels and money.' The entire system was disordered, Barclay suggested, as what more could 'be expected from children who marry so early and are kept in the seclusion of a home for their rest of their days'? 'Such is the state of our little heathen sisters', she concluded, condemning all Indian women to the place of a younger sister.[78] Older women too, however, were severely critiqued as Reverend Robinson, working in Salem, put it: 'The "power behind the throne" in every Hindu house is the grandmother. She is rigidly conservative.'[79] By the 1880s, older women were commonly identified as the 'chief obstacle' 'preventing the spread of Christianity' in India.[80] The presentation of younger women as victims and older women as villains served to construct a *cycle* of oppressed-oppressing women and was typical of missionary writing not only in India. In Africa, similar concerns were levied against 'heathen grandmothers'. When Mrs Thomas and Mrs Sykes's girls' school in Inyanti (Ndebeleland) was nearly closed in the 1870s it was attributed to 'the old grandmothers' and their fears that 'if their children were trained by the teachers they would be no more fit for wives for their own countrymen.'[81]

The frustration many missionaries felt with Indian women due to poor conversion rates also contributed to the sense that the zenana was a site where Christianity was being actively resisted. The evangelical belief that women had a natural tendency towards spirituality was always a double-edged sword as far as proselytisation was concerned. But during the second half of the nineteenth century, women were increasingly depicted as the chief opponents of Christianisation in India, thanks to what was described as their domineering orthodoxy and their intense ('heathen') religiosity. As Janaki Nair discussed of imperial discourses more generally, the zenana, optimistically depicted as a place of educational reform in the mid-nineteenth century, became emblematic of subversive female power, and later a 'site of resistance to "civilisation" '.[82] The collusion of older women with the forced marriages of young girls implicated women in the reproduction of their own victimhood. This led to a curious placing of agency, in which women, whose volition was usually denied in favour of their male relatives, or displaced altogether as power was vested in corrosive heathenism, were blamed for perpetuating their degradation. Whilst female missionaries continued to emphasise that 'no class of society in India suffers more from their position as heathens than the women of India', the image of the dominating 'women of India' was nevertheless undermined by their simultaneous presentation as 'powerless' or 'delicate'.[83] This paradox was a common one in missionary writing and encapsulated many of their thoughts about the home and family. Women were primarily characterised through their victimhood, but the home also gave them access to considerable strength, which missionaries found equally disturbing. It was the simultaneity of these discourses – of women's strength and women's victimhood – within the household that made missionaries so convinced that the 'heathen home' needed to be destroyed.[84]

Conclusion

Discourses of 'family' and 'home' performed several important functions in missionary thinking. They were used to organise complex issues about relationships, sexuality and domesticity around 'the household' and codify societal differences for their British readership in culturally resonant ways. Through juxtaposing images of heathen otherness to a universalising rhetoric, missionaries suggested a capacity, as yet unrealised, for human sameness, integral to their missionary project. By representing Africans and Indians not simply as 'heathens' but as 'mothers' and 'children', missionaries drew on a language of Christian brotherhood, and suggested familial links between 'home' and the 'foreign field'.

But as well as performing apparently inclusive functions, the representations of missionary and indigenous families that I have discussed in this chapter consolidated commitments to difference. Monopolising the normative for themselves, missionaries identified 'heathen' families as perversions of what was 'natural'. The tones of horror, shock or pity that shaped their descriptions of the families they encountered ensured that British responses to such peoples would flow from a position of perceived superiority. In describing the treatment of women in India as 'evil in a degree scarcely to be apprehended by one who has not actually seen it,' the LMS suggested that family life abroad was not only 'utterly wrong' but so very different to that 'at home' that it was impossible to convey there.[85] Through such representations, missionaries justified their endeavour to overturn and fragment indigenous families; in both India and Africa, indigenous families were suitably oppressive and horrifying to necessitate the dislocations of family life which the conversions they initiated could cause.

'The Missionary Family', 'The African Family' and 'The Indian Families, were tropes that derived their discursive power from their positioning as completely discrete from each other. Missionary families appeared in a different conceptual framework from indigenous ones. In published missionary literature, the only form of interaction that appeared to take place was that of the 'native' imitation of missionary families. This was part of the discursive work of published missionary genres; in other writings, it can be seen that the relationship between the idealised types, discussed above, was far more ambiguous than public ones suggest. In the following chapter, I explore some of these ambiguities.

2
Re-Making Homes: Ambiguous Encounters and Domestic Transgressions

Fluidity, fragility and the family

There is no doubt that families exercise strong social, economic and psychic binds, pulling their members together and suggesting shared identity and belonging. By presenting families as set types, missionaries exaggerated, almost reified, this commonality in their writing. But families are fluid constructs, whatever the illusion of fixity. Family members come and go, not least in missionary families where birth rates and death rates were high. Besides rooting identity and belonging, families are also characterised by instability, dislocation and conflict. Family members may have different race, national or religious identities, for example, as well as being of different genders and generations.

In the previous chapter, I explored how, in claiming that Indian and African homes were utterly unlike and completely separate from their own, missionaries suggested that families operated as sealed cultural types, which could be placed oppositionally. In this chapter, I examine how colonial experiences challenged this positioning, focussing on the production of a difference that was always fragile, always ambivalent and always unstable. Discursive constructions of Christian and 'heathen' families as discrete marginalised their many complicated overlaps and intersections. In colonial households, missionary ones included, anxieties around the home illuminated perceptions of difference and reconfigured them. As Stoler argues, racial classifications were 'defined and defied' or 'confound[ed] or confirm[ed]' through intimate encounters.[1] I argue that missionary families and indigenous families (even 'heathen' ones) were neither spatially nor emotionally discrete. The household was a location where ambiguities threatened to disrupt the discursive split between 'civilised' and 'uncivilised' in missionary writing. Yet as individuals entered into intimate relationships that appeared to threaten that cultural boundary, discourses of the domestic were also re-encrusted and difference recreated. The chapter is structured around three areas where essentialised understandings of 'us' and 'them' were challenged in the intimate sphere of the domestic: conversion; the interior space of the missionary household; and cross-cultural relationships.

Conversion and convergence

'Heathenism' was the operative word through which Indian and African homes were racialised in missionary discourse: whilst 'Hindu women', for example, were racialised and objectified within a specifically Indian context, such depictions were woven into a wider narrative of 'heathen oppression'. The label 'heathen' never simply evoked religious difference but also stood for cultural and, less candidly, racial difference, as 'heathen' was discursively aligned with 'African' or 'Indian' and sometimes with 'darkness'. Nevertheless, through framing their thinking in terms of a Christian–heathen framework, at least at one level, missionaries suggested that Christianisation would dissolve this principal manifestation of otherness.

Although the tropes powerful in missionary writing were often static ones, missionary thinking was premised on the potential for change. Indigenous people were to be 'transformed' by evangelisation. Conversion never simply meant a faith-based transfer of allegiance; it had to be embodied in cultural practices. The domestic was an important site where such change was to occur. 'We must get them to be cleaner and to put up better houses,' Reverend Wookey wrote from South Bechuanaland, and 'do more to make *happy homes*.'[2] Wookey's colleagues in India thought on similar lines. Back in Britain, the Foreign Secretary of the LMS wrote of the missionary imperative: 'to touch the domestic life of those great Eastern races who scarcely know what the word "home" means, and to teach and persuade them so to alter their ways that the women, the wives and mothers, shall... become the fountain of Christianity.'[3] Here, as elsewhere, missionaries portrayed themselves as the *only* harbingers of change, representing indigenous families as stagnant, and marginalising other colonial agents who were also taking European domesticity abroad. What were the implications of conversion, and the fundamental desire to induce domestic change, for the framing of difference in missionary writing?

As would be expected from the wider geographical differentiation of their civilising strategy, missionary approaches to transforming family life were tailored to both their understandings of the indigenous peoples involved and the specific historical circumstances of their intervention in different places. In the nineteenth-century Cape, the LMS used institutions and later settlements to try and 'recreate' San and KhoiKhoi families. In doing so, it responded to a combination of the hunter-gather mobility amongst the San and Khoi, the dislocating effects of slave regimes on indigenous families, pre-conceptions about Africans lacking domesticity and the early missionary influence of Moravians, who had drawn on their own historical persecution to create isolated Christian communities.[4] The aftermath of emancipation and the use of institutions and settlements by emancipated men and women put missionaries in a powerful position to engineer the 'civilised' communities they desired.[5] 'Cottages' reflected missionary understandings of privacy in their very architecture and were to be kept 'orderly', 'regular' and 'clean'. The power to allocate or withhold such a cottage was used to enforce a patriarchal family structure administratively.[6] As the LMS left the Cape, and as its missionaries encountered more sedentary, pastoralist, Bantu-speaking peoples further north, their approach to changing African families diversified. Some built houses for chiefs and other royalty (and in doing so tried to establish European dwellings as a status symbol); others encouraged traders to introduce the material culture of English domesticity into African homes. In Bechuanaland, missionaries encouraged Tswana men to construct buildings according to European architectural tastes and trained women as servants to work in missionary homes and as 'domesticated' wives to tend their own.[7]

Missionaries approached their task of engineering new forms of domesticity in India differently. Because they acknowledged that Indians already had strong understandings of family life, they focussed on abstracting individuals from existing homes rather than *constituting* homes from scratch. Orphanages and boarding schools were used to create alternative domestic spaces where children could be raised away from the damaging influences of 'heathen' homes and 'free from the contaminating influence of bad companions'.[8] By 1840, boarding schools and orphanages were an established element of missionary strategy in India and were popular amongst missionary supporters in Britain due to their combined educational, spiritual and humanitarian functions.[9] The idea of removing children from the family and into boarding schools would have been a familiar one to missionaries from Britain where institutionalised education was common. Many missionaries would have been educated in boarding schools themselves, and many more sent their own children to school in Britain. But when thinking about Indians, missionaries articulated the value of boarding schools in terms of the need to protect children (particularly girls) from the effects of 'the degrading and demoralising influences to which their parents were exposed'. Instead, they were to be placed 'under the fostering care of a mother in Israel', essentially a European Christian missionary wife.[10]

Missionaries anxiously hoped that 'the Christian' home was rapidly spreading across the world. By the early twentieth century, they claimed that:

> Greater than any other influence that is being brought against the Hindu family system is the Christian home that is being reproduced in India. All over the land, in the cities and towns and villages are ideal homes being founded by native converts. Marrying at a suitable age, the wife educated as well as the husband, the young people go to their own home, and the children are nurtured in Christian truth while the voice of family prayer and Christian hymns show that God the Father and His eternal Son are honoured beneath the roof... the influence of this new factor in the life of India cannot be over estimated.[11]

Not only is the imagery of reproduction striking here, but the alleged completeness of the transfer is striking. What constituted the domestic was layered, from the Christian ambiance, daily routine, education of its members, age of marriage to the conception of the Holy Family.[12]

Real and fictitious examples of indigenous families who had adopted British familial structures appear throughout missionary publications as hopeful reminders that 'true' conversion *was* possible.[13] Engravings of smiling, apparently happy, Christian families supported textual claims that converts formed monogamous marriages in which women were respected and partners faithful and that they lived in homes that were suitable to nurture children 'properly'.[14] In India, missionaries emphasised cross-caste marriage as evidence that indigenous culture had been abandoned.[15] In Africa, details of converts who lived in 'neat, well-furnished cottages and fully adopt the habits of civilisation', where one could see 'Ornaments, cooking utensils, furniture... ' demonstrated an altered domesticity that represented 'civilisation' as evidence of Christianisation.[16] But ambivalence was often latent. Whilst missionaries claimed that these new homes were 'wonderfully nice', it was added that it was 'only by contrasting them with those of other natives, that their cleanliness can be properly appreciated'.[17] To European eyes, it was suggested, their 'cleanliness' may not be immediately visible.

The presentation of *Christian* Indians and Africans challenged the simplistic alignment of African/Indian, 'Heathen' and 'Uncivilised', against British/European, Christian and 'Civilised'. To some extent, converted families became a new ideal type. The Datts, a family Mary Budden worked with in Almorah, are but one example. Dr Tara Datt was the superintendent of the LMS's medical work in the leper asylum in Almorah, and their eldest daughter also studied medicine in Edinburgh. But it was Mrs Datt, 'born and brought up in heathenism' but having 'imbibed all the principles of a Christian life and home', who had undergone the most radical change. She represented a complete break in the equation of 'Indian woman' with 'degradation' and, with her 'Christian influence and training', strove 'to inculcate these principles in her children'.[18] It was thanks to her that the family consisted of 'civilised' individuals in a well-ordered domestic sphere.

The accompanying photograph, showing off the Datts to the *Chronicle*'s readership (Figure 1), reflects some of these transitions. The western-influenced dress, Christian symbolism and the absence of Indian jewellery, earrings or nose-piercings (usually of great interest to missionary illustrators and early photographers) are striking. The names of the Datt's 9 children – John, Joel, Basanti, Lydia, Gracie, Mohani, Imogen and Daniel (the latter two were absent when the photograph was taken) – though mixed in origin, again suggest movement away from obvious Indian signification. The patriarchal composition (with the names of the male family members heading the photograph and female ones at its foot) and the central place occupied by a text, presumably religious, embodying learning and piety at the family's heart, also represented values which, despite their cross-cultural resonance, missionaries would have been eager to claim as 'western'. That it was a Christian *family* as opposed to Christian *individuals* is clear.

In these moments, it was possible to be Indian *and* Christian, Indian *and* 'civilised'. In unhinging 'heathenism' from Africanness or Indianness and apparently realising missionary endeavour, converts could embody a new opposition to 'heathenism'. Because they did not also suggest an unhinging between 'heathenness' and 'indigeneity, to some extent converts became 'brown Englishmen'. There was little 'native' about them. A deviation in skin colour was all that

Figure 1 The Datt Family
Source: *Chronicle*, July 1895, 180.

was left of an 'old' identity which continued to be associated with otherness.

Missionary publications tended to present Christian, or Anglicised, households as 'lights in the dark' coexisting alongside, yet apparently completely separated from, 'heathen' ones. This rupture was crucial to how missionaries narrated the process of conversion. There is no doubt that proselytisation introduced painful and fracturing strains on a convert's relationship with their natal family. In both public and private discourse, conversion was explicitly associated with 'forsaking father and mother for Christ'. The renunciation of family provided an emotional climax to highly formulaic conversion stories that appeared in missionary literature with astonishing frequency. In a typical example, Balraman, a young man of the 'Naidoo' [sic] caste, converted to Christianity through the LMS's Madras Mission. His family, like so many others, was devastated, and Balraman's parents, siblings and 'many relatives of the family'came to see the Reverend Hall who recorded the following scene:

> his mother wept most bitterly, and when she saw that she could not induce her son to go home, she turned to my dear wife... and prostrated herself before her, begging mercy. She pointed to *our own babe*, who was then in her mother's arms, and asked my beloved partner how she would like to lose *that* child, and entreated that she would pity her feelings as a mother, and send Balraman her first-born child home with her. A long while was thus spent, amid the most heart-rending scenes, and when the father of this youth saw that all their efforts were vain, he wept like a child, and calling on one of his gods, exclaimed, 'Rama! Rama! Rama!' After the relatives had left the mission-house, Balraman broke his caste by eating our rice, and had his kootamy, or sacred hair cut off.[19]

The focus on the renunciation of family ties helped 'Christian' and 'Heathen' to retain their oppositional positioning in missionary discourse by dismembering the kinship ties that ran between them. This rupture was crucial to missionary thought which relied on the differentiation of these states.

Missionaries found the transition and syncretism mediating 'heathenism' and 'Christianity' deeply disturbing. At least by the later nineteenth century, missionaries had become deeply troubled by the disassociation of some of their values from others. New forms of religion (such as Ethiopianism) proved formidable rivals for British Nonconformity and were feared to indicate a dangerous unravelling at a theological level. At the same time, missionaries agonised about converts 'backsliding' into 'old' forms of behaviour. Similar anxieties occurred around family formation. In theory, LMS missions were not to be syncretic. Unlike within Catholic missions (at least as characterised by their Protestant rivals), caste was not to be tolerated and professing Christians must nullify polygamous marriages and abandon indigenous customs. In practice, however, LMS missionaries varied widely in their tolerance of 'heathen' ways.

The family was a key site in which missionaries agonised over the boundaries between 'heathen' and 'Christian', and, in so doing, deliberated questions with no easy answers. What should be done with second and third wives? What should happen if the children of Christian parents participated in indigenous initiation ceremonies?

Could they be circumcised? Were all Christians respectably dressed, and what about those who dressed respectably in public but not at home? Could Christians share dwellings with non-Christians (a scenario particularly problematic in societies where communal living was practised) or did Christianisation absolutely demand the privitisation of the home? What was the place of dowry or bridewealth in Christian marriages? What about inheritance? Could Christians be buried with non-Christian relatives? In posing such questions, missionaries engaged with the intangibility of difference; in attempting to answer them they erected boundaries to define it.

Some missionaries were in no doubt about the answers to such questions. John Mackenzie, for example, firmly believed that '[A Christian] cannot continue to live in the habits of a heathen. The African who believes that Jesus is preparing for him a glorious mansion in Heaven, will endeavour to build for himself a decent house on earth.'[20] But what exactly constituted a respectable house, and what about those who lived in a home outwardly respectable yet dubious within? T.D. Phillip wrote of Hankey in the 1850s, that although the improvement of dwelling houses had brought 'changes in their social habits of great importance and a valuable auxiliary in promoting morality' that 'most assuredly, all these applications do not necessarily and apart from religion, lead to morality'. 'No amount of mere civilisation will produce a higher morality,' he wrote 'but yet where there is religion, civilisation aids its higher development.'[21]

Many missionaries appear to have been torn between the conviction that 'heathenism' and Christianity were absolutely different and the realisation that they could not be clearly differentiated. Reverend F. Baylis typically claimed 'the difference between heathenism and Christianity strongly shown' but also that new converts were 'weak Christians'.[22] Discussing the problems of retaining converts during processes of cultural transition, he continued, 'some of them long to keep up some of their old heathen customs, especially going in procession with tom-toms, &c., at their marriages, and when they find that these things are forbidden they may be disappointed and leave us.'[23] Baylis clearly considered that playing tom-toms at weddings, even 'Christian' ones, was inherently 'heathen'. Other missionaries were less certain, writing home for clarification on boundaries that seemed all too intangible.

These problems became intensified when missionaries encountered individuals who appeared to embody elements of both 'heathenism' and 'civilisation'. Sechele, King of the Kwena, was a flamboyant example of such a person. Sechele had first encountered Christianity through David Livingstone and had developed his faith through the Hermannsburg Mission and later the LMS.[24] He learnt to read easily and used his extensive scriptural knowledge to answer his missionaries back, using Bible passages to justify actions missionaries were convinced were deviant.[25] Sechele was also interested in 'western' material culture. He dressed in European clothes, collected European furniture, lived in a house made of bricks and endeavoured to acquire European food which he demanded his wife and servants cook in a European style. Missionaries who encountered him were fascinated by these collections of furniture and by his domestic environment, and impressed by the 'extreme cleanliness of everything'.[26] But those who worked closely with him, particularly the Prices and the Mackenzies, felt these trappings of a 'European' 'home' to be displaced.

Responses to Sechele exemplify what Homi Bhabha has explored as the profoundly destabilising ambivalence of colonial mimicry, the desire that is, 'for a reformed recognizable Other, *as a subject of a difference* that is *almost the same but not quite*' (emphasis original).[27] The ever-increasing influx of European goods into the southern African hinterland meant a proliferation of the commodities of 'western' domesticity, potentially not associated with their supposed spiritual dimensions, that missionaries could not control. Such familiar goods, often acquired as status symbols, were reappropriated in ways that were unfamiliar and as such became unsettling and subversive.

Although Sechele's commitment to Christian teachings fluctuated, and he never fully renounced indigenous rituals, it was his familial relationships that missionaries found most problematic and that eventually severed their relationship with him. Sechele's wife, Mma-Sebele, was long a source of comfort to the LMS, believed to have been a 'true Christian at Heart' having been educated by Robert and Mary Moffat at Kuruman.[28] At the time of his conversion, Sechele had 'put away' all his other wives, keeping a monogamous relationship with Mma-Sebele alone. In 1880, however, Mma-Sebele died, and Sebele's re-marriage shattered the missionaries' confidence in the king. At the age of 72, Sechele married Kholoma, the 19-year-old runaway daughter of the Ndebele King Lobengula. They did not speak the same languages (Kholoma only SeTebele and Sechele only SeTswana and English). More pressingly, Kholoma was 'heathen' ('barbaric' even, the Prices claimed), and they married in a 'heathen' wedding ceremony. It was these domestic concerns, rather than any spiritual disavowal, that rendered Sechele again 'heathen'.[29]

Sechele and other such individuals embodied an unhinging of values that was found humorous at best and dangerous at worst. They posed a frightening image of convergence between 'Christian' and 'Heathen' families and disordered the separation of markers of Englishness and those of 'nativeness' with which missionaries were at home. Whilst missionaries wanted to induce *change*, they feared *transition*, and wanted to move from one absolute to another.

Elsewhere, missionaries encountered more mundane manifestations of blurry boundaries that were equally disturbing. In particular, they found that professing Christians maintained indigenous family arrangements previously considered 'heathen'. For example, child-marriages amongst Indian *Christians*, as well as Hindus and Muslims, were very troubling (and generally attributed to Catholic converts).[30] Primarily these concerns were articulated through a discourse of 'weak Christians', which contained ambivalent manifestations of Christianity by framing indigenous people as the 'weak' followers of 'stronger' Europeans. Rather than engage with a plurality of interpretation, missionaries reasserted a commitment to a 'true' ('western') faith and practice.

These tendencies characterise colonial discourses more widely. As Partha Chatterjee argued, '[the] modern regime of power [was] destined never to fulfil its normalizing mission because the premise of power was preserving the alienness of the ruling group.'[31] The constant moving of goal posts was a feature of colonising writings and necessary to the justificatory logic of colonial discourse. In reforming discourse Indians could never attain the same level of 'civilisation' as their British teachers. Historians of missionaries have often noted the reluctance with which missionaries withdrew from their mission fields.[32] Porter suggests missionaries were reticent to leave peoples and places to which they had become attached, reluctant to 'declare oneself redundant' and deterred from moving on by the practical difficulties that starting again in a new field entailed.[33] Alongside this was the sheer inability to recognise the Christian communities built by Indian and Africans as anything other than 'dependent' and a fundamental disbelief that these new communities could generate future generations of Christians without 'sliding back' into 'heathen' ways of life.

Certainly, missionaries were reluctant to concede that the families of 'native Christians' ever 'developed' sufficiently to reproduce independently. Whilst individual Christians could be found in the present, flourishing Christian communities (at least those with which missionaries were happy) were always located in the future. A boarding school upbringing was thought to be as essential for the raising of the children of Indian Christians as it was for 'heathens' and was justified in surprisingly similar language. Writing in the late 1890s, Miss Barclay catalogued a list of disappointments with the Christian communities in India and went on to write of 'Our Christian Girls', that: 'It [was] simply impossible to allow them to remain in their own homes owing to the filthy language they hear from the heathen round about them and other indecent practices which they see.' Barclay advised that as soon as these Christian Indian girls were 'able to learn' they should be brought to a missionary home where they could be 'trained in ways of virtue and honour'. Barclay believed that 'the state of morality in India is such as to render it highly dangerous to leave any girl-child in the house without someone to protect her', regardless or not of whether it was a Christian one.[34]

Difference was remade upon conversion, difference that had less to do with 'heathenness' than with 'Indianness'. Barclay simply reproduced many of the same tropes for Indian Christian women which had been developed for Hindus that I explored in Chapter 1: not least in the association of the Indian home with 'indecent' behaviour.[35] Instead the English mother and English home were asserted as the superior model.

Missionaries were jealous of the position they had created for their own families as idealised Christian role models and could not easily share it with converts. Representations of the family in these complex moments of vision and re-vision created a layered picture, which formed an ambiguous patina across the images of 'Christian' and 'Heathen' families explored in Chapter 1. In the 'foreign field', missionaries often dealt with the fragmentation of binary systems, through discursively reenforcing difference. This 'othered' converts as well as reaffirmed their own domestic identities which could all too often feel at risk.

The missionary household as a site for convergence

Missionary households were in part defined through their colonial positioning. As Stoler discusses, colonial cultures are 'unique cultural configurations' and never a straightforward export.[36] In looking at Anglo-Indian domesticity, Procida argues that '[i]n creating a home in the empire…Anglo-Indians did not, nor did they intend to, faithfully recreate metropolitan British domesticity.'[37] Although as discussed in Chapter 1, missionaries often represented the movement from metropole to colony as just such a process of export, missionary families also adapted to colonial spaces. Missionary families were influenced by the transient lives of their members and the constant flow of guests from the wider family of missionary sisters and brethren through each station. Sometimes missionaries presented their domestic spaces overseas as exaggerated reifications of English domesticity. As a missionary wife in India wrote, 'all that may be said and urged from the Word of God, upon the duty and particular sphere of wives, in every position, applies with increased force to one occupying so elevated a standing in the church as a missionary's wife.'[38] These representations of the Missionary Family hinged on two things, firstly the insistence on its 'European' or 'English' identity and secondly its presentation as discrete from indigenous families. But, as I go onto explore below, there were many tensions between these desires and the experience of colonial living; tensions that had important implications for the creation of difference.

The household was a key site of missionary identity, embodying an ethnically *English* domestic identity, anchoring gendered familial roles and signifying the moral or religious meanings of a 'Christian Home'. This was not only a construct of missionary propaganda but an ideology that infiltrated their material, imaginative and spiritual worlds. Lacroix, a missionary to Bengal, for example, impressed his children with the importance of the 'sacred circle of the home'.[39] Lacroix's house and garden, set apart from 'Indian' Calcutta, was a place for the daily performance of this identity, through morning family prayers, the taking of tea on Sunday afternoon visits, and by the presence of the family members Lacroix delighted in 'seeing... gathered in an unbroken circle in his truly CHRISTIAN HOME'.[40] These multiple meanings family made, and was made from, worked together to reinforce European identity overseas. On the other hand, the centrality of 'home' to missionary identity meant that anxieties about (ethnic or gender) identity were often manifested in thinking about the home.

'Degeneration' was one such threat which was often configured around the household. Racial status was always vulnerable in the colonial sphere, particularly for children and adolescents. Like other colonial families, British missionaries in both India and southern Africa believed children must be sent back 'home' to Britain in order to maintain their 'racial' and 'cultural' purity.[41] In this case, the imagined national 'home' took precedence over the domestic 'home'. If relatives in Britain could not look after them, girls went to the LMS school in Walthamstow (and later Sevenoaks), and boys to Blackheath.[42] Schooling in Britain was believed to reinforce children's 'English blood' with 'English associations they have secured at home and English training such as their parents enjoyed'.[43]

Missionaries shared these anxieties about degeneration and childhood with other colonial families, but they articulated them through their own prism. Whereas Stoler has demonstrated that amongst Dutch Indies society, cultural interaction, or a child's familiarity with indigenous languages, was seen as an especial cause for concern, in missionary families such knowledge was generally valued.[44] Instead, it was the threat of 'heathenism' and religious interaction (mixed with, and reflected in, physical degeneration) that was particularly feared. Similarly, whilst missionaries used boarding schools from the start, their anxieties about 'degeneration' grew in the mid-century and thus coincided with a period of increased anxiety about the vulnerability of Europeans to a tropical location elsewhere. Again, the shift in missionary thinking was attributed to experiences within the movement. Discussing the practice of sending away children in 1880, it was noted that 'in the early days of the Society, and before a broad experience had shown the moral danger of keeping them among the heathen, they were in the most instances retained at our mission stations till they grew into men and women.' But that with 'a broader experience of the evil to be met with in all tropical countries it has become the habit to send the children home after they are seven years of age'.[45] The Foreign Secretary of the LMS emphasised the absolute

> necessity for sending their children away to this country when they reach the age of five or six, partly that they may escape the injurious effects of tropical climates on the constitution of the young, but chiefly that they may be separated from the polluting moral influence of contact with heathenism.[46]

Removing children from the home did not, however, mean home was any less important as a site of identity formation. The process of home-building was actively used to resist cultural degeneration and to maintain colonial difference. As ideas about degeneration intersected with age, so they did with gender. As I shall discuss in Chapter 4, the corrupting effects of 'the tropics' on the body were often constituted as a problem of women's health. Ideas about *cultural* degeneration, however, were often thought to threaten male missionaries more than their wives or female colleagues, and women were expected to keep their husbands civilised when abroad. 'Our chief work', Elizabeth Price wrote of missionary wives in southern Africa, 'is to keep the husbands *up* – up from sinking down down gradually into native style[s] of living – losing *heart & spirits* in that great work in which we but act as organ *blowers* to the musicians' (emphasis original).[47] Such an aim formed a colonial extension of the civilising influence British women were thought to have at home and was widely reiterated by missionary wives elsewhere.[48]

The performance of a missionary wife's civilising duties, however, differed across colonial sites. When Price wrote from Bechuanaland that it was her wifely duty to keep her husband 'comfortable & his home civilized & Christian-like', she suggested the crucial role of home-making.[49] Of Norwegian missionaries to Madagascar, Skeie notes the importance of 'material things', such as furniture, dress or food, in 'creating and maintaining a "Norwegian" environment'.[50] The same was true of LMS missionaries across southern Africa (beyond the Cape that is), where not only the *possession* of material paraphernalia but its constant washing, cleaning and ordering operated symbolically to embody the wider preservation of 'civilisation' against the corrupting effects of its situation in a 'heathen land'. The proper accoutrements of a civilised meal, for example, were hard to maintain. After a long discussion of the difficulties in laying a tablecloth in an environment where crockery became inexplicably 'speckled', Price concluded that her readers would 'see how difficult a thing it is in this country to keep up civilization & not to go slip-shod'; she continued that she found 'it necessary to be *over* particular rather than *under* for it [sic] one *begins* slipping little duties as of no consequence in such *hard* circumstances – oh how one runs downhill'![51] Maintaining a European identity overseas required constant work.

Missionaries in India faced different challenges around the home and anxiety about the domestic was less frequently expressed in terms of the sheer 'impossibility' of housekeeping. Jane Haggis remarked that '[d]omestic arrangements are notably absent from the surviving writings of the South Travancore missionaries,' something she considered a 'surprising omission', particularly when she compared her findings to that of Patricia Grimshaw on American missionary wives to Hawaii (who seem to have experienced many of the same domestic difficulties as British missionaries to southern Africa).[52] Haggis suggested the difference may be explained by the extensive use of 'suitable' domestic labour there.[53] Certainly, domestic labour was easier to obtain in India, and domestic workers more accustomed to European demands.[54] But there were also other differences between Indian and African circumstances. The procurement of the material elements of 'European' culture was easier in nineteenth-century India than in the southern African interior. Missionary work was less mobile in India than in Africa (where 'pioneer' missionary work continued further into my period and where, even once long-term work was secured, they were vulnerable to periodic settlement removals (the movement of the Ngwato capital from Shoshong to Palapye in 1889 was one such example, traumatic for the missionaries established there).[55] This meant in India less time was spent in wagons (notoriously difficult to upkeep), and home-making was easier. The acquisition of food and preparation of meals, however, proved difficult in India as well as southern Africa, and missionaries complained they had to train their servants personally to make 'puddings' and 'leavened bread'.[56]

The textual strategies through which missionaries to both India and southern Africa framed their domestic struggles were, however, very similar, not least because both used comparisons with 'natives' to reinforce their material performance of colonial home-building. As in Mrs Sewell's confirmation of her domestic role through her encounter with zenana women, discussed in Chapter 1, many missionary wives used their critique of indigenous domesticity to reaffirm their Europeanness. In her journals, Price outlined the 'innumerable things great & small wh. surrounded me & so many of wh. by their possession I found gave me great work, yet without wh. I shd. become as barbarous as Bantsan [her Tswana friend]'.[57]

The very walls of missionary houses came to represent boundaries between 'civilised' and 'uncivilised'. But they also represented the permeation of these boundaries both literally and imaginatively. Price described her home as a structure 'all crumbling away with the worm, the walls cracking, so that in one place we can nearly slide in our hands'.[58] More distressingly, the periodic invasion of her home by African insects embodied her struggle to insulate her 'European' home from 'things African'. She described how

> a nasty *largeish* red spider wh. had literally *haunted* our little table of an evening – coming down regularly from the bookshelf & promenading the cups & saucers, or books & desks, making *me* start off aghast & shuddering & leaving R[oger Price] each time utterly at a loss how to secure & kill the ugly beast – so rapid were its movements. Well, one morning *where* wd. I see the wretch but creeping up my Baby's little petticoats!! I sprang forward with a scream of horror, & smashed & thumped the creature till it was a spider no longer.[59]

In India, it was the heat more than anything else that was felt to pervade and corrupt the home.[60] As in southern Africa, however, attention often focussed on physical boundaries. Certainly those homes that appeared in missionary correspondence were those half built, half fallen down, needing repair, too unhealthy to inhabit, or abandoned altogether. The material fragility of the boundary supposedly demarcating the missionary home from its colonial location was so troubling, because it allowed into the very 'sacred circle' of the missionary home things considered 'other'. It was not only insects that invaded the walls behind which missionaries attempted to protect their identities, servants and visitors represented legitimate, yet also threatening, permeations of these spatial demarcations.

Relationships

When living overseas, missionaries operated in a contact zone of empire, where they intended to interact with and thereby change the peoples they encountered.[61] Many of these encounters occurred, or were predominantly represented as occurring, in public spheres both in indigenous spaces such as markets, bazaars or courts, or in missionary public spaces such as chapels, schools and orphanages. Such interactions were constructed as common, legitimate and desirable. Representations of private spheres are somewhat different.[62] Missionaries and indigenous Africans and Indians were usually constructed as occupying discrete domestic spaces, as missionary and indigenous families were discursively separated into very different homes. Where interaction was acknowledged between them, published writings overwhelmingly represented missionaries entering indigenous homes (the 'penetration' of the zenana being the most iconic example), as opposed to Indians or Africans entering missionary ones. The representation of the missionary home as a 'sacred space' often rested on the exclusion of indigenous peoples from it. However fragile Elizabeth Price's house may have been, she thought of it as a refuge from those with whom she worked:

> we live among these black people and make their cause our own, & their instruction our work & object, yet we count it our greatest luxury to be free fr. them – to retire a little fr. them, as of an evening & to be able to read & write & chat undistracted by their presence – that is, without having to be constantly guiding, checking, rebuking them, as one has where one is face to face with them, poor things.[63]

As such, her home appears to be, at least at certain points of the day, associated with 'whiteness', somewhere free of an intrusive 'black' presence. And yet, African people often came into and sometimes lived *within* Price's household, as they did with those of her colleagues. Here as elsewhere in the 'foreign field', missionary and indigenous families were spatially and emotionally entangled, and indigenous people were always present in the 'white' space of the missionary home.

Indigenous people entered missionary homes in many capacities, some welcome and others perceived as intrusions over the sensitive borders of the 'sacred domain'. Women, ideologically linked with the 'private sphere', felt, and were felt to be, particularly vulnerable to the transgressions of domestic space. James Hepburn, whose relationship with the Ngwato was seen by his employers as worryingly intimate, nevertheless attempted to demarcate the public sphere where he worked from his wife's private domestic sphere, albeit in her wagon. He insisted to an unwanted intruder that 'I should teach neither her nor any other person at my wife's wagon, which must be held to be as sacred from intrusion as her own hut.'[64] Here, Hepburn constructed the missionary home as beyond the normal sphere of missionary activity. Other missionaries, however, did not make this distinction in the same way and welcomed some indigenous people into their home as an intentional aspect of their missionary work.

Political and environmental refugees, converts rejected by their natal families, orphans and other 'destitute' indigenous people were, on occasion, welcomed into the domestic quarters of many missionary stations. Unlike white visitors (who also frequently inhabited missionary homes) these guests occupied an ambiguous role on the edge of missionary households. When Reverend Birt, of Xhosaland, for example, noted in a typically off-hand comment, that he had 'at present, four girls, *besides* [his] own household' (my italics), he located these women outside his 'own household' but within the bounds of his home.[65]

In many cases, this liminal status did not, however, stop such guests from becoming emotionally intimate with the missionary family, particularly, perhaps, children who grew up in missionary households. Annie Coles, for example, became very close to two Indian twins who had been found by the roadside beside their dying parents and sent to her family. Being too young to be sent away to school, it seems that to all intents and purposes, the Coles adopted them. Initially, they had engaged 'a woman' to attend to the twins, but the Coles found her treatment of the boys uncaring and dismissed her – instead the twins shared the attentions of their own boy's *ayah*.[66] The Coles took the twins with them when they moved to Bangalore, and again to Bellary; no mention was made of such an arrangement being temporary. Mrs Coles wrote of them with obvious affection. In many senses, they appear to have become part of the missionary's family. Not knowing their date of birth, Annie Coles wrote: 'I keep their birthday on 2nd May that being my own boy's Birthday. They were all 6 years old last week.'[67]

Despite these intimacies, however, the presence of these children did not mean the *convergence* of missionary and indigenous domesticity. Firstly because, as with the idealised converts discussed towards the beginning of this chapter, the boys were not presented as 'native' and, having been baptised George and John Angel by the Coles's friend, they no longer had Indian names.[68] So little mention of the boys' background was made that, if it was not for a comment that their ornaments and 'elegantly formed hands and good features' suggested they must have been 'high caste', I would otherwise have been unable from Coles's correspondence to know they were Indian.[69] In this sense, they may have been 'whitened' in Coles's writing – as she attempted to maintain a 'white' identity for her household, and the twins were co-opted within it. Following Sara Ahmed, a 'white space' does not necessarily mean a place occupied solely by people who identify as 'white' – places may maintain a cultural 'whiteness' despite the presence of 'non-white' people.[70]

Secondly, despite the emotional connections they clearly developed with the Coles, the status of the twins remained liminal to the family. Financially, they could not be included in the allowances the LMS provided for the Coles's own son. Annie Coles wrote to the Ladies of Carr's Lane, a women's philanthropic organisation in Birmingham, in the hope that they would sponsor the children.[71] Most poignantly, when Annie Coles died suddenly later in 1850, the twins were not sent to England like her own child. They appear to have counted for so little at this moment of crisis that there is no reference to them at all in her husband's correspondence.[72] That the boys were positioned inside the household but ultimately outside the family is also indicative of the peculiar public–private function of the missionary household more generally. The maternal role Annie Coles performed was born of her professional position as a missionary wife, as well as personal attachment. This positioning of children and guests as 'dependents' did not disrupt the missionary family as a 'white space', or a unit of European identity, but instead contributed to missionary projections of themselves as the 'mothers' and 'fathers' of Indians and Africans.

Other indigenous people worked in the missionary household as domestic servants. Despite propaganda images of missionaries as lonely pioneers and missionary wives as upholding the household alone, from their private correspondence, it is clear that, like other colonial families, missionaries were heavily reliant on paid domestic labour. This domestic labour was not always easy to come by. As I discussed above, in Africa, particularly Ndebeleland, missionaries often struggled to secure labour at all.[73] In India too, however, servants were considered 'not of course first rate', and domestic workers, 'whether they be professing Christians or heathens', were a constant source of anxiety.[74] Nevertheless, at the very least, most missionaries employed indigenous women to look after their children, 'ayahs' in India and 'nurses' in Africa.

As with Anglo-Indian families that have been discussed by Fae Dussart and Elizabeth Beuttner, domestic servants performed intimate tasks, from suckling children to washing adults.[75] Such bodily contact between self and other was potentially unsettling and, like other colonial writers, missionaries found that the relationships between their children and indigenous servants were particularly anxious ones.[76] 'Ayahs' were often treated as a destabilising influence, and parents pondered how 'to save the little ones around from the terrible influence of the heathen ayahs and bearers'![77] Indigenous servants were not necessarily Christian and brought 'heathenism' as well as indigineity into the missionary household.[78] Similarly, unlike that of converts, the presence of servants in the missionary home was always marked. Some missionaries felt the influence of servants to be polluting, and suggested their presence, sight, noise and even smell were unwelcome eruptions of 'heathenism' in their own domestic sphere. That missionaries in India believed employing 'Eurasian' and 'East Indian' women lessened the dangers of intimate servant contact with their children is suggestive of the racialised subtexts of such discourses.

The servant–employer relationship also generated anxieties about dependency and social order. In Britain, Davidoff and Hall argue that servants moved between public and private manifestations of the family, occupying a liminal space between the family and the workforce.[79] In the colonial sphere, such transgressions were liable to acquire racialised dynamics as well as the classed elements that shaped them at home.[80] As Dussart argues: 'Servants, though positioned as subordinates within the Anglo-Indian home, nevertheless had the power to subvert its order and disrupt its sanctity.'[81] Servants similarly inverted the established missionary positioning of indigenous people as dependents.

In the writings of missionary women, it seems that the help servants could provide was mitigated by the additional work they generated. Training servants was a discourse integral to any discussions of domestic labour which extended public conceptualisations of missionaries imparting knowledge into the private sphere and reasserted the alignment of English women with domestic authority and indigenous women with dirt and disorder. Elizabeth Price evocatively described literally scrubbing her new servant girl, Maméri, before allowing her to touch her baby:

> First I stripped her – or told her father to take every bead away with him – for reasons wh. I perhaps [had] better not state in a letter for my refined English friends, or they might get a horror of Africa – & never become missionaries... I popped her into a bath and set to scrubbing her till the perspiration streamed off me, such was the energy required – for there seemed layer after layer of dirt to come away ere I could call her fit to take my beautiful little one.[82]

This dehumanising description recalls Elizabeth's revulsion at the intrusion of insects, dirt and other transgressive 'things African' into her home. The difference Maméri represented was unimaginable and indescribable for Price's English readers. Managing servants was a means of controlling such interruptions and repackaging dependence as a task in which missionary wives could demonstrate both their Christian patience and their domestic authority. As Mrs Weitbrecht wrote of her servants from India, '[t]heir cheating, lying, pilfering, and deceitful habits, form one of our greatest outward trials, but yet they may be managed, and we may enjoy even take comfort from them, by understanding the best way of teaching them.'[83] In portraying themselves cleaning their servants rather than being cleaned by them, missionaries in both India and southern Africa re-encrusted the cultural hierarchy upon which their work depended, and re-presented themselves as invested with the moral associations of purity their servants were thought to lack.

Sexuality added another intimate and complicating dimension to relationships within the home. Phillipa Levine argues that sexuality was always 'prominent among the anxieties associated with imperialism', because it 'has constantly blurred those always unstable boundaries' constructed in 'modern Western societies' around 'public and private' and 'male and female'.[84] Sexual relationships were another site through which essentialised constructions of difference were problematised by the experience of coloniality. But besides *blurring* boundaries, discourses around sexuality also tended to clarify, or articulate, categorising agenda that were otherwise vague and unspoken. Some sexual relationships caused 'outrage' or 'disappointment' in the LMS as missionaries married below their class, or, particularly problematically, had relationships with 'native' women. Such relationships, subjected to the institutional scrutiny of the LMS (often in the form of tribunals), were 'breaches' or 'transgressions' that illuminated and codified the boundaries they crossed.

The locations of boundaries within which sexual relationships were to be contained, however, were unstable and varied over time and place. Emily Manktelow has demonstrated that in the very first years of the LMS, the society's approach to marriage was ambivalent.[85] Marriage was often discouraged altogether due to the expense and potential inconvenience of up-keeping missionary families.[86] When marriage was undertaken, a European wife was not necessarily considered advantageous over an indigenous woman. Indeed, members of the LMS argued that in the South Seas, missionaries 'would do well' to build 'matrimonial connexions' with early converts.[87] Marriages with indigenous women were, in this case, thought to be cheap, offer protection, and to produce the seeds for the development of new Christian communities.[88] By the end of the eighteenth century, however, such policies were rapidly changing.

In southern Africa, the scandals concerning missionary relationships with African women, discussed in Chapter 2, and the LMS's 'Synod' of investigation into them (held in 1817) consolidated race as a boundary between missionaries and indigenous women that should not be sexually 'breached'.[89] As Elbourne argues, although the 'disorder' the Synod identified was publicly defined as 'adulterous' or 'slovenly' sexual conduct rather than as miscegenation, it also made it clear that sexual relationships between LMS missionaries and African women were 'irregular' in their own right. The LMS was also re-thinking its approach to missionary relationships with indigenous women elsewhere in this period. Its reaction to similar sexual scandals in Tahiti indicated a broader LMS shift towards an ideology against cross-cultural marriage.[90] It soon became clear that European relationships with indigenous people could not be 'respectable'.

By 1840, the Missionary Family that I described in Chapter 1 as racially and culturally discrete from indigenous families was already entrenched. All missionary sexuality was expected to occur within marriage; LMS missionaries were encouraged to marry socially 'respectable' and constitutionally 'robust' partners who would act as 'helpmeets' in the day-to-day running of their missions. Usually, missionaries married before departure. Once abroad, however, those missionaries who faced the early death of a spouse might re-marry into colonial societies (to Anglo-Indians in India and to settlers in southern Africa), without incurring criticism, though many chose second wives from within the missionary community itself. Theoretically, such partnerships prevented male missionaries from forming 'unsuitable' relationships with indigenous women and this included *marriage* as well as extra-marital affairs. For all that cross-cultural relationships were forbidden, however, they continued to occur, though determining how frequently is difficult.[91]

In 1851, Mr Mead, a British Missionary whose second wife had recently died, decided to remarry again, this time to a 'native' woman.[92] It was immediately evident to Mead's colleagues in India and the Directors in Britain that in doing so he had transgressed a boundary: they were scandalised.[93] Marriage was a way of maintaining European identity in India, and in the eyes of his colleagues, Mead's choice of partner irreparably breached that identity. Little was said about the matter publicly, and it was Mead's colleagues, not Mead himself, who conveyed his news to the society, but the marriage was considered utterly 'inappropriate'. The religious or class status of the woman was not mentioned in the associated correspondence; it seems her 'race' or 'Indianness' spoke for itself. That Mead was otherwise well respected and had served the society a long time could not save his career. Although one colleague suggested he and his wife should be quietly re-stationed somewhere remote, in the face of his marriage to 'an Indian', his connection with the LMS was dissolved.[94] In 1850s-India, it seems that the racial difference of Indians had acquired the power of an unspoken rule, and that this must be retained in private as well as in public.[95] A mixed-race partnership was inconceivable as a basis for the Missionary Family. Race had become a boundary within which sexual relationships must be contained.

Just like other colonial thinkers, missionaries continued to find 'mixed-race' relationships unacceptable over the course of the nineteenth century, and the difference of Indians and Africans was thought to be self-evident. During a period of intense debate about 'native' Christians in India during the 1880s, Reverend Kennedy, an LMS missionary recently retired from work in Benares, summed up the LMS position:

> ...missionaries do not marry Indians, nor give over their daughters to the best converts. If they tried there would be rebellion against parental authority. I am not aware that missionaries to Madagascar

> marry Malagasy women, or missionaries to Africa, African women. There are good reasons why they should not. When they leave their native land they do not leave behind them their habits of thought and life; they might as well try to leave the colour of their skin behind them ...[96]

The difference between indigenous people and missionaries, whether that was expressed in terms of religion, cultural 'habits' or skin colour, had become insurmountable.

Class, respectability, religious piety, health/fitness and race were all lines within which the LMS attempted to enclose its missionary families. As race became increasingly present as a demarcating factor, this always fluid category had to be deployed as though solid in missionary practice. At the same time, missionaries had to confront race as a category that offered no such boundaries and one that was impossible to extricate from ideas about class and culture.

It was not only of dichotomous constructions ('us' and 'them' or 'white' and 'black') where boundaries were felt to need policing, far more often sexual transgressions clustered around more ambiguous categories. Two examples of how these slippages occurred (contemporary to that of Mead) can be taken from the Tamil mission in the 1850s. Documents for the Madras Tamil missions are a particularly rich source – as the LMS historian recorded, 'The District committee of those days was a curiosity ... it having been found that the brethren agreed better when apart than together ... all business was transacted by correspondence.'[97] The excellent bureaucratic record that developed in response to a set of relationships already tense allows for an interesting insight into less professional relationships that missionaries otherwise endeavoured to keep hidden.

In comparison with the muffled discussion of Mead's marriage, his colleague's (Mr Nimmo's) relationships were the subject of several enquiries, one missionary tribunal and at least two Supreme Court investigations concerning 'libel'. There were also many pages of official LMS correspondence, which told the following story. In 1855, a 'native woman' had come to Tripassore (where Nimmo was stationed) from Cambassum, bringing with her 'her daughter of whom she had openly asserted that Mr Nimmo was the father'.[98] When Reverend George Hall, the secretary of the District Committee, and his colleagues went to Tripassore to investigate, they 'heard so much that making every allowance for the native character' – they felt it their 'duty' to 'lay the matter before our Committee'.[99] The ensuing tribunals dragged up further tensions and allegations concerning the organisation of Nimmo's mission, caste practice on his station and a history of personal antagonism between Hall and Nimmo.

Part of what made Nimmo's case so complex was that he was not a 'British' missionary but a Calcutta-born 'East Indian', meaning that the case involved the intersection of two layers of racialisation: the relationship between an 'East Indian' and a 'native', and the relationship between the 'East Indian' and the 'British' missionary communities. The term 'East Indian' is an ambiguous one which changed over time and often coincided with alternative (also unstable) labels such as 'Eurasian' or 'Anglo-Indian'. The LMS sometimes used 'East Indian' to refer to missionaries of European descent who were born and raised in India (outside of the missionary community). At other points, 'East Indian' also referred to Indian-born people of mixed European and Indian ancestry – those discussed elsewhere as 'Eurasians'. These missionaries occupied a problematic place in the racial hierarchy, performing many of the same roles as British missionaries (unlike 'native' preachers, catechists or evangelists who always had lower status roles) but receiving less pay.[100] 'Racial' identity was often deliberately obscured by East Indians, unsurprisingly, given the status at stake in these racial namings.[101] Attempting to determine 'colour' in these patterns of racialisation is unhelpful. They were a distinct and substantial community which missionaries could easily identify and, in Madras in the 1850s, they mobilised as a group in Nimmo's defence.

In the course of the lengthy allegations following Hall's investigation into Nimmo's relationships, a personal battle developed between Reverend Hall and the East Indian community in Madras.[102] In Hall's writing, the issue was deeply racialised although it was hinged on the language of 'community' and 'class' rather than 'race'. 'There is a deep feeling against us especially among the East Indian Community which is very large here'; he wrote, 'they look upon the whole case as one of persecution against their class and they are certainly heaping the bitterest reproaches on me and the Society.'[103] Hall continued that the case served as 'an indication that East Indians cannot be connected with our mission.'[104] It is significant that the underlying racial antagonism latent between these communities was exposed and intensified at this moment. Intimate relationships (especially gone bad) marked the social boundaries between different groups. Hall's understanding of the racial status of 'East Indians' was complicatedly entwined with thinking about sexuality, as 'transgressive' sexuality blurred a series of boundaries between categories of difference missionaries liked to keep separate.

Almost concurrently with Nimmo's case, the same Madras subcommittee was investigating an alternative case of 'misdemeanours': those of Mr Paul. Paul was an 'assistant missionary' and a 'native' Indian who in 1856 had worked for the LMS for nearly 30 years. Three months after his wife died, he remarried a 'fair East Indian' woman – Rachel – who, although she could not satisfy the LMS with the depth of her Christian conviction, had attended an LMS girls school run by Mrs Porter until her marriage.[105] Only three months after their marriage, Rachel gave birth to a baby. Paul, denying the child was his, asked for a divorce. Again the Madras missionaries were anxious both to investigate and conceal the scandal.[106]

Attempts to determine the paternity of the baby demonstrate the ongoing struggle with the intangibility of 'racial' difference and yet they refused to abandon it as 'evidence' of identity. Rachel (herself racialised as a 'fair East Indian') accused a 'sergeant' of the nearby Deveton College of seducing her. But who exactly this man was remained unclear. An exasperated Reverend Gordon asked

> who and what is this Sergeant? We are not told. I presume he is either a European or East Indian (for I never heard of a native being so called). Now the colour of Rachel's child is said to be 'very dark'. It is strange that so dark a child can be the offspring of a European or East Indian![107]

As in Nimmo's case, there were several 'racial' hierarchies operating here, and Gordon, like his colleagues, looked to 'colour' as an indicator of race, class and cultural status. Yet information about 'race' was neither forthcoming nor visually evident. Discussions of the baby's exact 'colour', in the correspondence on this case, also point towards the perception of miscegenation as a threat to racial boundaries, deeply disturbing to missionary thinking. Like Nimmo, as an East Indian, Rachel was both racialised and sexualised, a characerisation compounded by her own illegitimacy.[108] It is typical that the discussion of difference was more anxious in situations where such status was already ambiguous and unstable than when difference was thought to be clear-cut.

The only charge the society could insist upon with any certainty in Paul's case was that, somewhere along the line, he had deliberately concealed Rachel's pregnancy. It was apparently due to these 'lies' that he was demoted to the inferior position of a 'catechist' with a reduced salary, at the outstation of Palucut – a change of scene where it was hoped, in time, he would 'redeem his character'.[109] Nimmo's case dragged on until he won a libel charge against Hall, which Hall found devastating. But despite Nimmo's efforts to maintain a position in the society, the LMS distanced itself from him, and his connection with the society was eventually dissolved. In both cases, the interplay of 'race' and 'sexuality' at the edge of 'family life' was considered damaging. Some missionaries transgressed boundaries that their colleagues were keen to maintain.

Conclusion

This chapter has explored conversion, missionary households and the relationships formed between missionaries and indigenous people as three sites where the boundary between missionary homes and 'heathen' ones was unstable. These experiences could both challenge essentialised constructions of difference discussed in Chapter 1 and reconfigure and solidify them. Difference and identity had to be constructed discursively and performed daily. Missionary families were not so homogeneously white, British, Christian and 'blood-bound' as they superficially appeared, and the boundaries between who was and who was not considered 'family' were in some respects permeable. But these discourses of permeability could only take place in reference to the essentialised discourses discussed in the previous chapter.

Missionaries developed many strategies for containing the threat posed by these permeations. Although Indians and Africans may have entered missionary homes, their presence was limited to subordinate roles which helped to limit their threat. That in some forms of writing their very presence was denied was another form of containment. Those relationships that could not be contained were perceived as transgressive. Transgressions could solidify boundaries that were otherwise vague and demanded the articulation of difference that was otherwise unspoken. Realisations of proximity provided new urgency to seal the boundaries policing identity. The home was a central place where racial difference could be re-stated, but it was not, of course, the only such location. Chapter 3 investigates how similar issues about the making and re-making of difference were configured on the body.

Part II

Sickness and the Embodiment of Difference

Overview

> The Gospel of the Christ of God is pre-eminently for the salvation of the soul, but it acts through the body, and must bring salvation to the *body* from all that is physically or spiritually impure.[1]

Thorne argues that 'by contrast to its humanitarian predecessor, missionary philanthropy ministered to souls and not to bodies, at least during the first half of the nineteenth century.'[2] Missionaries often claimed the same, that they were concerned with 'the soul', and thereby unlike 'mere philanthropists'. Yet much of their time was occupied with covering, cleaning, treating and describing the body. The body was also a site where difference was located. Universalistic conceptions of humanity were fragmented by a focus on bodily difference: 'women' were divided from 'men', 'adults' from 'children', 'black' from 'white' and 'sick' from 'healthy'. The body acted as a prism through which colonial and colonised societies were refracted and understood, suggesting that the discourses thereby produced were essentially discourses of embodied difference. Missionaries saw difference as inscribed on the body in a number of different senses. Their ethnological writings described the appearance of those they met in language which had some overlap with anthropological discourses on race. Missionary travel writing frequently evoked indigenous people in bodily terms, from encounters with 'poor naked bushmen' in Africa to those with Indian Garrows 'looking rather fierce'.[3] Their preoccupations with the regulation of sexuality, cleanliness, dress and child-rearing reflected other ways in which 'the body' featured in their thinking and practice.

Part II uses writing about sickness as a way into thinking about the importance of the body in missionary constructions of difference.[4] Sickness is a key theme in missionary thinking and an important discourse of difference that needs to be considered alongside those of gender and race. As Rod Edmond argues, 'the operation of a health/disease dichotomy was a crucial but, very unstable, marker of difference within and across these defining characteristics of race, gender and class.'[5] Not only disease but also medical knowledge could operate to mark difference. In her study of colonial medicine in East Africa, Megan Vaughan powerfully demonstrates that medicine 'played an important part in constructing "the African" as an object of knowledge.'[6] Missionary thinking about both sickness and medicine helped to construct both Africans and Indians as 'others'.

As noted in the introduction, postcolonial and disability theorists have drawn attention to the intersections between racism, colonialism and disability, both in terms of shared social and political subordination, and in the metaphorical linkages between them. Deaf activists have deployed the language of colonial resistance to claim members of the Deaf community as a linguistic minority, with a distinct culture, suffering the 'physical subjugation of a disempowered people' under 'the imposition of alien language and mores, and the regulation of education on behalf of the colonizer's goals'.[7] Colonising formulations have also drawn on this shared language – leper asylums as 'colonies', for example. From the opposite perspective, the language of disability has been used rhetorically by some postcolonial critics: Ato Quayson, for example, discusses processes of 'disabling the colonized' that have been created by economic and social exploitation.[8] Such imagery is powerful, but as Mark Sherry argues, the transfer of metaphors between disability, race and colonialism is potentially problematic.[9] A straightforward conflation is not only offensive, but conceptually confusing, blurring very different experiences and marginalising distinctive and divergent cultural constructions and patterns of stigmatisation. This chapter intends to explore rather than reproduce these rhetorical conflations and unpick the relationship between sickness or disability and race, gender and religion carefully. The metaphorical slippage between sickness and 'race' is taken as a useful subject of analysis in its own right, illuminating as it does the axes of power in the formulation of difference.

Related to discourses of sickness are those of medicine and 'cure'. Over the course of the nineteenth century, medicine was increasingly used as a 'tool of empire' to intervene in indigenous societies and to 'colonize the body' (in David Arnold's phrase) epistemologically, through the assertion of 'western' medicine's superiority over indigenous healing.[10] As I discuss in Chapter 3, from the 1860s, missionary societies also conceived of medicine as a 'tool', in this case to effect conversion. This represented a major change in policy. Engagement in medicine was shunned in the first half of the nineteenth century as a costly diversion from 'true' evangelisation, but such activities gradually became accepted; by 1900 medical work was enthusiastically endorsed (at least in some mission fields) as a key to the hearts and minds of potential converts.[11]

One reason why medicine became an increasingly popular area of missionary work was the growing western confidence in biomedicine (a biologically rooted form of therapy) in this period. The early nineteenth century saw significant innovations in the conceptualisation and design of medical instruments, such as the stethoscope, and pharmacological advances in drug therapy, which fuelled this confidence.[12] Developments in anaesthesia and antiseptics further changed the medical landscape.[13] Many of these changes can be seen in the work of medical missionaries who gradually endorsed new 'hygienic' practices, distributed newly developed powders and solutions and attempted innovative surgical procedures themselves. However, as I demonstrate in Chapter 4, this is only part of the story. There are strong continuities in the way in which missionaries thought about illness over the course of the nineteenth century. Throughout my period, the more subjective frameworks of climate, constitution and trauma were held up as explicatory factors that operated outside new biomedical frameworks.

Chapter 3 investigates sickness as a discourse of difference in missionary thinking by exploring how the wider language of sickness conjured up fears beyond those of biological disease. I use missionary treatments (textual and material) of disability and disease to explore processes through which 'heathenism' was pathologised and difference embodied in their thought. Chapter 4 uses sickness to think about the missionary experience as one that was also embodied. Missionaries had much less to say about their own bodies, made invisible through their normative construction, than those 'heathen' bodies they perceived as 'peculiar'. The historiography of missionaries, prolific on missionary interventions in indigenous bodies and quiet on their own medical experiences, has tended to repeat this pattern.[14] One of my aims in discussing sick missionaries is to move away from the missionary orientation of sickness/health around heathen/Christian constructions, respectively. This second chapter, then, explores how missionaries' own experiences of sickness in the 'foreign field' were mediated through and contributed to the sense of their own alterity.

3
Pathologising Heathenism: Discourses of Sickness and the Rise of Medical Missions

Sickness and the depiction of a dangerous 'foreign field'

In both missionary discourse, and wider imperial imagery, Africa was constructed as a 'sick continent', a 'wound' or a 'sore' upon the earth. As Megan Vaughan writes: 'From Livingstone onwards, reports from Central and Eastern Africa insisted that the continent was "sick" and suffering from the evils of the slave trade, from paganism and the creeping forces of Islam', images she suggests were important in demarcating Africans as people to be pitied.[1] The language of sickness also shaped conceptualisations of India. Sickness became part of the 'spectacle of heathenism' and was represented in missionary writing by crowds of sick, emaciated or dehumanised bodies, of 'but shadows of men' and 'mere skeletons, tottering along rather than walking' in the aftermath of famine and cholera.[2] The very real epidemics, famines and droughts that affected India and Africa in this period were discursively mobilised to position colonised peoples as vulnerable and dependent on the 'west'.[3] As missionaries evoked 'new and untouched fields of vast extent teeming with millions of the perishing heathen', they constructed 'the tropics' as places of bodily suffering, as well as of spiritual deprivation.[4]

Disease, disability, disorder and danger are related through complex webs of metaphorical associations.[5] On the one hand, disease can be experienced metaphorically – as an 'attack' or an 'invasion', for example.[6] On the other hand, the real or imagined experience of disease is so powerful that it is often used to conceptualise negativity *beyond* bodily boundaries. As Susan Sontag explored, 'the subjects of deepest dread ... are identified with the disease' so that 'the disease becomes adjectival'.[7] In Victorian Britain, the 'body politic' aided the conceptualisation of social problems as 'diseases'.[8] These processes often interact. Images of 'contagion' shaped both the conceptualisation of disease (as in the development of germ theory) and the pathologisation of social changes (such as racial integration).[9] 'Disorder' was conceptualised as disease, and disease, 'disorder'.[10]

In the nineteenth century, place became an important part of the metaphorical linkages forged between disease and disorder.[11] In Britain, the industrial city was understood to be physically diseased, rife with cholera and tuberculosis, and a disease to the body politic itself.[12] Overseas, similar thinking operated to construct Africa and India as places of sickness in their entireties. Particular climates or geographical areas became associated with particular diseases: for example, many believed that Bengal was the 'natural home' of cholera and was peculiarly unhealthy.[13] Africa was more abstractly imagined as the 'white man's grave'.[14] Significantly, increasing tendencies over the nineteenth century to conceptualise the tropics as places of medical danger was accompanied by a contemporaneous development of ideas about moral and social 'degeneration' in colonial spaces.[15] In missionary discourse, many such fears crystallised around 'heathenism' and were interpreted through an overtly moral framework.

More so than most colonial thinkers, missionaries contemplated the way in which disease and disorder were suggested to interact in scriptural texts. In both the New Testament and the Hebrew Bible, disease and disability are intimately linked to sin. Some texts suggest a causal relationship between sin and disability such as blindness as punishment.[16] Others use disability and disease to evoke sin figuratively: blindness, to continue with the same example, is often used to symbolise sin, wickedness, confusion, directionlessness and ignorance. Such metaphors play both on blindness as not-seeing, and on impaired mobility, depicting blind people as physically and spiritually lost and sinners as 'groping like those who have no eyes'.[17] In the New Testament, associations like this were compounded by the equation of Jesus with 'light'.

These images were intensely powerful in missionary discourse and often acquired racial dimensions. Not only were missionaries, as Christians, 'enlightened' but, through the complementary metaphor of 'darkness', dark skins were equated with 'dark' spirituality and, through this, with blindness. The Brahmins were described as 'a race of blind guides', 'heathenism' was itself depicted as 'blind', and indigenous critics of missionaries were claimed to have minds that were 'blindly prejudiced by their own religion.'[18] Christianity (like 'civilisation') was depicted as sightedness, and the giving of sight (like making light) was a powerful metaphor for conversion.[19] Reverend Mullens, a senior missionary in India, wrote that whilst 'Christianity, certainly, is a sun ... of great resplendency', it 'finds the Hindus so blinded by their idolatrous creed and their prejudices, that it shines upon them in vain'. Continuing in a vein reflective of mid-nineteenth century trends towards surgical treatments of blindness, Mullens proposed that 'A surgical operation [was] requisite to remove the cataract from their spiritual vision', an operation he believed would expose the errors of their system.[20]

Encountering disease and disability

Whilst Africa and India were metaphorically depicted as sick places, missionaries also read difference off 'actual' sickness, which they often found shocking. Elizabeth Price wrote that she would 'never ... forget the sight [she] beheld' when her family passed a sick woman on a journey to Kuruman in the 1860s.

> A creature – a human being – lay beneath the tree ... A very skeleton – emaciated to a terrible degree – yet bloated & swollen in some parts of her poor body and face! Oh Horrible! ... I also observed that her bosom was full – as of a nursing woman ... She gazed at us vacantly – half like an idiot. We all seemed struck motionless at the horrible sight ... I leant out and enquired what [sic] she was? ... we were horrified by the scene ... [21]

Perhaps because her comments were made in a personal letter, not intended for publication, Price's remarks deviate markedly from the benevolent approach to sickness which, as discussed below, was often projected in medical missionary propaganda. The visuality of the scene is striking and the women's body is objectified, rendered a spectacle in Price's memory. It is significant that the woman's own gaze was 'vacant': this colonial gaze was classically one-directional.

In this way, indigenous people who were ill became part of the visual spectacle of 'heathenism'. In contrast to the euphemistic way in which they wrote about their own illnesses (see Chapter 4, below), missionaries described sick Indians and Africans in crudely somatic terms. Textual depictions were frequently graphic. Discourses around leprosy spawned particularly explicit images: of 'crippled' lepers crawling to chapel and those with disfigured hands and mouths fumbling the communion cup.[22] By the later nineteenth century, photographs of a whole variety of suffering people were used to illustrate missionary magazines; images of emaciated famine victims making a particularly compelling form of voyeuristic viewing.

Both textual and visual images of the diseased and the dying reflected the horror often evoked by encounters with sickness. Although missionaries sheltered behind the hope that people who were sick were in some way 'different' to themselves, this form of difference was terrifyingly unstable: missionaries themselves were unavoidably vulnerable to pain and suffering. Fear of contagion generated vulnerability: sick people could represent a potential threat to missionaries' own bodies. Besides being frightened by the appearance of the woman discussed above, the Prices drove away from her because many of their party were 'unvaccinated'.[23]

But as fearful as Victorian missionaries may have been of the epidemics they found both epistemologically and theologically baffling, their fear was often displaced onto indigenous cultures, where the 'native' 'horror' at disease was presented as spectacle itself. Despite noting his own 'dread' of smallpox, it was the Indians, Reverend Bacon wrote, who were 'terribly afraid' of cholera. In the midst of the late 1880s' cholera epidemic, Bacon sympathised with 'the poor creatures' who must find it 'sudden and mysterious' because they stood on 'the brink of the, to them, great unknown, without light or guide.' Firmly distancing himself from 'Indian' fears of cholera, Bacon explained it not by the deadly disease itself but by their lack of Christian faith through which to experience it – a lack that was animalising. Unlike Bacon himself or, he supposed, his British readers, 'their hope [was] not brightened, nor their sorrow lightened, by the thought of Him.'[24] Indigenous treatments of illness were similarly reduced to a spectacle, caricatured as 'absurd and sinful': at best rendered curiosities, at worst treated with horror.[25]

Given the symbolic encoding of disability, the presence of people who were physically disabled in missionary writing become powerful embodiments of 'heathenism'. People who were blind were used to symbolise, in bodily terms, the 'dark' worldview of the East. One missionary wrote of the 'never-varying cry' of 'an old blind beggar' he passed each day: '"One pice! one pice! God has given you everything; give me one pice!"' For the missionary, the cry, evoked 'the East calling to the West', 'the East' he went on to state explicitly was 'old, blind, starving – begging from us – rich through the mercy of God'.[26] Blindness and age marked the colonial other as different: spiritual metaphors appeared embodied.

Although reports of blindness are common in both Indian and African missionary writings, it is perhaps unsurprising that they are particularly prevalent in accounts of the zenana, which was otherwise linked with 'darkness'.[27] In a striking instance, Mrs Mullens discussed a promising pupil, Jotee, and her identical twin sister, Abee, the latter of whom was completely blind. Jotee, the sighted twin, was depicted as intelligent, eager to learn about British 'civilisation' and open to Christian teaching. Abee, the blind twin, was constructed as firmly entrenched in 'heathenism'. Mullens described how she 'longed to pour the light of truth into' Abee; 'if only', she lamented, Abee would 'sit at the feet of Him who giveth sight to the blind, happy would it have been for her', but Abee was, she lamented, 'a worshipper of Krishno', doomed to a life of darkness, bodily and spiritual.[28] Blindness here as elsewhere was experienced through a metaphorical film which equated physical and spiritual disability.

People with disabilities could symbolise 'heathen' evil in the pitiful form that Abee appeared to embody. But it could also take less passive forms. 'Disease' or 'disfigurement' could be emblematic of a particular culture, as well as an abstract 'evil'. Foot-binding in China and female genital cutting in Africa were used to suggest that women were being actively 'disabled' by 'heathenism'. The woman injured in childbirth was another trope of 'heathenism' which recurred in missionary thinking across the globe and appeared to consolidate the assumption that indigenous cultures were damaging and cruel. In these examples, bodily disorder formed yet another way to articulate (particularly female) 'heathen' suffering. 'Where heathen systems...have their full sway, woman has always been more or less degraded,' Reverend Burman Cassin deplored, 'in some places she is crippled for life.'[29] The 'crippled' woman, foot-bound, mutilated or otherwise disfigured often became emblematic of the culture itself, as well as symbolising an abstract 'evil'.

The discursive relationship between race and sickness was, however, unstable. Disability often carries contradictory associations and certainly did so in Victorian culture. People with disabilities were not only used to represent evil, but also heroic or tragic struggles *against* it; they could embody virtue as well as sin.[30] Whilst the blindness of 'heathens' may embody that 'heathenism' in missionary texts, the blindness of *Christians* was used to emphasise spiritual sightedness.[31] Christians who were blind were often presented as suffering heroically and gifted with an unusual clarity of religious or moral 'vision'.

Missionary responses to leprosy sufferers can be read in this light. As Vaughan and Edmond have explored in different contexts, scriptural teachings invested leprosy with conflicting meanings. In *Leviticus*, leprosy is equated with 'pollution' and 'sin'. Conversely, Jesus' benevolence towards lepers provided a New Testament imperative to philanthropic action and presented lepers as needy victims. Missionary writers drew on both these trajectories, evoking sin as 'the leprosy of the soul', but lepers as pious converts.[32] In the LMS asylum at Almorah, the high numbers of conversions (by 1891, 79 out of a total of 112 inmates had converted to Christianity) meant that lepers often appeared in missionary writing as examples of the suffering 'saved'. Mausuwa, the first convert at Amorah, was described as giving 'clear testimony of his faith' and, though 'laden with years and frailty, and disease', as having 'a bright and cheerful spirit', with which to help his 'suffering companions' to 'bear patiently the sad load they have to bear'.[33]

Representations of sickness complicate the construction of ethnic difference in missionary thinking. Sometimes, sickness seems to usurp the ethnic differentiation paramount elsewhere. A person may be reduced to their disability: their blindness, deafness or disfigurement, for example, and this, rather than say their colour, may be conceived as the most striking thing about them. Vaughan discusses the construction of a 'leper identity' in missionary discourse around leprosy asylums in East Africa.[34] In the writings of LMS missionaries too, being a 'leper', especially a 'pious leper', could indeed absorb other forms of identity. Descriptions of the bodies of leprosy sufferers (which were detailed) were not explicitly racialised – there was no mention of skin colour, or other 'racial' markers, but only those of disfigurement. And yet race was still there, operating as a silent signifier. The fact that these bodies were being described at all was a marker of their difference – European bodies, diseased or otherwise, did not appear in this way (at least in writings produced overseas).

The language of sickness pathologised cultures as well as people. The disabled bodies of indigenous people could operate to signify the wrongs of that culture itself. The foot-bound woman evoked China, women with genital cuttings embodied Africa, women injured in childbirth evoked all 'heathen lands' and were, in missionary thinking, 'disfigured' and disabled. And yet, at other points, disabled people are presented as liminal to their cultures, as 'outsiders' occupying a marginal position, not least because disabled people were often recorded as having been 'forsaken' by their families and rejected by their communities.[35]

These very different meanings inscribed by and onto disability created the fluidity in missionary thinking about sickness that allowed people who were sick to be associated with both heathen otherness and Christian renewal. There was the suggestion that difference could be dissolved, and body and soul 'healed'. By equating indigenous African and Indian bodies with suffering, and metaphorically linking 'heathenism', sin and disability, the body was depicted as a site through which missionaries could work.

The rise of medical missions

From the 1860s onwards, medical missions became an important way in which missionaries interacted materially and discursively with the body. In the LMS, as in other British missionary societies, the development of medical missions was hotly disputed, as is reflected in their hesitant expansion. For some decades after the Edinburgh Medical Missionary Society (EMMS) was founded in 1841, it struggled to survive; attitudes to 'medical missionaries' were ambivalent, and they were often discouraged. Many argued medical work distracted from evangelisation, and the criticism that medical missionaries were prone 'to mix up medicine with religion', and 'sought to attract persons to religious services by the bait of cheap doctoring' was made both at home and overseas.[36] The quality of converts gained through medical 'bribes' was said to be poor, and they were costly converts to make.

During the 1860s, however, the sick body became an important site of missionary intervention. The LMS began to employ increasing numbers of missionaries with formal medical training – 39 by 1908, becoming the third largest employer of medics of British Protestant missionary societies.[37] The historiographical debate around this change of direction is substantial and unresolved.[38] Some claim it arose from a reconfiguration of the role of 'benevolence' in Christian thinking.[39] Others argue that medical work was a 'tool' to induce conversion; either through wonder healings or through strategically targeting people when they were at their most vulnerable.[40] Still others suggest medicine was most useful as a means to reach people who were otherwise inaccessible to them, such as women, to win the 'hearts and minds' of those uninterested in Christianity and to 'disguise' proselytisation.[41] Many LMS missionaries were motivated by several of these rationales simultaneously. They claimed that medical missions were successful because people were more susceptible to conversion when spiritually and physically 'weakened' by illness, when their 'heart' was 'softened by disease and pain and suffering'.[42]

The Travancore medical mission, developed in the 1860s, was the archetypical example of such a mission and its physical design and the daily routines it anchored embodied many of these desires.[43] It was one of the largest spheres of LMS medical missionary activity and by 1900 it was treating two fifths of LMS patients across the world. With Neyoor as its head station, it developed into a large network of hospitals and dispensaries. By 1895, the Neyoor hospital had 33 beds, saw 957 in-patients and, 41,363 outpatients a year, and had 15 dispensaries and 23 assistants, figures that made more satisfying reading than attendance figures in local churches, schools or other missionary institutions.[44]

In the hospital, bodily and spiritual healing were intimately connected. Patients would be read Bible extracts (usually parables and miracle stories) and the missionary staff would 'remind' the patients 'of the awful disease that afflicts their souls, and... point them to Jesus, the great Physician, who alone can cure them.'[45] All kinds of cases were seen, including cholera, injuries, small-pox, tumours, blindness and fevers. Though very variable in terms of expertise, method and success, the techniques missionaries used to treat these injuries and illnesses could be pioneering, with some discussed in the *Lancet*.[46] Surgery was also important in treating injury and, later, cataracts. Some patients were admitted and submitted to a rigorous daily routine of prayer, bathing and treatment. Others were treated as out-patients and given an appointment card which they were instructed 'must be kept clean'.[47] Printed on each card was the patient's name and hospital number, 'the rules of the hospital, eight appropriate passages of Scripture, and a short prayer.'[48] Such a card, and such a daily routine, can be seen as reflecting the combined aims of medical treatment, 'civilisation' and Christianisation, which were at the heart of the medical mission. Cleanliness, orderliness, treatment and prayer were combined in an overall process of *healing*.

Despite the globalised claims of medical missionaries, their work took different forms across different sites of empire, even within the LMS. The vast majority of LMS medical work was concentrated in the East. In India, the large medical mission in Travancore and a leprosy asylum in Almorah, in the North-west province of Kumoan, were established in the 1860s.[49] By the early twentieth century, India had 23 LMS-run missionary hospitals and asylums. From the 1880s, women were involved, both within the medical missions discussed above, and as 'lady zenana doctors' visiting Indian women who would not be treated by male doctors, usually in their homes.[50]

At the same point in the late nineteenth century, there were no qualified LMS doctors or nurses in southern Africa and, beyond an abortive attempt to build a hospital at Molepolole, there were no LMS hospitals.[51] Whilst some individual missionaries asked their employers to provide funds or trained men for medical work there, the society's directors were reluctant to do so.[52] Instead, (untrained) missionaries in southern Africa 'doctored' their patients, particularly in the royal and chiefly courts, on an *ad hoc* basis – more as an itinerant trade than a formalised professional activity.[53] In direct contrast to doctors sent to India, confident in their 'expertise', Sykes, a missionary to Ndebeleland with no medical training, felt profoundly insecure about the medical work he and his colleagues felt compelled to perform. 'Those of us who came here without any such knowledge', he wrote, 'have been obliged to acquire it by practice. We have had to perform such surgical operations at times, as the thought of at home would have made us shudder.'[54] Although medical work was attempted at the Lake Mission of Central Africa, and the LMS started a medical mission in Madagascar from the 1860s, in southern Africa, medicine was not institutionalised until the twentieth century.[55]

At the time (and to some extent historiographically) such a discrepancy was often explained by the argument that medical work was most strategically deployed in missions where all other means of evangelisation had failed. Medical work in the East, in particular, was justified by references to the low rates of proselytisation by more conventional strategies. But this does not explain either why medical missions were not adopted in particularly 'difficult' southern Africa missions, such as Ndebeleland, or why the LMS's largest medical mission in India was in Travancore, an area where missionaries had already been unusually successful. Other factors, therefore, must also have been important and can be used to think further about how and why colonial otherness could take so many different forms.

The divergent forms that medical missionary work took reflected broader patterns of missionary engagement with different regions. The performance of medicine in southern Africa as an itinerant trade, conducted in public, often with large audiences, reflected the public nature of missionary evangelisation in southern Africa more widely. In contrast, the treatment of women in parts of India by female medical missionaries occurred alongside the development of zenana visitation. The unbalanced adoption of medical missions between India and Africa was part of a wider differentiation of missionary practice across these sites, particularly in regard to institutionalisation. In the 1860s, when medical work was developing in an already well-established Indian mission field, the LMS in southern Africa was undergoing large-scale upheaval and could not have supported the establishment of similar institutions.

The discrepancy also arose from the differing positions that African and Indian people occupied in the missionary imagination. As part of the British Raj, more colonial thinkers were interested in working medically in India than they were in Africa. The idea that the Ndebele were a remarkably healthy people who did not suffer from the 'contagious diseases', 'consumptions', 'pulmonary complaints' or 'rheumatism' fuelled an LMS conviction that 'a doctor would find it 'difficult to live among the Matabele' and perhaps explains the lack of medical work there.[56]

Indigenous attitudes towards medical practice also shaped the form that medical work would take. In India, indigenous medical institutions set a precedent for institutionalised colonial medicine. That missionaries in Africa found their patients 'ungrateful' discouraged the development of further medical work there. So, conversely, did African enthusiasm for medical practice. This was particularly the case amongst the southern Tswana where, as Hardiman and the Comaroffs note, indigenous cosmology suggested a close relationship between spiritual and bodily well-being.[57] Missionaries who recognised that '[t]he priests are their physicians; their medical and religious superstitions form parts of *one* system' were wary of administering medicine to those they feared wanted not to cure illness but to achieve immortality.[58]

Varied medical practice produced as well as reflected divergent ways of writing about the body across colonial sites. Because more hospitals were developed in India, Indians were frequently represented in the subordinated role of in-patients. Africans, meanwhile, were depicted as difficult patients who 'wasted medicines' and 'stole calicos'.[59]

But, just as diverse discourses about the family were homogenised in missionary writing, so were divergent encounters with sickness woven into a common narrative, be that set against the backdrop of formalised medical missions in India or *ad hoc* and unqualified 'doctoring' in southern Africa. Africans and Indians were both depicted as recipients of this 'help', defined through their sickness, indigineity and 'heathenism'. Missionaries, meanwhile, constructed themselves as 'benevolent' people who would bestow humanitarian help and scientific knowledge.

Medical missions and discourses of difference

Just as the sick body acted allegorically for 'heathenism', so the representation of the missionary as healer was symbolically resonant. The patient–healer relationship, and the power dynamic it held, was itself constitutive of the colonial difference upon which the logic of the medical mission was predicated.

John Lowe, a Scottish medical missionary associated with Travancore, was influential in framing medical missionary work in these terms. In a text widely circulated in justification of medical missions, Lowe claimed that 'all barbarous and semi-civilized nations are ignorant of the fundamental principles of medical science.' Upon this basis, he argued, '[c]ommon humanity, therefore, to say nothing of Christian benevolence' should prompt missionaries to medical work thereby exposing 'the mercenary and heartless pretensions of the priest-physicians' as well as caring for and comforting 'the sick and suffering' and mitigating 'the cruelties inflicted upon them'.[60] There are two important points here. Firstly, Lowe's assumption that it could be taken for granted that Christians were in a position to help those trapped in 'heathen' superstition and that such acts were benevolent. Secondly, that Lowe conceived the spread of 'science' and 'Christianity' together: biomedicine, 'civilisation' and Christianity were all part of Britain's 'gift' to the 'heathen' world.

Peter Williams has argued that 'benevolence' was 'upgraded' in the mid-century.[61] Congregationalists, among other post-millennialist thinkers, shifted from focussing on saving 'heathens' from the eternal punishment they would face upon death, to creating a meaningful present.[62] The reconsideration of Jesus' life as a 'healing ministry' was both a cause and a consequence of such shifts and one which medical missionaries harnessed to powerful effect. They claimed that medical missionary activity was obedient to Jesus' demand to heal, imitative of his own work 'for the salvation of body and mind', and responded to the recognition of 'not only the sanctity of human life but the obligation to preserve its health'.[63]

At home, the philanthropic milieu in Victorian Britain made reports of medical work a useful fundraising tool believed to arouse 'the interest and sympathy' even of those 'for whom missionary work of other kinds has not attraction.'[64] Overseas, medical missionary work was valued as an 'object lesson' of Christian benevolence. Based on pity rather than compassion, the endeavour to 'lighten the burden of human anguish among the uncared-for millions of the heathen' produced a benevolent self-image, confirming of identity to missionaries abroad. Missionaries defined their work against indigenous attitudes towards disease which they depicted as 'uncharitable' at best, 'cruel' at worst.[65] Hinduism, for example, was said to teach that lepers were 'objects of divine displeasure', and to blame illness on 'wickedness' committed by the sufferer 'in a former birth'.[66] Such views were juxtaposed with Christian teachings which missionaries, ignoring the complex symbolism of leprosy discussed above, interpreted as stating that lepers were objects of pity that should be cared for. The idea of a God who punished, which was never far from the Congregational worldview, was marginalised in these discourses. When a mother's vice was used to explain a congenitally disabled infant, and veneral disease explained through 'sin', these morally laden explanations were re-routed through the language of biological causation.

The performance of benevolence was gendered. In India, female medical practitioners claimed that their medical work complemented feminine nurturing roles. As Francis-Dehqani argued of the CMS in Persia, framing women's involvement in medicine through discourses of 'maternal instincts' allowed women doctors to quell anxiety about their adoption of a public, professional role.[67] Tales of white Christian women, associated with bodily as well as spiritual cleanliness, rushing to patients, kneeling beside them in poor, 'dirty' homes, and touching their wounds, were used to exemplify a 'feminine' compassion.[68] Male missionaries also drew on discourses of benevolence, but appropriated them differently, particularly by emphasising their imitation of Jesus as a benevolent leader. T.S. Thomson, a doctor at the Travancore medical mission, was one of many who found that as a 'medical man' he was 'constantly besieged by the blind, the lame, and the sick... that he would be like the Great Physician who had "compassion to them all" '.[69]

In drawing on Christ's ministry in this way, missionaries articulated their impetus to benevolence in terms of a naturalised relationship between Christianity and healing. Missionaries returned to the Gospels to argue that they had 'not only our Lord's example' but 'His direct command; what He Himself did, He commissioned His Apostles and the first teachers of Christianity to do.'[70] The first disciples had, wrote Lowe, been given power 'to "heal all manner of sickness and all manner of disease" (Matt. X 1)', and it was Jesus himself who had demanded they ' "heal the sick that are therein, and say unto them, The Kingdom of God is come nigh unto you" (Luke X 8,9)'.[71]

Lowe's other claim that 'semi-civilised nations are ignorant of the fundamental principles of medical science' was a second key discourse of difference through which medical missions operated. Historiographically too, rapid medical developments in Europe and a post-Enlightenment urge to disseminate this knowledge as part of a greater project of 'civilisation' have been linked to the development of medical missions. This conjuncture was a powerful one but not perhaps a convergence inevitable in missionary thinking.[72]

Whilst a link between 'healing' and Christianity may have been longstanding (albeit one slow to manifest itself in modern medical missions), the use of *biomedicine* (that is the conceptualisation and treatment of the body as a biological organism that could be 'scientifically' understood) was not.[73] Tensions between 'science' and 'religion' could be strong in this period and Jesus' healing, which missionaries so often claimed to follow, was based on miraculous interventions rather than 'medicine' of any sort. Although some missionaries attempted to *stage* their healings as miraculous, dramatising the wonders of chloroform, or cataract removal, for example, LMS missionaries themselves did not attempt to perform spiritual healing on Pentecostal lines.[74] Indeed, whilst prayer *accompanied* biologically understood healings, suggestions of spiritual cures of bodily ills that had infiltrated revivalist Christianity at home were deliberately abandoned in the export of Protestant Christianity abroad. As Terence Ranger notes, in the late eighteenth century, Wesley had brought back a world of spirits, spiritual healings and exorcisms into Britain, but in Africa, such tactics were deliberately avoided.[75] In the 'dark continent' missionaries believed they were encountering 'a credulous, superstitious multitude' who may 'misunderstand any emphasis upon spiritual healing.'[76] Instead, LMS healing took a 'scientific' form and reflected the growing Victorian understanding of disease as a biological puzzle that could be solved. Consistent with Enlightenment thinking, nineteenth-century missionaries maintained a conceptual separation between 'scientific medical practice' and 'superstitious healing'.

Missionaries, and their secular contemporaries who were also attempting to introduce elements of biomedical practice across the empire, mapped the disjuncture between 'science' and 'superstition' onto metropolitan and indigenous spaces, respectively.[77] Imagining British practice as 'scientific' required considerable discursive work. Late nineteenth-century biomedicine still used techniques such as bleeding, later to prove unhelpful in material terms, and vast gaps in medical understanding remained. Furthermore, 'scientific' medicine was not consistently accepted, far less practised, in 'the west'. In a study of popular belief in Southwark, S.C. Williams demonstrated that 'superstitious' medical practice (carrying a rabbit's foot to ward off disease, for example) remained widespread in Britain well into the twentieth century, particularly amongst the working classes.[78] But in colonial thought, the complex medical pluralism of metropolitan Britain was subsumed under an elite, 'scientific' discourse. Emergent biomedicine stood for what was 'European' and was represented as a cohesive body of knowledge framed in opposition to other, 'less civilised', forms of thinking.

The geographical distance imagined to demarcate 'civilised' and 'uncivilised' understandings of the body was reinforced by the representation of Indian and African medical practices as embodiments of heathen 'cruelty' and 'superstition'. Indeed, many medical missionaries' chief goal was contending with indigenous medical practice, rather than tackling sickness directly. In Africa, missionaries encountered 'medicine men' and 'witch doctors' as alternative sources of bodily and spiritual authority. In India, it was male doctors and either their 'barbaric' treatment of women, or their prohibition from seeing them at all, which focussed missionary outrage. Childbirth was a particularly emotive concern, and missionaries wrote of women injured by 'barbarous' practices and 'half-murdered with native treatment'.[79] In a typical example of such writing, missionary doctor Bentall described 'a filthy, dejected, poverty-stricken, frightened-looking soul' who had been 'so injured' by 'maltreatment' during child birth, that she had had 'a most awful deformity ever since'. This woman, like thousands of others, it was suggested, found social isolation close on the heels of physical disability; she had been abandoned by her husband and banished from her 'old home', rendered thus wholly dependent on the medical mission.[80] In Africa too, injury during childbirth was a recurring theme, though there it was framed through racialised concerns about African midwives, particularly older women, who were demonised in missionary writing as superstitious, dirty and incompetent.[81] The very high maternal mortality rates in Victorian childbirth were conveniently absent from writings about the suffering of 'heathen women' abroad – here as elsewhere sickness became something that was 'other'.

Missionaries overseas also systematically ignored contemporary debates over the relative roles of midwives and doctors in Britain, which involved similar struggles between 'superstition' and 'science'.[82] 'Superstitious' working-class beliefs were used to justify 'home' medical missionary work but were articulated through the languages of class and gender, rather than race.[83] When overseas, medical missionaries not only overlooked similarities but explicitly and repeatedly reiterated the disparity between 'at home' and 'out there'. The opening of a maternity ward in Neyoor, for example, was contextualised not within the late nineteenth-century medicalisation of child birth but within the missionary project of rescuing Indian women from the 'immense amount of needless suffering' found in 'Hindu households'.[84] Missionaries in the 'foreign field' explained the frustrations of their work (and the non-compliance of their patients) as derivative from their racial difference and their colonial location. Alice Hawker complained of the 'unlikeness to medical work at home' she found in North India. 'At home one attacks disease by the methods which one has been trained to believe are likely to be most successful,' she wrote. 'Here one attempts to do the same, but is thwarted at every turn'.[85] Patients who refused to come to hospital, objected to 'special diets' on 'caste principles' or were unable to procure the prescribed foods through poverty, and the sporadic consumption of medicine necessitated, Hawker wrote, a 'disappointing' relinquishment of the 'cherished ideas' of medical practice.'[86] For Hawker, resistance to 'western' medicine was born of the 'ignorance' and 'superstition' she expected to contend with in the colonial sphere more widely. Sykes made similar comments about his patients in Ndebeleland, whom he found 'ungrateful' and 'troublesome'.[87]

In India, scientific discourses were embodied in missionary hospitals, which were constructed as 'clinical' places, utterly unlike the superstitious disorder outside. Particularly from the 1880s, when discourses of hygiene proliferated, hospitals were envisioned as sterile environments through which patients could be cleansed and concealed from 'heathen' influences.[88] The missions' 'large healthy wards' were dramatically contrasted to the conditions patients were claimed to face at home where they would be confined to 'a dark, stuffy room, fed with unsuitable foods or starved, and with medicine given or withheld, or replaced by native preparations at the caprice of friends'.[89] Associations between sanitation and (moral) purity, dirt and sin meant that a sojourn in a sanitary environment was believed to be 'civilising' in itself, as well as a welcome opportunity to remove people from 'heathen' environments.[90] Hospitals created spaces where missionaries could police the daily lives of Indians to an extent they could never do outside. Moveable screens, curtains and segregated wards, were used to enforce western conceptions of the privacy that missionaries struggled to instil in private homes.[91] Hospitals were places where patients could literally be held captive to Bible teachings, where they were forced to listen to Christian services, sing hymns and read religious tracts.

Visitors and patients would have been in little doubt when they came into the medical missions that they were entering 'western', Christian, spaces. 'Native' ways of organising peoples were to be abandoned. In the Travancore hospital, John Lowe wrote, one could see 'sitting side by side, the Brahmin and the Sudra, the Shanar, the Poolah, and the Pariah, men, women, and children, of all castes and creeds, sitting under the same roof.' Such plurality was an achievement in itself, Lowe expounded, in 'a land of caste prejudice'.[92] But despite Lowe's pride at the abandonment of caste and creed distinction in favour of a system that reflected 'common humanity', the division of space in the medical mission was also hierarchical and marked by social difference, structured around race and gender, instead of caste.[93]

Medical missions functioned through the evocation of difference; 'us' and 'them' were positions onto which other dichotomies (such as science versus superstition and benevolence versus cruelty) could be mapped. At the same time, the articulation of these overarching discourses was accented by the specificities of different colonial sites. In India, as discussed above, these discourses were embodied in clinical hospitals. In Africa, where many missionaries candidly discussed their work as an 'incessant pottering with medicines' for which they were little trained, they nonetheless claimed to possess an 'understanding' that was 'scientific', if only by virtue of their Europeanness. A similar phenomenon occurred in leprosy asylums where the inability of missionaries (or almost anyone else in the late nineteenth century) to *cure* the disease meant scientific discourses were tempered. There, missionaries implied they were scientific *in approach* – that they recognised leprosy as a bodily disease, not as a 'punishment'. Yet, despite these differences, all medical missionary practices were bound together through the logic of difference.

Embodied conversion

Whilst constructed through difference, medical missions, like other missionary endeavours, were also premised on the potential for change. 'Difference' was never imagined to be so great that it could not be dissolved upon conversion. Medical missionaries believed their work was to 'heal', and this carried spiritual as well as bodily connotations. As discussed above, it was hoped that medical work would ingratiate people to Christianity who were otherwise suspicious of it, expose those to Christian teachings when they were at their most vulnerable, use scientific 'miracles' to awe indigenous people into adopting 'western' ways and provide an 'object lesson' of Christian benevolence that would be welcomed and appreciated.

Interestingly, given this rationale, many of those who went to the mission for treatment were in fact already Christian.[94] In 1866, out of the 4862 patients treated at Neyoor, 2346 were 'professing Christians', a further 505 were Roman Catholic, and only 1930 were 'Heathens' and 81 were 'Mohammedans'. It is unsurprising that willingness to subject oneself to biomedical practice often reflected a wider familiarity or sympathy with 'western' culture. It was, however, a tendency completely obscured in medical missionary literature. In all missionary writing, it is reiterated that medical work could and did bring about conversion. Medical work had the power to make those who were 'unlike', 'like'. The central place that the body played in realising these conversions is significant.

One of the most striking things about missionary writings about medical work is the predominance of conversion narratives. Conversion narratives were very formulaic and usually structured around three elements. Firstly, the prospective patient, suffering from physical illness, would seek help from 'traditional' sources, be that through praying to 'false gods', or attempting indigenous healing techniques. These methods would inevitably fail, and the afflicted person (or sometimes their family) would turn to the mission in desperation. Secondly, in the medical mission the 'true God' was put before them, usually in the form of the 'Great Physician' and Jesus' Ministry, and they would again pray for help, though this time to a 'good' and omnipotent agency. Thirdly, the patient was *both* physically and spiritually 'healed'. The intimate relationship between body and soul in the process of healing was emphasised throughout: the processes were intimately integrated.

The ambivalent relationship between 'body' and 'soul' in missionary thought is clearly evidenced in the position occupied by prayer in missionary healing. Prayer played an important element in conversion stories, despite being rather at odds with the emphasis elsewhere in medical literature on 'science'. Missionaries prayed for their patients to recover, and many patients made explicit prayers to their 'new' God. On his way to the mission, one patient, typical of such stories, was claimed to have prayed ' "O, only true God! I trust in thee and go to the hospital for treatment. If I recover and return in health I shall abandon the worship of all my former gods and worship Thee only." ' He received treatment at the hospital, got better within a few days and convinced he had received an act of Divine benevolence went on 'to embrace Christianity at once'. He continued to attend missionary services on his recovery.[95]

For many missionaries, the power of prayer was as solid a fact as that of the medicine they used to effect cure. At the same time, when confronted with indigenous explanations for sickness, they insisted that disease could only be understood in scientific terms. That is, they believed both that it was 'science' not 'superstition' or belief that explained and cured illness and that they were utterly dependent on an all-powerful God for the bestowing of health, for whose help they could pray.[96] As Ashton advised his colleagues, missionary doctors should ' "Trust in God," yes, but also "keep your powders dry." '[97] God not only directed the enactment of this medicine through missionary activity, but had, many argued, bestowed 'superior' medical knowledge upon Christian Europeans.

Missionaries found it difficult to convey the complex relationship they saw linking 'science' and 'prayer', body and soul, to potential converts. Dr Alice Hawker, for example, complained she was often asked by patients whether they should eat the paper the prescription is written on. She was yet more exasperated by women who having missed the pre-surgery prayer and hymn service prepared to leave without being treated, saying ' "But what is the use of the medicine if you don't sing to us first?" '[98] The close relationship between prayer and science was easily taken further than missionaries felt comfortable with. Such issues occurred in Africa as well as in India. As Megan Vaughan notes of east Africa, apparently miraculous cures (particularly cataract removal) were problematic for missionaries, anxious that their patients and witnesses did not understand western 'science' as 'magical' in the same way as indigenous cures had been.[99] In both Bechuanaland and Ndebeleland, missionaries complained bitterly that they were asked to perform medicine as though it were 'magic' and begged to bestow eternal life (literally) rather than treatment. 'The old chief has a strong belief in the power of the white people's medicine', William Sykes complained of Mzilikazi, 'He seems to think if he can only get plenty of it, it will make him immortal.'[100] However, whilst missionaries found these misunderstandings difficult to deal with, this fluidity between body and soul was an important part of missionary thinking; difference would always be read through the body and soul together.

That LMS missionaries demonstrated a systematic ambivalence between the concept of 'body' and 'soul' in their thinking is important, flagging both concepts as unstable and fluid. This ambivalence had important consequences for the conception of colonial difference, not least in regard to constructions of 'race' which, as I have discussed above, could be articulated through registers of both biology and culture. Accepting western medicine, like undergoing the other transformations that missionaries demanded accompany conversion such as changes in dress or sexuality, made the body a crucial signifier of theological belief. As one missionary put it, '[t]he Gospel of the Christ of God is pre-eminently for the salvation of the soul, but it acts through the body, and must bring salvation to the *body* [italics original] from all that is physically or spiritually impure.'[101] One consequence of this slippage was that an ideological commitment to human universalism always had the potential to be disrupted by the perception of bodily difference. Missionaries may have asserted that all humans were the same in the eyes of God, but they also perceived bodily differences which they found spiritually significant.

Conclusion

Missionaries used discourses of sickness to other the peoples and places they encountered. The discursive construction of India and Africa as places of sickness was used to pathologise 'heathenism', as was the reduction of indigenous peoples in the missionary press to spectacles of sick or starving bodies. These tropes contributed to wider images of dependency and helplessness in missionary writing that have problematic legacies today. They also contributed to the conceptualisation of colonial others in somatic terms. But, of course, 'sickness' was not only experienced by 'others' but also by Europeans and missionaries themselves. Given the symbolic encoding of sickness, and the association between 'sickness' and 'otherness', I will use the next chapter to explore how missionaries thought about themselves, their families and their colleagues, when they too were sick.

4
Illness on the Mission Station: Sickness and the Presentation of the 'Self'

> Missionaries generally are sent to unhealthy and uncongenial regions.[1]

Sickness and missionary activity

In the previous chapter, I explored how missionaries responded to sickness overseas and how they developed a framework that powerfully linked sickness, 'heathenism' and 'otherness'. In claiming a healing role for missionaries, they indirectly aligned themselves with 'healthiness'. In this chapter, I ask how, given this framework, missionaries responded to their own illnesses and those of their friends and colleagues in the 'foreign field'. In doing so, I use sickness to explore discourses of difference (principally those of gender, age, health and location) internal to the missionary 'self' and think about how the experience of sickness overseas could both potentially threaten the lines around which missionaries constructed colonial difference and re-encrust them. Sickness provides a useful way into these 'internal' differences not only because of the anxiety it generates, but because it is a subject that utterly pervades missionary correspondence.

Despite the potency of illness, much historical writing represents it simply as an interruption of a healthy 'norm', a condition resulting in a 'lapse' of productivity or an uninteresting hiatus in career, rather than a formative or valid experience in its own right.[2] Greater historiographical attention is warranted, however, not least because of what experiences of sickness can reveal about everyday life, social experience and identity. Periods of sickness form important points of rupture which can force introspection, or, in the case of long-term illness or disability, periods of continuity which embed themselves in identity. Using the language Stoler reserves for sexuality, I read sickness as a 'dense point of transition', or a 'privileged' site through which one can access questions of identity. This is partly because of the intimacy involved in discussing, treating and experiencing sickness and partly because of its ability to pervade many areas of lived experience. Illness prises open all kinds of anxieties – about life and death, religion, social relationships and dependency. Writings about sickness are revealing of how missionaries lived their lives and what they expected from them. Experiences of sickness have, therefore, a profound effect on the way in which difference is imagined and constituted.

Sickness always shaped the course of missionary activity. In the early years, very high death rates severely hindered growth, and employers struggled simply to replace dying missionaries with new recruits. In some places, so many missionaries died before they had even learnt the vernacular that evangelisation was minimal and the missions abandoned. Sierra Leone was a notorious example where only 6 of the CMS's 15 missionaries survived their first few years, and the Wesleyan and LMS missionaries met with similar fates.[3] The struggles of the pioneer missions in 'the white man's grave' were mythologised in the founding narratives of many societies, allowing bodily weakness to be recast as spiritual strength or adventurous heroism.[4] Although particularly characteristic of the earliest movements, catastrophic losses remained an occasional fact of missionary venture throughout the nineteenth century. The 'Kololo Incident' in 1858, when almost the entire Helmore and Price families died of Tsetse fly fever within a few days of each other, was one such tragic episode which punctuated the history of the LMS. In the 1870s and 1880s, the surge of Protestant missions to Lake Tanganika proved 'one long tragedy in the sacrifice of life', devastating for all the societies that were involved, including the LMS.[5] Many missionaries and 'native' guides died from a range of unidentified diseases and from malaria.[6] However, although the narratives constructed around these events attempted to contain sickness within discrete dramatic boundaries, the reality of sickness in the foreign field was, although more mundane, far more pervasive: seeping through periods of banality and 'progress', as well as characterising the disastrous.

Illness was a chronic part of the missionary experience. Sickness and health preoccupied a huge proportion of missionary correspondence as missionaries detailed their own illnesses and those of their colleagues and loved ones; applied to take leave, or to return to Britain; outlined and justified medical expenses; explained slow work, or lack of work; and suggested health risks connected with particular areas or seasons to those with little experience of their location. Chronic illness patterned everyday life. When illness was critical and immediate (that of self, spouse, parent or child), it transcended all other matters, creating ruptures in missionary biographies by compelling them to leave their stations and return to Britain. Many of the journeys missionaries made between metropole and colony were prompted by illness, either in necessitating leave or compelling retirement. Illness and health shaped perceptions of the self and of others and channelled social relationships. It helped to construct difference because of its power to inscribe itself onto the body and the mind, shaping imagined worlds and social performances.

In June 1841, Reverend Crisp concluded his letter with a summary of news from the other stations in and around Bangalore of south India, an account which merits long quotation:

> ...It may be satisfactory to you to hear in brief a few particulars from the stations – Mr Leitch goes to relieve Mr Caldwell, and will be requested also to preach at Davidson's Street once on the Sabbath for Mr Porter, who I regret to say has been obliged to leave Madras and come up here for his health. Mr Beildbeck has left Nallajah Pettah for the coast in greatly impaired health, and there is considerable difficulty in finding a temporary supply for his station. Mr Regel though better than he was is still so poorly that he has felt obliged to decline going either to Nallajah Pettah or Madras, at either of which places his help would just now have been very acceptable...Mr Rice has returned to Bangalore and is in pretty good health, but is obliged to be very careful not to over-exert himself, I think that neither his health nor Mrs Rice's will admit of any longer entertaining the idea of his removing to Bellary. Mr Miller of Nagercoil has had another rather serious attack and though somewhat better is still no further [and is] very weak. He is recommended to remain here and make further trial of the effects of this climate but a sea voyage is the remedy ultimately contemplated by the Doctor and I have no idea that any thing short of that will afford him full relief. He bears his long affliction with much cheerfulness and resignation, and is patiently waiting for a clear indication of his duty, which he is quite prepared to follow. We have heard with great concern that Mrs Campbell (of Mysore) has suffered very seriously from the failure of her sight that she is obliged to leave Mysore for the Hills and there is but little hope entertained that even that will afford her much relief.[7]

Whilst Crisp was writing at a time of particularly acute affliction for the Canarese missionaries, such round-ups occur at unhappy intervals throughout LMS correspondence. Notes about the health of fellow missionaries were included in most reports, and there was generally at least some bad news to tell. As evident from the passage above, ill-health dictated the manning of the missions, with stations frequently left unoccupied due to the missionary's health or 'healthy' missionaries rotated to cover vacancies. Such occurrences were clearly inconvenient for the LMS as were the long periods of leave illness necessitated.

Indeed, the costs that sickness incurred for the missionary society were so substantial, particularly taken as a proportion of tightly calculated budgets, that they often caused considerable friction within the organisation. As discussed below, requests made by sick missionaries for doctors' fees, voyages to Britain or convalescence in the hills or coast were often contested by the Directorate in Britain. Wrangling over costs delayed many actions deemed by missionaries and their doctors to be 'urgent' and generated long-lasting bitterness.

With this in mind, it is hardly surprising that the LMS was concerned to regulate the potential for illness amongst its missionaries and their prospective partners and attempted to identify and discard candidates believed to be physically or mentally 'weak' before any training was invested in them. Potential candidates were examined by LMS physicians, and prospective missionaries had to provide a detailed certificate of their personal and familial medical history. By the 1880s, substantial medical interviews and examinations had been established.[8] Occasionally, the directors would take into consideration a candidate's constitution in order to determine where to send them, but usually, candidates with any detectable weakness were not accepted at all.[9] Candidates who had, or had a family history of, epilepsy or mental illness were automatically rejected, as were those who had speech impediments or were deaf, conditions believed to impede a candidate's ability to learn a foreign language.[10] Endfield and Nash have explored the ways in which the LMS extended its control over the health of missionary women and the wives of missionaries through the Candidates Examination Committee. Deploring 'the serious evils resulting from the early failure of the health of the wives of missionaries', the society demanded that its own physicians must attest to the 'fitness for the missionary service of every intended wife of a missionary founded upon his personal examination'.[11] When it was impossible to examine potential wives at first hand, a lengthy series of questions had to be answered by a qualified person in written form.

However, whatever measures the LMS adopted to screen out sickly recruits, it could not, of course, manufacture an 'actual' distinction between the overlapping states of 'sickness' and 'health', still less control the potential for them, and no measure the society ever took prevented its missionaries from becoming ill. The extent to which we see how, in India and Africa, these 'healthy' recruits were transformed into people often characterised as 'sick' is striking. As a discourse of difference 'sickness' had to be endlessly remade.

Intellectualising the experience of illness

In their correspondence, missionaries named a considerable range of afflictions from which they believed they themselves, their families or their colleagues to be suffering. Bowel and liver disorders, heart disease, rheumatism, fever, headaches, fatigue, weakness, smallpox, cholera, epilepsy, nervous disorders, and hysteria were among the most common afflictions in India. In southern Africa, coughs, chills and infections were also frequent complaints. For women across the empire as well as in Britain, problems stemming from miscarriage, pregnancy and childbirth accounted for a large proportion of sickness and were not infrequently fatal.[12] Infant mortality was attributed to 'teething' (which was held responsible for infant fevers, rashes, convulsions, coughs and diarrhoea, irritability and restless sleep).[13] Naming the disorder however, whilst important, was only the tip of the iceberg. Beneath the labels lay a complex web of associations which further reveal the complex slippages between mind and body in missionary thinking, and the ambiguous ways in which they perceived their bodies as entangled within their colonial environments, and their location in a place of 'difference'.

In the mid-nineteenth century, medical knowledge was in a transitional stage. Eighteenth-century developments in morbid anatomy had generated increasingly structural understandings of the body. In the nineteenth century, such knowledge was mobilised as survival rates following surgery were transformed with the development of general anaesthesia in the 1840s and antisepsis in the 1870s.[14] Strides were also made in pharmacology: between 1800 and 1840, morphine, quinine, codeine and iodine, among other drugs, were identified, isolated or created.[15] Disease identification and classification were also becoming increasingly specific, developments that quickened later in the century with microbe isolation.[16] And yet, throughout the nineteenth century, other illnesses remained symptomatically defined, 'weakness', 'fatigue' or 'hysteria', for example, were understood as illnesses in their own right. Missionaries borrowed promiscuously from all the various sources of medical knowledge they encountered rather than simply 'converting' to the biologically orientated understandings gaining dominance in medical discourses in Europe.[17] The three most common causes of sickness in missionary thinking were 'disease', 'constitution' and 'climate', explicatory frameworks that were intimately and intricately connected.

So-called nervous conditions, from which missionaries suffered to a staggering degree, powerfully demonstrate the complexities surrounding mid nineteenth-century illness, illustrative as they are of the many slippages between mind and body that ran through missionary thought. As I discussed in Chapter 3, the boundaries of the 'physical' body were unstable in missionary thinking, but, whilst for the 'heathen', ambiguity was primarily articulated in terms of a fluidity between 'body and soul', when talking about their own health, the slippage primarily occurred between body and *'mind'*.[18] A 'nervous condition' was characterised as a disease of the bodily nervous system, and thus as a physical problem that could affect any organ. Nervous conditions would 'imitate' the bodily symptoms of other diseases, presenting themselves as anything from dyspepsia or constipation to typhus or delirium. 'Hysteria' or 'nervous conditions' could thus be fatal.[19] Links were also often drawn between 'nervous disorders' and conditions labelled 'neuralgia', 'insanity' and 'epilepsy'.

The experience of such conditions was gendered. Male missionaries tended to somatise their 'nervous conditions'. For female missionaries, 'hysteria' was a common and openly acknowledged idiom of distress expressed through crying, anxiety and agoraphobia. John Lowe (a medical missionary at Travancore) described his wife's symptoms, which he attributed to 'hysteria' and 'neuralgia' as: 'constitutional' and 'bodily' 'weakness', 'intense suffering', an 'utter inability to help herself', and a 'depression of spirits'. He claimed that, for 8 months, she had 'never once been out of the Bungalow, seldom indeed out of her room'. She had shrank from seeing anyone but Lowe himself, refusing to see even her 'best and most loved friends'. At night she suffered terribly, resting only 'under the influence of sedatives'.[20] Such conditions ruptured the idealised image of the 'missionary wife' discussed in Chapter 1, yet also reinforced gendered understandings of women's fragility, not least in Mrs Lowe's total confinement to the domestic sphere.

Like their contemporaries in Britain, missionaries explained these breakdowns through a combination of constitutional weakness and mental anxiety, from the traumatic loss of a child to concern about loved ones to the inability to preserve 'tranquillity of mind'.[21]

Overseas, however, the explanation of sickness was also informed by a complicated and evolving dialogue about the environment.

During the early modern period, ideas about hot climates were ambivalent. Karen Kupperman has illuminated a longstanding belief that the West Indies were unhealthy and argues that English people expressed 'profound anxiety' about visiting what they considered a 'hostile' environment.[22] Whilst perhaps unsurprising given the devastatingly high death rates amongst early European travellers, Mark Harrison suggests that in regard to *India*, it was far from inevitable that the tropics would become associated with medical danger.[23] Indeed, he argues that between the fifteenth and eighteenth centuries, many travellers to India were impressed with what struck them as a salubrious landscape lacking (smallpox aside) the numerous diseases prevalent in contemporary Europe.[24] Kiple and Ornelas make a similar point about seventeenth-century attitudes towards parts of the West Indies, which were also considered relatively healthy.[25]

From the early nineteenth century fear of hot climates grew and 'the tropics' were increasingly seen as unsuitable for long-term European residency. Images of India are axiomatic of this shift. The vast majority of illnesses missionaries experienced there were attributed to the climate. It is not coincidental that in Indian missionary discourse, references to 'the burden and heat of the day' were used both metaphorically and literally, to capture the trials and tribulations of missionary endeavour. Not all colonial spaces, however, were tropical, and quite different ideas about health and environment developed around temperate climates. Areas of the Cape Colony, for example, were sometimes seen as a 'regenerative' haven for sick Europeans (Cecil Rhodes among others), particularly for those with 'nervous break-down' and tuberculosis sufferers.[26] Nevertheless, there was much overlap in missionary responses to southern African and Indian climates, particularly in the interior. Beyond the Cape, missionaries wrote of a land infested by tsetse fly, malaria and 'heat'. Bechuanaland was often considered unhealthy and, for Europeans, Ndebeleland generally more so despite the good health enjoyed by the Ndebele themselves.[27] Hostile climates (ones too cold as well as too hot) characterise the accounts of journeys across the subcontinent. Even in the apparently wholesome Cape, Reverend Williamson was not alone in complaining that he was persistently 'affected by the climate which is not at all, especially in the Karoo District, as is usually supposed in England'.[28] Both India and southern Africa were considered different from, and more 'adverse' than Britain, they were considered to be 'wearing' for individual missionaries, who needed periodic removal to the coast or to the metropole in order to maintain good health. Noticing their responses to a 'foreign' environment, Indian or African, was a way in which missionaries 'felt' their difference from those they encountered there. But such ideas, though common across many sites of empire, were formulated in ways particular to different locations.

Williamson's suggestion that the climatic hardships he experienced in southern Africa were not appreciated in Britain was part of a wider fault line between metropole and colony. Overseas, missionaries were aware of localities that were healthy and ones that were dangerous, but these subtleties proved difficult to convey to those with little experience of their regions of work. There were also tensions between the LMS as an organisation which drew from a collective body of knowledge and the understanding individuals held about their own health. The LMS Directors, cautious from repeated 'disappointments' and incapacitations, hoped that rigorous medical examinations would determine whether a candidate could withstand adverse environments. But such measures were not very successful, in part because individuals were more optimistic. In the records of application, it is difficult to find a single example of a (metropolitan) applicant who actually thought that a foreign climate could possibly adversely affect their health. 'My constitution is excellent', Mary Wallace wrote in her application, 'I am not subject to any diseases and I think that my health would not be materially impaired by change of climate.'[29] Nor did the metropolitan physicians that provided medical certifications of fitness consistently suggest that removal to the colonies was always perceived as a bad thing. One doctor, certifying John Thompson's fitness for missionary work, suggested that, although the prospective missionary had suffered from a slight attack of bronchitis, it was his opinion that 'so far from suffering inconvenience from the warm climate, his health would be improved by it.'[30] Such assertions were no doubt prejudiced by the nature of the application process and the applicants' eagerness to be selected. Yet such assertions, all of which were backed up by supposedly independent medical certification, suggest that 'fear of hot climates' was not so common amongst those with no direct experience of them as the historiography of colonial medicine often claims.

Images of the environmental spaces of empire were filtered through thinking about racial difference. Missionaries thought Indians and Africans were resilient to the climates to which they were 'native'.[31] It was missionaries' Europeanness which made them vulnerable. The relationship between climate and race has a complex history, much of it concerned with ideas about 'adaptation': the belief that, given time, Europeans could 'acclimatise' to a new environment through a temperate lifestyle and by adopting 'native habits'.[32] Mark Harrison, amongst others, suggests such beliefs were related to monogenistic thinking which, structured on the understanding that racial difference was fluid, posited an interactive relationship between 'race' and 'environment'.[33] During the 1840s, such ideas started to shift. As racial difference was increasingly conceived as 'fixed', the belief Europeans could 'adapt' waned and fear of 'hot climates' grew.[34] Change that *was* seen to occur in the tropics was increasingly perceived as 'degeneration' rather than 'adaptation'. As Warwick Anderson notes, 'polygenistic' understandings of climate and well-being were reflected in post-1850 colonial literature, where 'the monotonous heat and humidity drive Europeans to despair, murder and suicide.'[35] In some respects, the physical experience of sickness in India or Africa represented an extension of the imaginative association between colonial spaces and moral 'sickness' discussed in Chapter 3.

In missionaries' reports and letters home, a huge proportion of the illnesses and deaths they recorded were explained by the 'intolerable' and 'excessive' heat, the 'glare of heat of the sun' or 'trying climate'; and colonial spaces were constantly contrasted with 'the comparatively genial climate of England'.[36] The more explicitly 'racial' dangers associated with climate that increased in other colonial discourses, however, developed only hesitantly. Even in the later nineteenth century, missionaries believed that they could adapt so successfully to hot climates that they feared returning to the metropole and the risk of chills there.[37] Nevertheless, when illness did strike, missionaries in both southern Africa and India alike were unwavering in deeming a return to the metropole essential for complete recovery. Both in Britain and overseas, it was repeatedly implied that missionaries in India or Africa got sick because they were European. It was in part because of this that it was often believed that, ultimately, evangelisation should be handed over to those 'native' to the climate. In these ways, sickness attributed to climate was used to mark racial difference and fed into other discourses about the relationship between sickness and race. Missionaries in southern Africa, for example, often claimed that race determined the experience of illness and that black Africans, for example, appeared to experience pain 'differently'.

Despite the importance invested in climate and race, however, they were usually believed to exacerbate existing conditions or weaknesses in an individual's 'constitution', rather than as operating on missionaries *independently*. Because of this, race and climate intersected with other discourses of difference, notably gender.[38] Trials of climate seem to have affected female members of the missionary community more severely than males. Believed to have weaker constitutions, women were seen as less resistant to tropical climates and more easily corrupted by them.[39] As Morag Bell argued, discourses constructing women as the 'weaker sex' suggested that they would be 'more easily upset' by tropical heat.[40] Both race and gender not only explained illness but also structured the way in which it was experienced and performed.

Identity and the experience of illness

Missionaries interpreted their sicknesses through a framework of race and gender. In so doing, they reflected, absorbed and consolidated wider colonial discourses which treated European bodies as fundamentally different from colonial ones, men's from women's. Sickness was performed in ways that reflected identity: men, women, adults and children presented their illnesses distinctly. At the same time, the performance of illness fed back into the *creation* of identity. The nervous conditions of missionary women, for example, were anticipated by their gender and enacted in ways that were gendered. Records of these experiences then fed back into images of the feminine in the colonial sphere. The women who had been deliberately selected by the LMS on the grounds of their fitness, their 'robust' constitutions and physical strength were soon depicted as weak, emotionally fragile, and physically and mentally vulnerable.

The experience of sickness could also fracture, erode or dismember identity. Physical and social changes wrought by illness, such as changes to appearance, or changes to personality yet more so, could threaten an individual's very self. The inability of 'hysterical' missionary women to look after their children, or of men to work, could challenge gender identities. They also disrupted the self-images missionaries wanted to convey both to indigenous people, and to their friends and colleagues in the missionary community and at home.[41]

One example of this unravelling of identity can be seen in the case of Ebenezer Lewis who, in the spring of 1862, suffered a breakdown which was to end his 20-year missionary career in South India. He experienced a 'great debility and depression of spirits', 'convulsions', outbursts of tears and became 'insensible', having 'apoplectic fits' characterised by 'violent struggling, foaming at the mouth, distortion of features, rolling and quivering of the eyes'.[42] Such symptoms demonstrate the challenges sickness posed to both the model of the 'manly Englishman' and of the 'suffering missionary' sometimes found in published missionary writings, where illnesses were calm, spiritual affairs. Indeed Lewis's condition was so disruptive to such images that it needed to be contained and the fits hidden. In a community that equated epilepsy with 'madness', Emily Lewis was left to care for her husband alone despite the 'physical and mental strain' this placed on her. 'Such was the distressing nature of Mr Lewis' complaint', she wrote, 'that I could not have a female friend with me to assist me, though some of the Misses Littens were anxious to help me but I could not permit them to come as the sight of them would have been injurious to Mr Lewis and the sight of him in one of those fearful fits would have been too much for them as none of them are strong.'[43] Whilst the anticipation of such a response suggests a [conformist] gendering of the Littens as weaker than Lewis yet, the sickness nevertheless challenged the ordered and self-controlled masculinity of an English missionary, as much as Mrs Lowe's 'hysteria' may be imagined to have challenged her ability to perform the role of missionary wife or mother.

At the same time as the symptoms threatened Lewis's gender–race identity, however, the diagnosis of his illness was rooted in understandings of his being an Englishman in India. Lewis's illness was explained through the damaging effects of climate on his European body, and Lewis himself attributed his symptoms directly to 'the excessive heat'.[44] All in Travancore deemed his immediate removal from South India 'indispensable' to his recovery.[45] Departure from the colonial sphere was a typical climax (alongside death) in the accounts of missionary illness and, indeed, Lewis returned to the metropole.

Narrative and the remaking of identity

Unlike Africans and Indians, who were thought to suffer from simple complaints that Europeans could 'cure', missionaries believed their own bodies to be extremely complex. There were multiple possibilities for the collision of different weakening factors (disease, climate and constitution), meaning that all illnesses were perceived as individualised, and reflexive of social as well as medical history. With the new discoveries in micro-bacteriology mostly absent from missionary discourse, even in the late nineteenth century, diagnostics remained a subjective process, and 'feelings' of medical as well as social value. Understanding sickness rested on a detailed knowledge of the sufferer and their circumstances, information which was organised into narrative form.

As the medical anthropologist Gay Becker argues, narrative holds a powerful constructive capacity to allow people to reconfigure an identity ruptured by illness.[46] Letters about Ebenezer Lewis's illness, for example, helped construct a narrative of his illness grounded in his identity as a white, British man. Such letters also emphasised the ways in which sickness had interrupted his *work* and how his wife was both reliant on him and nurturing of him, which placed the illness in a gendered framework. In the missionary community, the sick person, their doctors, family and colleagues all helped to weave a narrative that closed the ruptures sickness potentially posed to their gender, ethnic or even 'missionary' identity.

Narratives told about illness were also important in explaining, de-mystifying and containing the destabilising effects of illness itself. In her investigation of Gulf War Syndrome (GWS), Suzie Kilshaw argues that veterans use narratives as strategies to make sense of a diverse and disorganised group of symptoms that are little understood. She argues that by 'assimilating the stories of other sufferers', veterans learn a 'culturally specific narrative form', which in turn 'provides a framework for the reflexive re-interpretation of one's past and helps to construct a narrative of GWS.'[47] A similar process can be seen at work in the writings of sick missionaries and their families. Given the importance of letters as a means of communication in this community, *textual* narrative was crucial to how the missionary experience of illness was both represented and understood.

Missionaries narrated illness linearly, with a beginning, a climax and a resolution (recovery, retirement or death). Such narratives were often protracted; whilst organic diseases could strike with frightening speed (cholera was particularly terrifying in this respect), they were situated in wider time-frames than the illness-crisis itself. When the illness materialised, a retrospective interpretation of earlier minor afflictions was read back onto the sufferer's life, linking a series of episodes, possibly spanning several years, to provide a coherent narrative through which constitution, climate and disease interacted. In doing so, missionaries actively transformed medical knowledge to reflect their own understandings of the body in ways that may appear incoherent as medical discourses but which formed unified narratives of the self.

The relationship missionaries saw between trauma and illness, and the gendering of trauma, meant that the narrativisation of illness was frequently pinned by gendered markers. For women, the death of a child (or the beginning of a long separation from them) was often placed at the beginning of the narrative, even if this occurred some time before the illness actually developed. In 1866, Reverend Samuel Mateer wrote to the Travancore District Committee (TDC) about his wife. She had been in India 7 years and had enjoyed excellent health until 2 years before, when she had become subject to 'severe and wearing attacks of nervous illness'. This had originated, Mateer believed, in the Indian heat but had been 'greatly increased' by the death of their child and her brother at that time and recently exacerbated by their separation from their two eldest boys.[48] Grief, interwoven with the weakening effects of climate, could make both men and women immediately and seriously ill. For women, however, narrative links were also forged between such tragedies and illness over considerable lapses of time.

For male missionaries it was the equally gendered diagnosis of 'overwork' that explained long-term physical 'decline'. The labours of missionary activity, the learning of languages, the demands of preaching and excessive travelling were claimed to exhaust constitutions already weakened by the climate. Work was gendered 'masculine' in missionary discourse. The work of social reproduction that missionary wives and daughters performed managing their households and caring for children was not understood as 'labour', and the missionary duties they performed, acting as amanuensis for their husbands, and running schools and orphanages, were quietly subsumed in LMS thinking as the activities of a 'helpmeet', not as 'work' itself. As such, women were not thought to suffer from 'overwork' like their male relatives. Neither were Indian and African men, characterised as 'lazy', thought to be overworked nor were their illnesses vested with the kind of masculine kudos sickness from overwork might engender.

The need to keep colleagues informed of developments, to preserve a record of a potentially terminal illness for family at home, and to justify any medical expenses to the Directors, meant that missionary records of illness were thorough. Such accounts also presented the opportunity to heal some of the troubling ruptures illness presented. The 'patience', 'stoicism', 'fortitude' and 'resilience' with which missionaries were claimed to face their illnesses helped reaffirm their missionary identity.

Narratives of terminal illness were particularly notable in this respect. Those missionaries who recorded the final illnesses of their colleagues weaved between descriptions of physical deterioration and ones of spiritual growth. In doing so, they rendered each step of the illness meaningful. Dying missionaries, male and female, made religiously laden speeches affirming that they were ready to meet their 'Heavenly Father' and were accepting, indeed welcoming, of their fate.[49] Such spiritual engagement was important for a 'good death' generally in Victorian thinking but, perhaps, particularly necessary for a missionary overseas where the gift of the 'fearless' and even 'joyful' Christian death was a potentially powerful object lesson in attracting converts to the faith.[50] It was at death that the body and soul were finally disentangled as the spirit 'rose' and the body, no longer needed, 'sunk'. Missionaries could little fathom the 'mysterious ways' of the 'Heavenly father' who 'cut down' missionaries 'at their height', ending their attempts to spread 'the Word' in 'His name'. But in narratives surrounding death, a liminal space was discursively created where the spiritual and the medical were brought together.

On the hastily written letters recording tragedy in the archives, editorial markings flag the elements of such narratives deemed acceptable for circulation amongst the missionary public. In reproducing a letter from Bechuanaland, it was Mrs Brown's 'peaceful smile which showed that she knew she was going to that which is far better' that the editors chose for public consumption, not her 'great and prolonged suffering' or her husband's 'wounded spirit', and 'aching, lonely heart'.[51] Although such accounts were clearly stylised and intertextually informed, the consistency of death narratives in missionary writing, and the strength their colleagues drew from actually witnessing them, suggests that some missionaries were able to perform (as well as textually construct) this cultural narrative. Spiritual beliefs could be embodied in these moments, the 'ideal' death acted out and social and spiritual identities re-enforced.

The missionary community and the missionary 'self'

Determining what was distinctive about the *missionary* experience of sickness in the empire from a demographic perspective is difficult. Missionaries suffered from what were apparently many of the same conditions as their contemporaries and understood them similarly to those in epistemologically related communities. Medical knowledge and accounts of personal experiences of sickness travelled through networks which joined the 'missionary community' with other colonial groups. Dr. John Lowe of the Travancore medical mission, for example, was trained in the same Edinburgh medical schools as lay colonial doctors in India and non-imperial doctors at home. Lowe's work in Travancore was discussed in the leading British medical journal, *The Lancet*. When his wife's ill health forced him to return to Britain, he continued to practise medical work with 'the heathen at home' and to write about 'the heathen overseas'.[52] In missionary writings, however, the experience of sickness was often filtered through an exclusive lens of particularity whereby illnesses were constructed as a specifically *missionary* experience. Illness became reflexive of and contributory to a specifically missionary identity.

Richard Price has argued that missionaries were 'mentally unbalanced' due to the 'unstable mix of values' inherent in missionary culture, such as what he describes as the yoking of their 'naïve expectation that the world could be moved by individuals inspired by the word of God' with 'a recognition of the helplessness of the individual before Providence'. He claims that colonial encounters (with the Xhosa, in his example) exacerbated this 'cognitive dissonance', and that the physical hardship and isolation experienced on the frontier deprived missionaries from 'access to much therapy of the sort one could seek in Britain'.[53] Price's consideration of how the 'social psychology' of the missionary movement played into their colonial encounters is interesting, but I have some queries. Whilst the isolation of many missionary lives would have been very difficult, I believe Price overestimates the amount of help their contemporaries *could* have sought elsewhere (beyond comfort, perhaps, from their immediate families who would have accompanied them anyway) and underestimates the stigmatisation of such breakdowns in both Britain and abroad. Further, the heightened emotionalism that Price describes was, at least in some manifestations, a valued part of nineteenth-century religiosity and experience and understood as reflexive of a spiritual relationship, not as a sickness. Pathologising spiritualism, or any other form of cultural experience, is something of which to be wary. Whilst to Price it seems obvious that the missionary worldview was an 'unbalanced' one, this could only be argued to have created 'unbalanced' individuals in a complicated way, not least because individuals have a powerful capacity to make sense of a disordered world. My concern in this chapter is not with the retrospective diagnosis of mental health problems in order to explain the actions of nineteenth-century missionaries. Rather than considering whether or not missionaries *were* more prone to mental and emotional difficulties than their contemporaries, I take here an angle that Price does not consider, that missionaries *themselves* thought they were unusually susceptible to debilitating nervous conditions and used this to define their own community as distinct from other colonial groups.

In the 1840s, unusually high mortality rates amongst the missionary communities of South India generated a debate about the relationship between illness and the missionary profession. 'The Lord is at present dealing very painfully with the Missions in this part of India', Reverend

Crisp, the secretary of the district commission, wrote to his directors. All the missionary societies in the district had lost members through illness and death, he lamented, and 'every successive month has appeared to bring with it fresh afflictions.'[54] Crisp looked for Providential answers for suffering, but medical explanations were also offered.

Dr Birch, a doctor not himself connected to a missionary society but who had often treated missionaries, decided to offer some advice. In a letter to the Madras District Committee, he addressed the problem of the extent of illness within missionary societies, which he saw as out of proportion with disease suffered by the British in India generally.[55] He wrote that 'having had but too frequent occasion to observe the ailments of those devoted to Missionary labour', he had been 'led to meditate on the causes of such frequency of sickness among a class of persons whose temperate and orderly habits should lead one to look for very different results'.[56] Ultimately, Birch placed the blame on overwork, enumerating the 'fatiguing demands' made on the 'mental powers' of missionaries, such as the pressure to learn new languages quickly, to be a preacher of the Gospel, a publisher of tracts and papers, to translate various works, to teach children, adults and catechists, and besides all this, to 'keep money accounts and a history of all his proceedings'.[57] He went on to elaborate the dangers of this schedule for 'the mental and physical powers of the missionary'.[58] Birch believed missionary work led to the 'overexertion of the brain', a problem worsened 'by want of wholesome exercise to brace the enfeebled condition of the body, which from its comparative inactivity has its powers diminished and a train of unhealthy phenomena arises which increases the cerebral disorder'.[59]

In Birch's professional experience, missionaries were particularly prone to 'enfeebling' conditions and acquired more 'disordered states of the brain' than the civil or military functionaries he also doctored. The letter, the diagnosis of missionary illness and Birch's various recommendations for a reduction in workload were welcomed by the missionaries of South India who claimed that they were 'convinced of the truth of his statements' and enthusiastically sent Birch's report to their employers in London.[60] Although Sewell urged the Directors to give their 'most serious attention' to 'Dr Birch's sensible letter on the failure of health among Missionaries', despite a follow-up letter sent several months later pressing for a reply, it seems, they never passed comment on his findings.[61]

Such a letter suggests that missionaries sometimes linked their illnesses to missionary activity itself. This is certainly supported by the number of medical certificates that cited overwork, the travel involved in missionary itinerancy or most simply the positioning of missionaries overseas as a cause of sickness. More dramatic episodes of missionary sickness often incurred criticism of the LMS from outside and implied an association between missionary work and ill health. The deaths of Mr and Mrs Helmore, three of their children, Mrs Price and the Prices' baby on the Kololo Expedition incurred widespread criticism of the society for a 'want of prudence', incompetence and for the callous casualness with which they were claimed to have let these families die.[62] Unsurprisingly, the LMS firmly rejected such criticisms, but accusations of neglect could come from within as well as from outside.

Time and time again, the experience of illness overseas generated heated divisions within the LMS, particularly between metropole and periphery. Requests from the directors for sick missionaries to suspend their return until administratively convenient led to bitterness and threats that, if the patient were to remain abroad, they would be permanently incapacitated. Mrs Mabbs's doctor, for example, was concerned to emphasise that her 'naturally... delicate constitute and nervous temperament' had been 'excited' by her 'considerable residence in the plains of India' and urged her speedy departure from the plains before her nervous strength was weakened to such an extent as to 'considerably injure her general health'.[63] The failure of the LMS directorate to pay for missionaries to travel at a class they felt necessary to stay healthy made many furious. Murray's chilling accusation that his wife's death was brought on 'chiefly through the effects of the voyage from England to Africa in such miserable accommodation' (underlining original) is a painfully raw articulation of this.[64] If the society had paid for a second-class steamer, Murray charged the LMS, 'I have little doubt that my dear wife would have been this day alive and my heart would not have been torn with grief.'[65]

For their part, the Directors of the LMS appear to have been suspicious of the measures demanded by missionaries abroad and repeatedly called their employees to account for the time they were absent from their stations through illness. In South India, Samuel Mateer, for example, was strongly reprimanded by the Directors for leaving his station to spend time with his wife in the Neilligey Hills after she suffered a miscarriage, leave for which they accused him of having undue certification.[66] Mateer was distraught, writing to express his 'great grief and astonishment' at the Directors' reaction.[67] Mateer emphasised to his employers his 20 years of good service to the LMS, as did the TDC, the local LMS auxiliary, which unanimously supported him. Other TDC members also claimed that they received the Directors' rebuke with 'deep regret and astonishment'.[68] More was at stake here than Mateer's personal career, and the TDC missionaries pleaded with their Directors 'for the work's sake and for our own and our families' sakes' that their good 'character' could be assumed, and they would be granted 'the Englishman's privilege of being reckoned guiltless till proved guilty'.[69]

The 'Missionary Character' idealised in missionary discourse always had to be constructed and defended, not only from indigenous peoples and colonial critics but from within the missionary family itself. Anxiety around illness exposes the ongoing sensitivity around 'character' and the hinging of that 'character' on a missionary's Englishness and the performance of their work *as a missionary*. Mateer and other missionaries who were similarly doubted felt betrayed when challenged by the Directors – challenges which they perceived as questioning their personal and professional integrity.

The debilitating effects of illness were particularly threatening to a missionary's professional role, a role and an identity that were formed through active engagement. Illness could literally render an individual unable to *be a missionary*, to preach, teach or even to remain overseas. Back in Britain, former missionaries unable to recover their health became almost invisible to the LMS. In contrast to those who left missionary work on grounds of age, or men who retired because their wives were ill, male and female missionaries who retired due to their own health were unable to partake in deputations with their colleagues and did not make speeches at missionary meetings. Appeals for money to provide for these missionaries kept them anonymous and represented them only through their impairments:

> Most of those dependent on the fund are in enfeebled health, while not a few are sorely afflicted and in great suffering....One – a veteran of forty-four years service – through a most painful and protracted illness has been confined to his bedroom over twelve years; another is subject to epilepsy; another is stone deaf; another is totally blind; another is imbecile.[70]

Until the 1890s, the annual collection for missionaries who had been disabled during missionary service was subsumed in the 'Widows and Orphans Fund', which the LMS had to remind contributors each year that 'Though actually called the WIDOWS AND ORPHANS FUND' it sought the comfort 'not only of the families of DECEASED MISSIONARIES, but also of RETIRED MISSIONARIES themselves...who, by length of service or through broken health, have been compelled to retire from their accustomed work...'.[71] Retired missionaries actually made up a substantial proportion of the recipients of this aid – in 1870, 20 of the 66 recipients of the 'Widows and Orphans Fund' were (male) invalided missionaries, yet missionaries disabled from missionary work were not only categorised alongside women and children as dependents but nominally subsumed under them.[72]

However, as I have discussed above, sickness could make as well as unmake identity and be binding as well as unravelling of the wider missionary community. In the recruitment literature for new missionaries, the risk to health involved in missionary activity (articulated in terms of climate, not nervous conditions) helped render missionary work heroic. When experiencing illness, missionaries claimed the tensions of duty between work and family were peculiar to their vocation. Furthermore, missionaries repeatedly dealt with sickness as a community – illness within that group was *imagined collectively* – as a blow to *the missionary enterprise*. At an individual level too sickness was performed in ways that reaffirmed the missionary identity of the patient. At least textually, it was claimed that missionaries struggled to maintain work to the last minute, were made unwell by the demands of missionary work itself and suffered illness in a patient, 'Christian' manner.

The way illness was narrated, recorded and disputed was shaped by local and international missionary networks and by the bureaucratic channels of the society. Because of the location of missionaries overseas, images of missionaries available in Britain were often textually created. Through illness, some missionaries became invisible because of their inability to represent themselves, others became more visible as letters circulated about their intimate bodily and mental states. In *published* texts, which were available to the supporters of missionary activity, all representations of ill missionaries were very limited, restricted to almost saintly illustrations of patient suffering, self-sacrifice and the relinquishing of life. Instead, it was primarily Indians and Africans who were represented as 'sick' and 'suffering' in published discourse, and the numerous and graphic illustrations of their sickness were used to consolidate representations of the colonial 'other'.

Conclusion

Missionary experiences of sickness complicated the discursive structures discussed in Chapter 3, by exposing more ambivalent statements of 'the self' and the potentially divided nature of the missionary community (especially around gender and location). To some extent this underscores the arguments made in Chapter 3: the ways in which missionaries discussed their own illnesses were so very different to how they described those of Indians and Africans as to reaffirm my argument that discourses of sickness were racialised and othering. But the vast differences between representations of sick Indians and Africans and those of missionaries and their families also contextualise, and so modify, that argument. It is not just a question, as it first appears, of indigenous people being objectified and reviled when they are sick and missionaries being treated more sympathetically. Although this is true, the difference runs far deeper. Even the scientific frameworks which missionaries wanted to embody when doctoring Indians and Africans appear to have been far less useful in their thinking about their own illnesses than were less tangible concepts of nerves and temperament. Whilst in Chapter 3, I demonstrated that sickness and health could operate as a binary opposition, In Chapter 4, I also argued that the way sickness shaped missionary thinking about their own bodies was not so clear-cut. Here the ambiguity and grey areas between those who can be considered 'sick' and those considered 'well' was far more evident. All discourses of difference were contingent and could shift.

Part III

Violence and Racialisation

Overview

Missionaries operated in spaces that were inscribed by violence. Colonial conquest was invariably violent, and the subordination of indigenous populations and the imposition of new disciplinary regimes often marked the coming of colonial rule across the globe. Patterns of colonial exploitation, from the expropriation of land, to the imposition of taxes to the creation of famine-inducing ecologies, were violent economically and had violent effects on the body, not least starvation. The rhetorical and epistemological dimensions of imperial violence subjected indigenous peoples to a violating European 'gaze' which wounded the psyches of individuals and communities, as well as violating the cultures of which they were a part.[1] In missionary writings, these forms of colonial violence coexisted alongside images of 'native' violence, of 'heathen cruelty', cannibalism, *sati* and infanticide. Violence structured colonial societies and pervaded colonial discourses.

In the following two chapters, I explore representations of violence in missionary writing and think about how violence was used to construct difference. As Rachel Standfield recently argued, violence was a site of colonial intimacy and was central in shaping cross-cultural encounter and producing a particular kind of European knowledge about the colonised.[2] As such, violence, like sexuality and, I have argued, sickness operated as a dense point of transfer, a powerful discourse with the potential to 'other'. Besides hurting the body, the experience of violence shapes thought patterns (generating fears, anxieties, memories and fantasies) and affects the ability to form, or not to form, relationships – dynamics crucial in thinking about processes of 'othering', colonial and otherwise.[3] Such processes do not only influence the victims and perpetrators of violence but also those witnessing, recording or consuming images of violence, experiences with their own power to evoke distress, horror and bodily feelings.[4]

Despite the pervasiveness of violence in colonial spheres, it is only recently that violence has emerged as a major topic of analysis in postcolonial and colonial history.[5] For the most part, the scholarship that does exist focuses on particular themes or catastrophic upheavals. The Indian Rebellion, Amritsar Massacre and transatlantic slave trade, for example, have been widely recognised (even by apologists of empire) as violent and troubling episodes.[6] Recently this has begun to change with scholars inspired by Foucault exploring disciplinary violence, for example.[7] But substantial connections are yet to be made between historiographies of violence and explorations of colonial societies ostensibly about other subjects, missionaries for example. Work on the striking case of excessive corporal punishment and execution conducted by Scottish missionaries at the Blantyre mission in Malawi, and the scandal these atrocities generated, remains unusual in its readiness to examine violence in relation to missionary activity.[8] But, as I will explore below, missionaries wrote about violence all the time and used it to characterise their colonial experiences and the 'others' they encountered. There are obvious ideological motivations for the historiographical reticence to explore violence in the British Empire. For British historians, it has been more comfortable to see Belgian, Dutch and German colonialisms as responsible for the most violent imperial regimes, and French and Portuguese decolonisation as representing a withdrawal from empire far bloodier from that of the British. As I shall explore in Chapter 6, such tendencies had long roots and formed a staple of colonial discourse. The sensitivity of violence as a subject matter more generally and the psychological and linguistic 'inexpressibility' of physical pain add to the difficulties surrounding the exploration of violence.[9] Further difficulties in analysing violence stem from problems of definition.

When trying to define violence (as with other discourses), its meanings start to unravel. For one thing, 'violence' appears only to denote what is 'illegitimate'; the same form of behaviour can be described as 'force' if legitimate and 'violent' if not.[10] The bestowal of legitimacy is socially and politically determined. Social context, the relationship between perpetrators and victims and the location in which violence takes place (at home, for example, in public, or during conflict) dramatically change the way in which a particular form of behaviour is interpreted.[11] Violence is also culturally constructed and, in moving between cultures, misunderstandings about the meanings of physical practices abound. British missionary and indigenous Indian or African interpretations of what was considered 'violent' did not always coincide (missionaries considered Indian forms of smallpox vaccination to be violent, for example, whilst practitioners considered it therapeutic).[12] It is this contingency of definition that gives violence its discursive power. In a colonial context, 'violence' would always be constructed through racialised understandings of its perpetrators, as well as constructing of them. For the purposes of this monograph, I explore 'violence' as identified (and therefore defined) by LMS missionaries as informed by their cultural background, colonial assumptions and personal experiences.

Further complications ensue from defining which forms of illegitimate behaviour may be seen to constitute *violence* as opposed to other forms of destructive or deviant behaviour. Violence does not necessarily have to be physically inflicted on the body *directly*; violating an environment, for example, can have very severe, yet indirect, bodily consequences (e.g. starvation resulting from herbicide). Verbal acts can be violent, particularly if such words have physical as well as psychological implications (as in witchcraft, for example).[13] Violence can be cultural or epistemological, as perpetrators attack belief systems, material culture and ways of life. My focus here, however, is on direct physical, or 'bodily' violence, as the form most emotively represented in missionary discourse *as* violence.

Over the course of the nineteenth century, missionary interactions with colonial violence shifted considerably. In the early nineteenth century, close links between the missionary movement and 'humanitarianism' meant that the report of settler violence perpetrated against indigenous people surfaced as a missionary concern across the world. In southern Africa, missionary humanitarian networks facilitated the flow of LMS reports of such violence to the imperial metropole via the Aborigines Select Committee. Missionaries were associated both in the Cape and back in Britain with the exposure of European violence overseas and an antagonistic relationship with settlers as a result of such disclosures.[14] By the mid-nineteenth century, however, such patterns had shifted and the report of settler violence steadily muffled. At the same time, however, missionary attitudes towards 'heathen' violence remained unchanging and resilient. The fears, language and images of 'heathen' violence were literally repeated decade after decade. Indeed, the extent to which these images endured was often at odds with the changing nature of indigenous societies – missionaries clung onto the horrors of *sati* and hookswinging as current concerns long after their decline and abolition. I shall be exploring some of these trajectories in the chapters that follow.

Chapter 5 explores the way in which violence was used to construct a colonial 'other'. Although the imagination of Africa as a 'dark continent', or *sati* and female infanticide in India, have already been much examined by postcolonial scholars, 'violence' as a concept is seldom used to think about such phenomena *together*. In taking violence, or more specifically bodily violence, as my category of analysis, I hope to draw out similarities in the representation of indigenous people performing very different cultural practices in different sites of empire and explore how missionaries understood such practices through a broader framework of 'heathen cruelty'. Chapter 6 uses the concept of violence to explore representations of *European*, or colonial violence, and the complications and ruptures this posed to missionary thinking about their own identities.

5
Violence and the Construction of the Other

> In China, Persia, and Arabia, in Phoenicia and Egypt in Aethiopia [sic] and at Carthage, in Peru and Mexico, in Greece and Rome, in Germany and in almost every country of the world, men have similarly, in the name of religion, deluged the earth with the blood of their fellow men... Yet even all these frightful enormities appear less surprising to us, when we hear of the horrors practised in their religious rites by the ancestors even of the present race of our English Rulers. Among them, on the commencement of a war, when some great chieftain was attacked with disease, or when any other calamity affecting the public occurred, the Druids, who were the priests of their religion, in order to secure the favour of the gods, presented them with the offerings of human victims, attended with circumstances of peculiar cruelty and horror.[1]

> *The dark places of the earth are full of the habitations of cruelty*, and... the power of the Gospel alone is adequate to the removal of the wills by which they are oppressed.[2]

One of the most pervasive tropes in missionary writing is the prevalence of 'heathen' violence. Cannibalism, human-sacrifice, tribal warfare, circumcision, ritual suicide, hookswinging, foot-binding, widow-burning, infanticide, self-flagellation and scarification, to take just some examples, operated in missionary discourse to identify 'heathenism' with violence, barbarism and savagery. In locating violence in the European past and in the non-European present, violence became a contributory discourse to stadial understandings of human progress and a powerful discourse of difference. Missionary periodicals presented tales of human sacrifice in England as sobering reminders of British history and as imperatives to proselytise further. Missionaries overseas conveyed endless images of 'heathen' violence back to Britain through letters, journal articles and lectures. Besides being the *subject* of articles and lectures, violence was part of the backdrop to many more mundane occurrences: depictions of violence woven between prosaic discussions of school-building and preaching kept missionary accounts vivid and made fundraising easier. Engravings also frequently carried undertones of violence, often presenting African, Polynesian or Aboriginal men armed with spears or other weaponry. Many cultures and 'tribes' were depicted as 'savage' and defined through their violence. Even the labelling of certain peoples as 'peaceable' consolidated violence as an axis upon which 'heathen' societies could be placed. This helped to justify missionary work: Christianity alone, it was argued, could end these cycles of violence. Violence in missionary discourse was an important subject through which 'heathenism' was 'othered', and indigenous people were racialised.

In this chapter, I examine how violence operated as a tool of racialisation, and how its report could undermine, denigrate or demonise those whose violence was represented. I argue that the very association of people of colour with violence, whoever the perpetrator, focussed attention on the somatic and defined those racialised 'others' through the body. It is not, however, simply the case that missionaries saw all 'heathens' as 'violent' (though this was a powerful theme); the kinds of violence in which indigenous people were expected to engage varied across different sites of empire. The ways in which southern Africa and India were imagined to differ was reflected in and inflected by missionary descriptions of the violence they encountered there.

Violence and the 'dark continent'

As Patrick Brantlinger powerfully demonstrated, images of Africa 'darkened' over the nineteenth century. A product of the 'transition, or transvaluation, from abolition to Scramble', the 'myth of the dark continent' enveloped the Victorian imagination, and Africa was increasingly associated with a dystopian savagery. By the end of the nineteenth century, British travel writers, explorers, missionaries and novelists represented Africa as a 'center of evil, a part of the world possessed by a demonic darkness or barbarism, represented above all by slavery, human sacrifice, and cannibalism, which it was their duty to exorcise.'[3] Inherent in all these characteristics, though not stated explicitly by Brantlinger, was the centrality of *violence* to this 'darkness'. It was not simply that Africa was unknown, disordered or chaotic, but the darkness was threatening, brutal and carnal; a turbulent and threatening (far from passive) colonial space.

Missionary literature formed a widely read genre through which violent and disturbing accounts of Africa circulated in Britain.[4] In private writings, missionaries recorded encounters with new forms of violence in accounts which suggest considerable unease with their location in the 'dark Continent'. In published missionary media, where uncertainties expressed privately appeared with exaggerated intensity, 'Africa' evoked and was evoked by images of 'barbaric' violence. Its very landscape was associated with dangerous animals and adverse climates. Graphic descriptions were provided of bloody 'tribal' warfare, of men hacked to death in vengeful killings, murdered women, abandoned babies eaten by wolves, prisoners of war tortured to death, awful punishments, indigenous and Arabic slavery and grisly animal sacrifices. In this sense, the images that missionaries painted and those of other travellers, literary tourists, colonial explorers, geographers and scientists, bear many similarities.

Christine Bolt goes further, arguing that missionary writings not only fed into the general colonial construction of a 'barbaric' Africa but that 'all too often, in fact, the missionary accounts are indistinguishable in their generalizations and their sense of moral superiority from the verdicts of British travellers.'[5] Like other travellers to Africa, missionaries were anxious to assert their heroism, mobility and 'objective' authority as they recorded 'horrors' which could little be imagined 'back home'. There is indeed much evidence in the writings of LMS missionaries to support such a claim. The travel writings of David Livingstone or Robert Moffat, for example, form significant links between missionaries and other explorers in their self-obsessed accounts of arduous journeys framed against a turbulent African backdrop. Such accounts emphasised the author's heroism by detailing the dangers they faced in violent spaces of empire.[6]

However, whilst there were many shared motifs between groups of colonial writers, the dynamics and purposes of textual production differed slightly between them. Firstly, whilst itinerancy was an important element of missionary work, most missionaries resided with specific groups of people for substantial periods. This led them to witness, negotiate and engage with indigenous violence in different ways to travelling spectators whose experience was ephemeral. Secondly, the periodical genre, which missionaries used more systematically than other travellers, lent itself towards concise, vivid writing and meant that violence was less embedded in other commentary than it was in lengthy books. Thirdly, in describing themselves seeing, touching and healing injured Africans, missionaries depicted an intimacy with the violence that their contemporaries often lacked, and this altered the nature of the spectacle their texts evoked. Fourthly, missionaries had a personal and professional stake in qualifying images of a 'dark' Africa with ones of peoples that could be 'enlightened'. Although these differences in the representation of violence are subtle, they fed into the particular way in which difference was created in missionary thought.

Some missionary writings were deliberately intended to refute other more sensational forms of travel writing and the violent and pessimistic images of indigenous people they produced. Alongside images of 'irredeemable savages', missionaries were compelled to provide for their public and supporters, alternative depictions of 'civilised' Africans, and Christian African communities, which, if only appearing as dim lights in the darkness, provided something to show for the money poured into their work and a rationale to continue to do so. Above all, the ultimate image that missionaries were creating was not one of the horrors of a dark continent in and of itself, but the horror of '*heathenism*'. As such, the explicatory framework upon which missionaries hinged their accounts of indigenous violence was distinctive.

When Robert Moffat contemplated his work in southern Africa he wrote that the 'sights witnessed, mental and physical' demonstrated 'the reckless prodigality of human life' he believed characterised 'heathen' societies.[7] It was not only violence he claimed to be witnessing but, held in this violence, 'barbarism' and 'heathenism' itself. 'Heathenism' was the most powerful line around which missionaries orientated 'civilised' or 'uncivilised' societies, and it was heathenism's violence that was used to validate their own actions in Africa and elsewhere. 'Heathenism' connected the experience and interpretation of violence across colonial sites; it was not simply that Africa was a 'dark continent' but that the whole 'heathen world' was horrific. Naming the horror as 'heathenism', however, did not mean it was discrete from those other frameworks of difference: 'heathenism' was always also racialised.

Violence was one of the many discourses in missionary writing where 'body' and 'culture', signified by 'blackness' and 'heathenness', operated together to register difference. When the Reverend Sykes claimed to be 'earnestly praying to the Lord' to end the 'turmoil' amongst 'these dark, benighted, fearfully savage people', he suggested the *embodiment* of a cultural 'turmoil' in that 'dark' people.[8] His slippage was a common one. The perpetration of violence by Africans was often explained through racialised imaginings of 'barbarous' intellect: more prone to irrationality, jealousy and crimes of passion, Africans were infantilised, de-masculinised and racialised through their 'need' to resort to violence. The figure of the 'savage' in whom violence was always implicit was the embodiment of such concerns.

The construction of the 'savage' in missionary writing is complex. The idea that African people were 'biologically' different was never openly embraced by the LMS and the kinds of anthropological descriptions of race commonly associated with a polygenistic 'hardening' of racial attitudes were openly scorned.[9] However, the way in which missionaries wrote about African bodies, which differs greatly from how they wrote about their own, demonstrates the importance of the body in registering difference in their thinking. For one thing, the bodies of Indians and Africans were *more visible* than European ones in missionary writings.

Descriptions of 'heathen' violence were often detailed, graphic and gruesome and therefore fed into wider colonial tendencies to define Africans through the somatic. 'The *Machaga* sprang on their victims as tigers on their prey', John Mackenzie wrote of the Ndebele warriors' attack on Kirekilwe, a Tswana Chief. He went on to elaborate on rumours that 'they did not kill him outright, but hacked off his hands and feet and left him thus on the ground, to pine in anguish, or to be torn to pieces by wild beasts'.[10] The image is horrifying: the animalistic representation of the perpetrators followed by the victim's further dismemberment by animals themselves. It is notable that injured Africans were denied the protective wrap of euphemising rhetoric that usually surrounds injury in missionary writings. The physical injuries of white groups, both Afrikaner and British, were not recorded in the same way.[11] This discrepancy contributed to a brutalisation of Africans in missionary discourse, not only in the violence attributed to them but by reducing them to bodies. In appearing broken and mangled, black bodies were objectified in missionary writing; the experience of violence, however articulated, was inflected on the body, leading black people to be seen as black bodies and black bodies to be seen as different.

The representation of the Ndebele in missionary writing demonstrates the use of violence as a racialising discourse and the ever-present slippage between 'race' and 'culture' within it. The Ndebele were repeatedly described as being *inherently* 'barbaric'. King Mzilikazi was portrayed as the personification, as well as the director, of extreme violence, a violent despot who 'having effectively crushed all the neighbouring tribes, rules over an immense extent of country with an iron despotism' where he was 'adored as a god by his prostrate vassals.'[12] His life story, Robert Moffat wrote, 'formed an interminable catalogue of crimes', inscribed onto the very landscape of Ndebeleland where 'scarcely a mountain over extensive regions but bore the marks of his deadly ire'.[13] Ndebele raids were claimed to be 'cruel', their methods of killing and their slaughter of women and children were particularly condemned and suggested to have a savage, animalistic quality.

Images of the Ndebele were so deep-rooted that the way in which they were described demonstrates remarkable consistency over time. In 1856, Moffat described the Ndebele as a 'nation of murderers, whose hand is against everyone'.[14] In 1863, John Mackenzie wrote of them as 'savages, every one of whose spears had repeatedly drunk the blood of the aged and the decrepit, the defenceless female and the tender infant'.[15] In 1889, Cousins, writing from London and entirely reliant on secondary sources, confirmed their 'bloodthirsty extravagance'.[16] Towards the end of the century, when the new medium of photography extended into missionary periodicals, photographs of Ndebele weapons appeared in *Chronicle* to illustrate articles on Ndebele missions (see Figure 2) and photographs of Ndebeleland itself were mounted on the tools of violence.[17] In this way, missionary writings fed into wider ethnographical discourses marking national character, body and 'race' onto African 'tribes'. Similar tropes, for example, appeared in exhibitionary discourses: the Ndebele played a central role in the 1899 'Savage South Africa' show (London), which promised its audience 'a horde of savages direct from their Karals', including 200 'Matabele' and 'wild animals'.[18]

Christine Bolt suggests the British 'admired' (perhaps feared) the 'warlike' Ndebele as a 'martial race'.[19] Whilst also keen to emphasise the physicality of the Ndebele, missionary writings allowed no such admiration – 'strong' or 'manly' behaviour could only be recognised if it was also Christian. Rather than 'brave' or 'heroic', missionaries wrote of the Ndebele as 'cruel', 'cowardly', treacherous', 'lustful', 'lazy' and 'grossly superstitious'.[20] They also constructed the Ndebele as emasculated, not least through their sexuality and their 'impure lives'.[21] Ndebele soldiers were suggested to be emasculated before their king, 'a nation of warriors ... vociferating language disgustingly puerile to one in whose presence they dare scarcely express a thought or speak a manly word'.[22] At the same time as Mzilikazi was represented as the personification of barbarity, he was infantilised before the power of missionaries themselves. In particular, it was claimed he was 'in love' with

Figure 2 Ndebele Weaponry
Source: *Chronicle*, December 1893, 307.

Robert Moffat, before whom 'the tyrant... made to do the bidding of the missionary with the pliancy of a child'.[23]

Crucially, the LMS linked Ndebele violence to their rejection of Christianity and determined 'heathenism' which continued despite Mzilikazi's apparent veneration of Moffat. The LMS had been exceptionally unsuccessful amongst the Ndebele (it took nearly 30 years to make their first two converts), and missionaries often had to account for the failure of their mission to their employers. In explaining why he had failed to convert a single Ndebele in his 13 years of missionary service, Reverend Thomas claimed Christianity went 'dead against... everything that dinstiguishes them as the Amantabele Tribe'. Their distinctive identity was organised around violence, for 'the Gospel', according to Thomas, 'destroys entirely their military standing, whose sole object is bloodshed and death, to devour and live on other tribes'. Wracking up the emotional intensity of the piece, Thomas concluded with the chilling statement that 'every year they send marauding parties to the weaker tribes, to kill the aged and very little children.'[24] Ndebele culture was claimed to be particularly brutal, characterised by despotic rule and a military structure. Missionary representations of a dark and dangerous

Africa were filtered through their own spiritual battles and reflected their particular concerns about 'heathen' violence: a link was often drawn between being 'peaceable' and being 'convertible'.[25]

Missionaries had a professional stake in claiming the violence they were fighting was 'heathen': it kept open the possibility for change. Representing the missionary struggle as one against violence also allowed them to draw on emotive humanitarian justifications for missionary work when scepticism at home as to the benefits of proselytisation grew. Both victims and perpetrators of violence were depicted as vulnerable people in need of European benevolence.

From the late eighteenth century onwards, missionaries wrote about violence using a discourse of sympathy. Constructing African people as mutilated victims dependent on European pity was clearly othering in effect but, in its emotional identification with the victim of violence, also carried a commitment to human universalism. Multi-sensory descriptions of violence suggested the viewer's own suffering through the act of witnessing physical pain. In one case, an example taken from the 1880s when such discourses were becoming increasingly confined to missionary circles and to what Hall calls the 'Abolitionist public', Reverend Hepburn responded with horrified compassion to hearing a slave being beaten 'mercilessly' by his African owner near Lake Ngami. Hepburn described his own body as damaged imaginatively by the experience of witnessing violence. 'Our hearts were lacerated by hearing the heavy blows', he wrote, 'my heart bled.'[26] This is reminiscent of Thomas Laqueur's argument that humanitarian discourses drew on the understanding of 'the personal body' as both the 'locus of pain' and the 'common bond between those who suffer and those who would help'.[27] Hepburn linked his own body with that of the slave. Many other missionaries went further to demand that their readers too 'feel' what the victim 'must have felt'. Such techniques lessened the tendency towards detached, voyeuristic, possibly morbid but otherwise uninterested responses to violence found elsewhere in colonial discourse, which reflected a sense that those victims and perpetrators were too distant or too different to engage with.[28] To some extent, the echoing of violence in the body of the witness allowed violence inflicted on others to be reconceptualised by missionaries as part of their own struggle against heathenism.

Encounters with violence were often formative moments of a missionary's experience of the 'foreign field'. They were also emotionally traumatic ones that made present their own bodily vulnerability, as well as the 'otherness' of those they encountered. Unlike in India, where violence was discursively confined within a 'Hindu' system of which they were not a part, missionaries in Africa were often caught up in turbulent geo-political dynamics. During the Cape Frontier Wars of the first half of the nineteenth century, and the Ndebele war towards its end, missionaries and their families were displaced, and their stations occupied and destroyed. Inter-communal as well as colonial conflicts were profoundly disorientating both physically and psychologically. In the midst of an Ndebele attack on the Ngwato, amongst whom he was living, John Mackenzie found himself dispatched to the mountains along with the Ngwato women and children. 'Matebele warriors did not make nice distinctions,' Chief Sekgomi had told the missionary, and 'the colour of a man's skin was not easily discovered in the darkness of the night.'[29] As the only man to flee the scene of conflict, the manly self-image Mackenzie projected in his other writings was troubled by the experience, and the status his race and gender usually conferred undermined.[30]

Violence can not only both confirm and alter power dynamics but is sometimes about the performance of power itself. Some missionaries, paranoid about the degree of dependence they had on the African chiefs they constructed as all-powerful leaders, interpreted violent episodes as intentional performances of power they were intended to witness.[31] In 1848, Mr Edwards witnessed an exchange he interpreted in this way. The missionary had been summoned from his home by messengers from the (unnamed) Chief of the Mabotsa in connection with a man who had stolen food at a time of famine. Arriving at the court, Edwards found the Chief 'full of rage'.[32] Members of the court 'smiled contemptuously' at his efforts to move the Chief to forgiveness, and he was interrupted in so doing by the arrival of a messenger who announced that the accused man, his wife and baby had been killed. Edwards was horrified, 'intimated [his] strong misappropriation' and left. His disapproval, it transpired, had been anticipated, and Edwards learned later that the Chief, 'fully conceived' of his opposition, had acted before he could arrive, 'aware that he had caused us much sorrow by the dreadful punishment he inflicted for a comparably trifling offence, without giving us an opportunity of redeeming them by offering a ransom'.[33] The humiliation Edwards felt at this display of power, and other similar incidents, fed into missionary paranoia about their vulnerable positioning in indigenous societies.[34]

Representing violence as something 'other', 'heathen' and 'dark' provided a way of negotiating some of the physical and psychological dislocation that missionaries experienced in colonial spaces. It also fed into a frightening picture of the 'heathen world'. Whilst missionaries abroad wrote from specific local situations about personal experiences of violence, editors, publishing their letters for dissemination in Britain, enwrapped these accounts in a broader framework of 'heathen cruelty'. Introducing Edwards's account in the *Missionary Magazine* the editor wrote that the incident demonstrated that '"the dark places of the earth are full of the habitations of cruelty," and that the power of the Gospel alone is adequate to the removal of the evils by which they were oppressed.'[35]

In missionary depictions of Africa, violence operated as a discourse of difference. 'Heathen' societies were explicitly claimed to be more violent than Christian ones, and Christianity was claimed to quell such violence. At the same time as drawing on ideas about 'heathenism', these images of 'savages', warfare, the lack of burial rites and attacks on women and children were tropes which were evoked in relation to specific *African* violence. Violence, interpreted simply as 'savage', was stripped of its political context, explained instead through 'corrupt' morals and effeminate or infantile chiefs governed by jealousy and 'passion'. Such representations of violence not only reflected the missionary inability to recognise 'culture' or 'civilisation' in Africa but also contributed to this tendency. As such, Africans were depicted waiting for European help. Only Christianity, it was claimed, could end their violence.

India

Images of violence were similarly pervasive in missionary accounts from India which also detailed the somatic injury of indigenous people and interpreted violence within an essentialist explanatory framework. In both continents, descriptions of violence were heavily influenced by race and gender assumptions, and 'heathen cruelty' was evoked in stark opposition to 'Christian love' and British ways of life. The forms violence took, however, and the way in which it was imagined, differed. Whilst violence in Africa evoked 'heathen' *disorder*, in India, violence was principally constructed through 'heathen' *civilisation*.

Islam, in missionary thinking, was readily identified with violence, 'tyranny' and 'fanaticism'. In keeping with the established colonial narratives of Indian history, missionaries associated Islam with a 'violent' Moghal past of 'despotic' Muslim rule.[36] Again like other colonial thinkers, the LMS partially attributed the Indian Rebellion to an unleashing of this hunger for power and blamed the violence on diabolically inspired 'Mohammedans'.[37] Attacks against European women in 1857 were also seen in light of the 'cowardly' 'Muslim' violence which, missionaries believed, Indian men inflicted on their own womenfolk. It was Hinduism, however, which occupied most missionary thinking about India and about the violence they saw residing there.

'Hinduism', interpreted by missionaries variously as a religion, a cultural system and a race, was claimed to be saturated with violence. Religious festivals were seen as particularly violent occasions, rituals and rites of passage were treated with horror, and cultural customs, such as *sati*, were found abhorrent. Violence was used to demonstrate that Hinduism was 'evil', and self-inflicted violence was cited as evidence of Hindu 'irrationality' and 'perversion'. Violence was thus located within the very essence of Hinduism.[38]

Idols were troubling sites of violence. In particular, Śiva and his wife Kālī were crucial to missionary representations of Hinduism and often used symbolically to evoke a violent religious system.[39] That Śiva could both bring death and conquer disease and that Kālī could represent what missionaries considered to be a contradictory combination of maternity, sexuality and violence made them troubling figures.[40] As Hugh Urban notes, the British generally abhorred Kālī due to early nineteenth-century associations between the goddess and *thuggee*, and she came to operate as 'a projection of everything that frightened British citizens in a foreign land, all the disorder, savagery, and unrest that threatened to unravel the fragile order of their rule'.[41]

Missionaries found material icons of Kālī violent visually, and believed her worship evoked violent spirituality and other violent actions (such as *thuggee*).[42] 'Everything calculated to inspire terror surrounds her', wrote Reverend Hacker of Kālī in the 1890s, 'She drinks blood like water. She wears a necklace of skulls. Her clothing is dead men's hands. Her earrings are two dead bodies. Her eyes are red, like those of a drunkard. Her face and breast are besmeared with blood'.[43] A complex slippage occurred between textual descriptions of Kālī as an icon; of Kālī's actions as described by her followers; bodily violence either performed in her name (or thought to be); and bodily violence believed to have been supernaturally inspired by her. At one and the same time, missionaries ridiculed her worship as the veneration of a 'piece of wood' and gave her diabolical agency capable of inflicting 'real' violence. She 'delights in sacrifices', Hacker wrote, 'taking great pleasure' in 'the blood of human beings'. Although the British had banned 'murderous sacrifices', hookswinging, and other 'abominations', he continued, 'horrid rites' were practised yet, 'in out-of-the-way places' beyond the gaze of imperial rule.[44] Hinduism as an organisational framework was used to explain the 'violent' behaviour of otherwise 'peaceable' Indians.

Missionaries experienced Hindu festivals as a terrifying extension of these concerns.[45] The crowds, the iconic material culture, the noise, smells and 'chaos' associated with festivals marked them as disorientating and frightening events quite unlike missionaries' own observances. Rituals involving self-inflicted pain were taken as bodily evidence of the power 'cruel' cultures had over Indian people.[46] These anxieties often manifested themselves in denunciations of practices missionaries read as 'violent'.[47] Descriptions of hookswinging, a ritual (that become increasingly popular during the nineteenth century) where a person (usually a young man) volunteered to be 'swung' publically either from ropes or through hooks driven through the flesh of their back, were particularly graphic.[48] Missionaries wrote of the 'swollen' and 'tortured body' of 'victims' who were 'beaten black and blue' and suspended in 'agony' and paraded through the streets; depictions which have the same somatic quality as descriptions of violence from Africa.[49] Violence was described in such a way as to dehumanise the participant altogether, as in Edith Fooks's claim when referring to the practice a few years earlier when '[s]ometimes the poor, mangled body was so torn, that before the progress of the car was completed *it* would fall from the hook' (my italics).[50] The criminalisation of hookswinging in the 1850s (after which effigies were substituted for people) did little to curb its condemnation in missionary periodicals.[51] It is significant that Fooks's account, produced in the 1890s, is based on practices abolished before she had even arrived in India and which she had never seen. Her account was illustrated by rumours that 'only two years ago this fiendish festival still boasted a human victim!' 'I forget in what part of India it was', she added – where the incident had been does not seem to have mattered, it simply contributed to the general understanding of India as a 'heathen' and violent place.[52]

In trying to rationalise hookswinging whilst simultaneously refusing to enter into the conceptual framework in which it operated, missionaries struggled with the allocation of agency; how willingly *did* Indian men and women submit to such practices, and to what extent were they simply 'victims' of a culture apparently vested with its own volition? Missionaries could little grasp voluntary participation in such practices, preferring to search for external forces. As Nicholas Dirks explores, agency was a key issue for other British groups in imperial India as well as missionaries in the controversies surrounding hookswinging.[53] Doping was one explanation offered to explain participation and was used to circumnavigate the enigma of voluntary involvement.[54] This had the effect of heightening the violence of the ceremony in representations. Hookswinging was represented as a coercive spectacle where 'the poor victims are drugged and intoxicated until they are not only frantic' but 'almost insensible to the sufferings inflicted upon them'.[55]

Societal and family pressures were also offered as explanations for the practice and were imagined to take many forms running from taunting or encouragement to genuine (if misguided) religious conviction to sheer sadism. One missionary reported that participants in the *charak puja* festival, which involved hookswinging, had claimed that such practices were performed to 'gratify the women'. Such an idea was profoundly disrupting to his conception of womanhood. 'What a monstrous state of morals must pervade that community where such barbarities are practised to gratify the females!', he deplored.[56] Significantly, the author continued by expressing his particular astonishment that such practices were conducted by 'the amiable and kind Hindoos!'[57] It was not only gendered expectations that were undermined by these acts but the racialising framework through which Indian people were understood. Indians were not 'savages'; they were usually understood in more feminised terms than black, African, men; they were not spear-wielding 'tribesmen'. Yet at the same time, whilst Indians were indeed constructed as 'gentle', their entire social fabric was also claimed to be saturated with violence. Violence was located in the very essence of Hinduism, and therefore, in 'Hindus'.

Given the preoccupation with Indian domesticity, it is not surprising that missionaries saw the family as a site of violence. Postcolonial feminist scholars have demonstrated the power of the paradigmatic assertion in colonial discourse at large that white men needed to rescue Indian women from Indian men in colonial discourse at large.[58] Both imperial officials and missionaries powerfully mobilised this construction to justify all kinds of colonial interventions. Nancy Paxton has discussed how Parliamentary reports cast Indian women in the position of victim and Indian men were associated with the gothic villain.[59] Missionary periodicals can be added to these genres. Violence was suggested to loom behind the lives of Indian women, so the missionary phrase ran, from 'her birth to her grave, increasing as she advances in age'.[60]

Sati was the archetypal example of this, and was used to imagine the 'degraded' state of Indian womanhood long after its abolition in 1829. Throughout the nineteenth century, memory, rumour and very occasional acts of *sati* themselves were used to assert a *sati* 'type' and to embody the ongoing horrors faced by Indian women. Evocations of *sati* were also used to underline other forms of violence, abuse and deprivation faced by Indian widows. As in the case of hookswinging, explanations offered for a practice that missionaries found 'contrary to reason' varied enormously. Some accounts focussed on male violence (represented by male relatives who threw women attempting to escape the fire back into the flames); others drew on an uncomplicated notion of 'irrationality' or 'superstition', and yet others recognised that many women actively chose their *sati*.[61] But even those who killed themselves willingly were not simply 'misguided', missionaries suggested, rather they were victims of a system constructed through violence.

Discourses of female infanticide also encapsulated the sense that the lives of Indian women were structured around violence. Writing from Madras, Mrs Porter, a missionary wife and advocate of female education in India, claimed that 'in Rajastan and Guzerat, and some other places, female children are daily seen lying dead in the streets,'places outside or peripheral to British rule or newly conquered.[62] Porter's explanation that 'mothers kill their female children and throw them into tanks and rivers to preserve them from future misery' is typical of missionary writings where Indian mothers were often depicted as helpless children themselves.[63] Locating infanticide within a paradigm of both 'Hindoo degradation' and one wider yet of 'heathen' violence against women, Porter drew on a logic, typical in missionary thinking, of double vulnerability where both the recipient and the perpetrator of violence were victims of a cruel culture.[64] The gendering of violence masculine, and the commitment to the idea that mothers love their children, led missionaries to reason that a mother who killed or hurt her children was herself victim of 'heathenism'.[65]

This pattern was extended beyond infanticide to depictions of more banal incidents of violence. Speaking at the LMS's anniversary meeting, Reverend Simpson, a Wesleyan missionary stationed in Madras, gave a graphic description of smallpox inoculation (portrayed as 'violent' despite its therapeutic purpose).[66] He described how, during the 'Festival of the Splinter', a mother 'deliberately thrust the thorn into the child's fat side' and, writing that she 'clasped her bleeding child against her bruised and bleeding heart,' bound them metaphorically in the evocation of pain.[67] Contradicting the general claim that 'heathen' parents lacked affection, Simpson continued:

> do not tell me that she did not love the child, she loved it to the heart's core; but she so loved it that she dreaded the touch of the fever; she dreaded the infliction of the small-pox; she so loved the child that she rent her own heart in throwing the charm around it.[68]

Reverend Goffin, in a fictional account of the branding of a small boy, drew on similar ideas, taking on the voice of the boy's sister to cry 'the cruel demons *had* got the child – had got my father and mother too, and were making them torture my little brother.'[69]

Throughout missionary writing perpetrators of violence were depicted as 'the poor victims of superstition and cruelty'.[70] The conceptual severing of the physical perpetrator of violence from the moral one allowed missionaries to maintain, despite the horrors they recorded, that Indian people themselves were worthy of salvation.[71] As David Savage discussed in regard to the question of female education in India, the ultimate oppressor of women in India was neither Indian men nor, in the case of infanticide, the Indian mother acting of her own free will but cultural practice and the Hindu religion itself.[72]

Besides strategically salvaging the morality of potential converts, the location of blame in 'culture' rather than 'people' also reflected wider ambivalence in missionary thinking. As in other strands of colonial discourse, missionaries saw 'uncivilised' cultures as reflecting the capabilities of a 'backward' people and thus closely linked culture with 'racial' human development. But missionaries also interpreted the different cultures they encountered with reference to theological frameworks. When missionaries described India as a 'hellish land', or as 'Satan's kitchen', they were not only talking metaphorically but were also reflecting ideas about real demonic agency. Goffin's discussions of 'cruel' 'heathen' parents being 'possessed' was also made in this context.

For missionaries, India was, like Africa, nightmarish, dark and violent. Missionaries were much less shocked than their contemporaries by the violence of the Indian Rebellion which confirmed rather than ruptured their expectations. Whilst some elements of Indian civilisation had been portrayed positively in Britain, particularly in early nineteenth-century orientalist writings, in missionary periodicals India had always been constructed as a 'hellish' land of violence, *sati* and infanticide. The shared language of a violent 'heathenism' enjoined the representation of Africa and India in missionary thought.

Violence, 'heathenism' and the British Empire

'Peace, universal peace, has been established from Cape Comorin to the Himalayan Mountains', Reverend Edward Porter wrote in the 1840s, claiming that 'peace and security' had been brought to 'one hundred millions of our fellow-beings and fellow subjects' in India. It was British colonialism that had brought this security, Porter continued, claiming 'the Hindoos in general rejoice in the rest and security which they experienced under our dominion in comparison with the anarchy and bloodshed which they suffered under their former rulers.'[73] That violence in India was located beyond the boundaries of British rule, either temporally, that is *before* British rule, or geographically, in either the 'Native States' or in isolated rural areas, was paradigmatic in missionary thought. The presentation of *sati* in missionary descriptions of India was typical of this. In the early part of my period, it was claimed that 'the burning of the Hindoo widow... still prevails in several of the countries of India not under the control of Britain, nor yet traversed by the messengers of peace', and, throughout the nineteenth century, *sati* evoked the memory of a violent pre-British past.[74]

Although missionary attitudes to empire were often ambivalent, the belief that British rule had the potential to rid the world of violence, and protect colonial others from 'heathen' cruelty, was almost universally upheld and often used to validate imperial expansion.[75] As the editor of the *Missionary Magazine* wrote in reference to *sati*, 'whatever may be thought of the policy of extending our conquests in that country... every friend of humanity and religion, must rejoice, that, wherever the power of Britain rules, these dark and murderous deeds are known no longer.'[76] Forms of colonial rule that failed to take an active part in the suppression of 'heathen violence' were deeply problematic to missionary thinking. The EIC was roundly condemned for its reluctance to intervene in hookswinging rituals, and, worse yet, for its collection of pilgrim tax at Juggernath, actions that represented complicity with 'heathenism' and a failure in imperial duty.[77] In contrast, its 'abolition of female immolation', 'suppression of human sacrifices', 'extinction of the Thugs and of slavery' and 'establishment of liberty of conscience' were held up as 'the great safeguards of our empire'.[78] Such policies had, one writer believed, sprung 'from a liberal, humane and enlightened policy' characteristic of British rule.[79]

The colonial structure to which missionaries in southern Africa could refer was notably less stable. In the early nineteenth century, the LMS had been very critical of British settlers and governance in the Cape, but (as I will discuss in Chapter 6), over the course of the century, imperial rivalry with other European powers, Boer expansion and an influx of white emigrants meant formal British rule was increasingly favoured as the least bad scenario (indigenous self-rule was not considered as a serious option). British influence in Africa, however, was of a very different nature to that in India and much less interventionist in the day-to-day lives of the inhabitants. Nevertheless, here also, many missionaries became convinced that only the British Empire could bring 'peace' to a troubled continent.

John Mackenzie, the LMS missionary, colonial commissioner and great advocate of British imperialism in southern Africa, argued repeatedly that *only* the expansion of the British Empire could pacify the violence which was otherwise endemic in the sub-continent. Whilst very critical of unregulated colonial settlement, Mackenzie remained committed to a 'vision of the future' that 'ends in peace', '[a]ssuredly, as England has abolished duelling, and still retains her honour and her self-respect', he wrote, 'so will the savage arbitrament of war be discredited and disused the world over.'[80] Whilst Mackenzie acknowledged that 'trouble [was] inseparable from empire', his construction of an idyllic 'Austral Africa' was nevertheless one of 'pax Britannia'.[81] Evoking the powerful language of an empire of 'liberty', Mackenzie claimed that 'England' had 'bestowed' 'liberties' and 'rights' to 'her colonists' and peace and 'civilisation' to the colonised.[82]

As in Mackenzie and Porter's imagery, violence in Africa and India was used to confirm and consolidate European identity as superior. Brantlinger argues that the nightmarish constructions of Africa in colonial literature suggest that Africa was used to locate elements of European fantasy.

> The Dark Continent turned into a mirror reflecting on one hand the heroic and saintly self-images the Victorians wished to see, but on another casting the ghostly shadow of guilt and regression ... shaped by ... a psychology of blaming the victim through which Europeans projected onto Africans their own deviant impulses.[83]

Brantlinger locates the guilt driving this reflexive fantasy in slavery and its legacy. Europeans, he suggests, performed a retrospective not fully articulated negotiation of the horrors of transatlantic slavery by reproducing the dehumanised images of Africans upon which it had depended. In missionary writing too, slavery haunted violent depictions of Africa, with the violence of African and Arabic slaveholders emphasised as though to redeem the behaviour of Europeans. The continuing violence of nineteenth-century colonialism across the world can be usefully added to enslavement as a source of such guilt.

'Tribal' warfare was a recurring trope in missionary representations of Africa and one they constructed as 'traditional'. Although the introduction of mechanised weaponry had rendered long-established cattle-raiding patterns more deadly, missionaries argued the converse: that 'the introduction of guns among the natives ... puts an end to most of their petty wars, and renders such as do occur much less bloody than they formerly were'.[84] Similarly, whilst the pressures of European colonisation had had a destabilising effect in southern Africa and generated much inter-communal conflict between disintegrating polities, missionaries refused, for the most part, to acknowledge its impact, instead constructing such conflicts as 'tribal'.[85] In doing so, they deflected attention from European violence. As I explore in Chapter 6, encounters with continuing British colonialism were troubling and fed into missionary anxiety about Africa.

Missionaries asserted that European expansion both in terms of formal imperialism and their own missionary project could end 'heathen barbarism'. In such thinking, the British Empire, Englishness, Christianity and whiteness all operated together in their antithesis to 'heathenism'. In writing about Mzilikazi's death, and the anticipated succession of the exiled Ndebele heir, Sykes wrote of 'the Zulu custom', whereby a chief would 'kill out of the way all other sons of his father from whom there was the slightest possibility of future opposition', juxtaposing this image of paranoid tyranny with 'English' patterns of succession.[86] Projecting his own desires onto the Ndebele, Sykes claimed that the people hoped: 'The new chief during his exile would have come in contact with English people, and have learned the white man's book; then he would know better than to kill them like dogs'. 'For, the little light which has dawned upon their own minds through the influence of Europeans generally, and their missionaries in particular, had led them to detest that horrible system of wholesale murder.'[87] Christianity was vested with the power to bring change, and 'white men', the 'English' or 'Europeans' were associated with peaceable, 'civilised' values. In India too, Christian widows were not to experience the violence inflicted on their Hindu and Muslim sisters; the female children of Christian parents were not to be thrown to crocodiles; Christian children were not to be branded, or sacrificed to horrifying idols; and men were not to be emasculated by hookswinging.

Conclusion

Because experiencing and witnessing violence is so distressing, violence operated as a very intense discourse of difference. It was not only Indians and Africans who were constructed as violent in missionary writing; violence was an important way in which *all* non-Christian or non-'western' peoples were marked as different. Violence played a powerful part in the missionary imagination of 'heathenism' and was used emotively to undermine, denigrate and demonise the diversity of cultures missionaries encountered. Situated 'out there', violence was described in such a way as to associate both the victims and perpetrators of 'heathen violence' with which was 'dark', 'distant' and 'different'. When missionaries did choose to evoke common humanity in their depictions, it was with the victims of violence, not with the perpetrators, they claimed to identify. But of course, in both India and southern Africa, missionaries encountered violence conducted by representatives of that 'superior', 'civilised' culture they claimed themselves to represent, thus posing a potential rupture to the alignments their writing attempted to forge. What, then, happened when, in order to preserve one's own identity, it was necessary to redeem the perpetrator of violence? It is these processes that I turn to next, as I examine the perpetration of violence by those whom missionaries considered 'should know better' and within, and as part of, the 'civilised' British Empire.

6
Colonial Violence: Whiteness, Violence and Civilisation

Confronting the violent self

> Sometimes 'civilized' Christians, like those African Dutchmen, hungry for land, are capable of tying a dozen Bechwana Christian men together by ropes, and then firing a broadside into them.[1]

In a long and eccentric speech given at the LMS's annual meeting in 1883 Reverend Edward White described the 'world of unreasoning heathens' in which he saw himself living. This world was violent and cruel, and missionaries were engaged in 'warfare' to spread the story, as White put it, of 'the shame of the gibbet, the pain of the race, the disgrace of the pillory... said to have been inflicted, nearly 2,000 years ago, on a Carpenter of Nazareth in Galilee'. The war was a difficult one to win, 'the conversion of the heathen almost everywhere', he wrote, 'is followed by trouble, persecution, family or tribal disunion, often by loss, depression and death itself'. Furthermore, battles had to be fought on many fronts. Sandwiched between diatribes against the 'Asiatic races', White reflected on the 'Christians', whose actions, he claimed, were to the missionary movement like 'being attacked in the rear by your own reserve while you are fighting on the front'. From Pope Leo XIII's recent condemnation of Robert Moffat as 'no properly authorised missionary of the Gospel', to antagonistic relations with 'Boers', White's account outlined a world where Christians as well as 'heathens' could be cruel.[2]

But whilst the paranoid forcefulness of White's speech was unusual, the substance of his diatribe was well-worn ground. The extract above strikingly demonstrates the ambiguities and apparent contradictions which seeped through colonial discourse. It was the Christianity of the 'Dutchmen' (or, by the 1880s, more commonly the 'Boers') that was problematised, not that of the Bechuana. And not only were these 'Dutchmen' cruel, but they were 'African'. Violence operated to other 'white' groups as well as indigenous ones and to formulate the unstable and ambivalent nature of 'coloniser' as a category of identification. As such, reports of violence are revealing of how missionaries positioned themselves in colonial discourse, and how difference was forged internally as well as externally to the colonial self.

Whilst missionaries were most vocal in decrying 'heathen' violence, they also encountered violence perpetrated by Christians, Europeans and Britons. In establishing 'pax Britannica', Britain engaged in a series of wars in southern Africa, Nigeria, India, Burma, New Zealand, Sudan and elsewhere, albeit ones they euphemistically dismissed as 'little' wars in colonial rhetoric.[3] India's northern frontiers were long contested, not least during the Punjab Wars. In southern Africa, missionaries witnessed nine Frontier Wars over the eastern border of the Cape Colony; the violent formation and colonisation of the Transvaal; the Zulu War; the Transvaal or First 'Boer' War; the Ndebele War and Rebellion; and the South Africa War. But as Fanon memorably put it, colonialism 'drummed the rhythm for the destruction of native social forms' ceaselessly, and the violence it brought extended well beyond conquest.[4] The maintenance of colonial authority always rested on the coloniser's potential to deploy further violence. Resistance to colonisation was often itself violent and was invariably followed by violent suppression. Non-state actors such as traders and settlers were entangled with colonising processes in complicated ways and were often reported to commit criminal violence both within colonial frontiers and beyond them.[5] Violence conducted by agents of the state, by British colonisers, by individuals and by groups such as the 'Boers' or Portuguese who had a more complicated relationship with the British Empire yet are just some of the very different manifestations that 'colonial violence' could take. Violence conducted in the 'lawless' places beyond the reach of the colonial state was not part of an 'official' imperial strategy, but it too was characterised by expansionist power-dynamics and often functioned to shape informal colonisation and, very often, to pre-empt formal colonial rule.

In this chapter, I discuss how the associations between 'savagery' and violence discussed in Chapter 5 were contextualised within, and unsettled by, confrontations with the perpetration of violence by Europeans and 'fellow countrymen'. I explore three forms of colonial violence: criminal violence; cross-colonial violence; and conflict and conquest. In each case, I suggest colonial violence troubled the missionary insistence that violence was linked to 'barbarity' and consider the ways in which the witnessing and experience of colonial violence drew on, threatened and re-encrusted, discourses of difference.

Violence and humanitarianism in missionary thought

Throughout the nineteenth century, missionaries responded to colonial violence with an uneasy prevarication between the acknowledgment that Europeans perpetrated violence against indigenous peoples and the insistence that 'heathens' were more violent than Christians. Missionary condemnations of colonial violence did not so much rupture a dominant discourse of 'heathen cruelty' but co-exist and cross-cut as an alternative formation in their writing. Whilst missionaries may have claimed that 'heathen' violence was 'barbaric', from their earliest days, they had also encountered and publicly represented the violence of Europeans.

Indeed, reporting that violence had been a defining part of early missionary identity, and images of the *colonial* relationship as one where people of colour were the victims of violence, not its perpetrators, were widely circulated, not least during the anti-slavery campaigns.[6] Images of 'native' victimhood at the hands of 'civilised' Europeans were widespread across the empire, from the subordination of the KhoiKhoi in the Cape to the destruction in Van Dieman's Land. In the early nineteenth century, missionary literature, and forums such as the Aborigines Select Committee, discursively wove these examples into a common humanitarian understanding of the ability and readiness of colonial settlers to inflict violence abroad.[7]

Over the course of the century, however, discourses about Europeans perpetrating violence against indigenous people started to occupy less space in the public imagination and missionaries claimed to embrace a more 'apolitical' stance (misleadingly, 'apolitical' in this context primarily meant a refusal to intervene either for or against colonial regimes, which therefore often implied endorsement).[8] The success of abolition, and the 'failure' of the Great Experiment in the Caribbean; the preoccupation with colonial resistance in New Zealand, India, and Jamaica; and a widespread 'hardening' of racial attitudes, altered the way in which the colonial relationship was framed. The violence in that dynamic was increasingly located with the colonised, rather than the coloniser. These shifts were not uniform and the report of colonial violence did not cease altogether in the mid-century period, but it came to be managed differently in missionary writing.[9]

The violence of 'fellow countrymen' – 'criminal' violence

As missionaries moved towards their 'apolitical' stance of the mid-nineteenth century, 'white', 'British' or 'European' violence appeared less frequently in their writings. At the same time, the violence that *was* represented tended to be presented as sporadic and exceptional rather than as part of a wider social problem (as it was in earlier discussions of settlers). Violence committed by Europeans in southern Africa outside the structure of formal warfare was depoliticised, and acts of assault, murder and robbery were understood simply as 'criminal' rather than as racially motivated, or rooted in the inequalities that colonialism generated. Whilst missionaries do not seem to have actively sought to 'hide' violence perpetrated by British subjects, or 'Europeans' in general, in their very tendency to record episodes of violence with shock and horror, they entrenched an unspoken 'norm': that the British Empire was not a violent concern in itself, and that 'Englishmen' were (usually) 'civilised'. Missionary outrage at European violence drew on ideas of 'racial', national and religious 'superiority' that suggested that 'fellow Englishmen' should 'rise above' behaviour fit for 'savages'.[10]

In 1893, missionary William Hinkley reported to the *Chronicle* a spate of violence occurring around the hill-station of Ramadrug, home to a sanatorium for British troops and English Residents, and surrounded by villages. 'Will it be believed', Hinkley wrote of a mango orchard owner, 'that one midnight this poor defenceless man was assailed by ten British soldiers of the Somerset Regiment, armed with three guns, and their heads covered with sacks to escape recognition? Two soldiers seized him, beat him, and held him, while the others plundered and destroyed the trees, breaking down some 300 of the best fruits.'[11] The orchard owner was badly beaten and left 'with three wounds on his face, and cut lips and spitting blood'.[12] Hinkley's disbelief and outrage, so apparent in his reporting of the incident, was fuelled by his shame that such behaviour had been perpetrated by British men. A few months later, Hinkley was even more horrified to report an attempted sexual assault where five British soldiers had attempted to 'capture' two 'native women' and had murdered a man trying to defend them.[13]

The language of shock structured Hinkley's reporting. The attack on the women was a 'case' he described as 'too sad for an Englishman to think of, much less to mention', re-encrusting the understanding that English people (note, for Hinkley, it was the 'English' who would be shocked by these 'British' soldiers) should know better.[14] In this way, it appeared that the violent occurrences in Ramadrug had erupted into the *Chronicle* through their very exceptionalism.

But these were not isolated incidents. 'The same thing occurs', Hinkley himself acknowledged, 'almost every fruit season, and not at such times only.' 'Within the last six weeks', he continued, 'in my own district of Anantapur, there have been, to my knowledge, three cases of robbery, violence, and murder even by British soldiers, and all have escaped punishment'.[15] Whilst no attention was drawn to the violence, or the threat of it, that these men represented in their professional capacity, Hinkley did contextualise these events within a wider public discourse about 'the conduct of British soldiers in India'.[16] Amongst other things, soldiers were associated with sexually transmitted infections in the controversy surrounding the Contagious Diseases Acts ongoing in this period and, although the trope of the 'Christian Soldier' was also developing, soldiers still occupied an ambivalent place in Victorian thought.[17] As will be seen in other examples in the chapter, violence often spotlighted groups with whom missionaries had frequent contact abroad but who seldom made the pages of the missionary propaganda: British soldiers certainly occupied such a position. As G. M. Bulloch, a missionary working at the military station of Benares complained, 'it is not usual in the pages of the CHRONICLE to take much notice of the work done amongst our fellow-countrymen in foreign lands' (perhaps, they did not fit the exotic images the editors generally preferred).[18] But encounters between missionaries and British soldiers stationed abroad were not only common but formed a staple part of missionary work in many parts of India, particularly the garrison towns. In writing of work in these places, Bulloch and other writers framed British soldiers as a non-native, yet equally needy, and in many ways equally 'foreign', target for missionary work.[19]

Members of the British Army were represented in missionary writing as class others marked as 'different', in part, by poverty and drink.[20] They were depicted as young men who were physically and emotionally vulnerable and were described in the patronising and critical tones otherwise reserved for indigenous people. As with Indian and African domestic spaces (particularly those that were homosocial), military barracks were described as degraded places of 'disordered' sexuality (sex-work and homosexuality were often hinted at), and 'disgusting and loathsome habits and conversation'.[21] Class and a military/civilian divide operated as alternate lines of identification which demarcated such men from idealised evangelical 'Christians Soldiers', either those like Havelock, who embodied their beliefs on the battlefield or (metaphorically) missionaries themselves.[22] What was expected from these men as 'Englishmen' conflicted with what could be expected from them as 'soldiers'. Discourses of aberration and containment appeared to resolve the disturbing potential of uncontrolled British behaviour without it challenging too deeply other missionary discourses that relied on the British being 'more civilised' than those they encountered, and the British Empire as a 'civilising' force.

There was no southern African equivalent to the huge standing army the LMS encountered in India. Whilst armed forces in the form of mercenaries and militia abounded, these were formed locally and performed quite a different role. As Jon McCulloch argues of later in the century, it was perhaps the *weakness* of the colonial state in southern Africa that explains the proliferation of small-scale violence there between indigenous peoples and local white groups.[23] Nevertheless, many tropes in the reporting of colonial violence appear in writings from across the empire. In particular, beneath the processes of identification which recoiled from violence committed by *'fellow countrymen'*, missionaries marked other social distinctions, such as class, youth, drink and insanity, to identify groups amongst whom the perpetration of violence was less surprising after all.

In 1866, Jean Fredoux, a missionary of the Paris Protestant Missionary Society working at Motito (near Kuruman), was dramatically killed by Nelson, a 'trader'. Nelson had apparently 'fallen in' with 'a couple of men of the same stamp from the Transvaal country' had 'obtained brandy from them' and 'becoming more or less intoxicated' had 'conducted himself in the most shameful manner on the station so much so that he was instantly ordered off by the natives'.[24] Fredoux attempted to demand Nelson return to Motito or Kuruman to be 'judged' for his wrongdoing, but when he approached the trader, Nelson had 'blown both himself and Mr F "to atoms" with about 175 pounds of gunpowder'.[25] Several Africans were also killed.

It seems to have been the fact that it was a missionary who was killed here, and Fredoux's personal connections to prominent LMS members (he was Robert and Mary Moffat's son-in-law and thus brother-in-law to both the Prices and the Livingstones) that brought Nelson to the attention of the *Chronicle*, but the event exposed the ambiguous missionary relationship with traders more widely. Not only were members of the LMS devastated by the 'agonising tragedy' of an untimely death, the LMS as a body was outraged at the spectacle of European violence before indigenous people. Because they believed Africans to be childlike and impressionable people, and Europeans overseas to be potential exemplars of 'civilisation', from southern Africa to Australia, missionaries worried that indigenous people would be undiscerning in the kinds of behaviour they imitated, and that 'bad habits' would be absorbed as well as good ones.[26] In this context, LMS missionaries feared Nelson, and traders like him, 'exerted a baneful influence on the morals of the natives with whom they came into contact'.[27] Furthermore, in exhibiting violence overseas, traders disturbed other missionary images of Christians as god-loving 'civilised' individuals and Europeans as having morals to which Africans should aspire. These images were the ones missionaries wanted to convey to potential converts and ones fundamental to their own sense of identity and cultural superiority. In representing the Nelson episode as an 'atrocious and horrifying event', the LMS suggested it disturbed the 'natural order of things'.[28] However many times traders demonstrated violent behaviour, missionaries clung to the abstract notion that Europeans were 'more civilised' than Africans and that any reversal of this was not only peculiar but shameful.

There were other elements that made the violence of traders in southern Africa and soldiers in India disturbing – the threat they were not only an *embarrassment* to 'their race', but they were actually a *corruption* of it. The racial status of Anglo-Saxons overseas was never secure and the disorderly, impassioned and apparently uncontrolled behaviour that often went with criminal violence generated anxiety about identity. One missionary, stationed in India, reported the 'sad scenes' caused when 'Sergeant A', a British soldier (unrelated to those Hinkley encountered), after 'recourse to his brandy flask', had heard a noise, become confused, accidentally shot an (Indian) man and run away into the night.[29] The missionary, accompanying the Sergeant's distressed wife, found the man's body after following rumours that 'a white man, very lightly clothed and barefooted, wild and haggard in appearance, and thoroughly prostrate', had entered the village and, 'apparently in utter despair, had thrown himself into and had been drowned in a neighbouring tank or large pond connected with the temple'.[30] The visual image such an account evokes had resonance with other accounts of those driven to 'madness' overseas.[31] 'Degeneration', brought on by the heat and sustained immersion in a 'heathen' land, was always a latent threat. For missionaries, that Sergeant A drowned in the tank of a *temple* may have carried the symbolic resonance of immersion in 'heathenism'. In the context of anxiety about moral and physical degeneration, the Sergeant's 'whiteness', like that of Nelson, became problematic.

What 'race' and 'whiteness' meant differed across colonial sites.[32] For one thing, it was contingent on the extent to which that colony could itself be considered a 'white space'. Writing of twentieth-century Britain, Dyer has argued that the 'power of whiteness' is lodged in the fact that 'the position of speaking as a white person is one that white people now almost never acknowledge', that whiteness is not marked, that white people do not need to specify that they are 'white' because that is considered 'normal'.[33] Sara Ahmed makes a similar point, claiming that whiteness occupies the 'normative'.[34] This makes sense; hegemonic categories are unmarked in this way. Given this, that the points at which whiteness *became* marked were often linked to episodes of violence is significant and points to the diverse meanings whiteness evoked. As Matt Wray notes, 'scholars of whiteness have become extraordinarily sure-footed and nimble when the word that follows *white* is *supremacy, power, privilege,* or *pride*', but have had harder problems dealing with 'poor whites' or 'white trash'.[35] In the colonies, new meanings of whiteness were created as European men and women defined themselves against those who were 'black', 'brown' or 'yellow'. Furthermore, as Stoler demonstrates, the colonial making of whiteness was played out 'not only the bodies of an immoral European working class and native other, but against those of destitute whites in the colonies and in dubious contrast to an ambiguous population of mixed-blood origin'.[36] Missionaries seem to have been speaking for 'whiteness' but even when named 'white' (or because of the very act of being named so), traders did not evoke the same connotations. In being marked, whiteness in colonial discourse was often used to identify a 'problem group', rather than an unspoken hegemonic identity, and 'whitemen' was used as a label more complex than simply the gendered embodiment of 'whiteness'.

Race and class together constituted 'white traders', such as Nelson, as another uneasy colonial group whose presence overseas was often illuminated in missionary writing through violence. Whilst early 'traders' had often been small-scale peddlers selling everything from medicine to gunpowder, or were linked with those pursuing ostrich feathers, following the mineral discoveries of the 1860s and 1870s many more 'fortune-seekers' had entered the interior. During the mid to late nineteenth century, these people seem to have displaced 'settlers' in missionary concerns about their corrupting European effect on indigenous people, through their 'swindling, falsehood, and filthiness'.[37] The association between traders and alcohol was also troubling. For many missionaries, drink, which nonconformists had long condemned both at home and abroad, signified irreligion and class otherness.[38] Ambivalence about the materialistic pursuit of wealth that fortune-seeking represented further compounded the class prejudices that underpinned hostility to traders.

Nelson was seen as 'not a solitary instance of the degradation exhibited in the character of European travellers in South Africa', but, as Moffat put it, as belonging to a 'class of men, who, by their example, teach the natives the most appalling forms of vice and misery'.[39]

The *Chronicle*'s editor drew attention to traders as a wider social problem:

> The influx of so many white traders in pursuit of ostrich feathers has exerted a baneful influence on the morals of the natives with whom they have come into contact. The conduct of most of these is a crying disgrace to the name they bear, as well as to the colour of their skin... and they do things which make the natives themselves blush. Had we here Burtonians of the Anthropological school, we should like to point them to this and then to that, and ask them when savages are to be civilized under the system they so shamelessly advocate.[40]

Such a diatribe evoked the uneasy relationship between missionary thinking and emergent anthropological thought in this period and appeared to suggest that the behaviour of Europeans beyond colonial frontiers complicated and undermined increasingly rigid understandings of racial hierarchies.[41] Missionaries claimed to be committed to a hierarchy based on 'morality', rather than biology. However, they also implied that the behaviour of Europeans (because of the 'colour of their skin' not, at least explicitly, because of their Christianity) *should* have been more 'civilised' than the 'natives'.

Rather than explaining colonial violence through racism, the structural dynamics of the British Empire or the experience of operating in a colonial field itself missionaries responded to these encounters through discourses of difference. On the one hand, excusing 'criminal violence' as an exceptional perversion (of 'white' people acting 'the savage') confirmed rather than disturbed existing categories of racialisation. On the other hand, missionaries recoiled from people they were embarrassed to acknowledge as 'fellow countrymen' and marked 'other others' within the colonising self.

Cross-cutting colonialisms: the Boers

In writing of the violence of 'white men' or 'white traders', it appears that missionaries valorised different 'white' ethnicities present in southern Africa. British, Dutch, Portuguese or German men and women, for example, were named simply as 'white' under a monochrome pattern of racialisation. As such, missionaries articulated one way in which they thought about southern Africa; as divided between colonised and colonisers and between 'black' and 'white'. But this 'whiteness' is misleadingly embracing. 'Whiteness' (like 'blackness') was cross-cut by ethnic as well as class identities that did not so much shelter beneath it, or subdivide it, but overrode it. Across the world, the LMS defined itself against other colonising groups, British and otherwise. In southern Africa, missionaries had another 'other' through which to explain and contain colonial violence: the Boers.

Boers shared many ostensible characteristics with British settlers: both had come from Europe, both were 'white' and both identified as Protestant Christian. And yet, missionaries often insisted on their difference.[42] As Antoinette Burton noted, the British had long considered Boers to be 'innately barbaric', 'brutal' and 'cruel' particularly in their treatment of Black Africans.[43] Violence was a central discourse used by missionaries to construct Boers as 'different'.[44]

In missionary discourse, Boer violence was conceptualised as systematic and as an inherent part of their national character. When missionaries told the story of the expansion of Dutch-speaking settlers, they constructed a narrative of violence in a rolling process of history writing. They claimed that when the British first came to the Cape, they had 'discovered' a barbaric slave society created by the Cape Dutch. In 1834, slavery was abolished in the British Empire and, after a period of 'apprenticeship', was forbidden in the Cape. Missionaries claimed that this had proved unacceptable to the Boers, who 'uniformly evinced the strongest prejudice against the aborigines of the country, regarding them as an inferior race, brought into the world to serve the purpose of the whiteman.'[45] Because they were no longer allowed to keep Africans as their 'vassals', missionaries claimed, the Boers trekked beyond British influence. This unleashed a chain of violence in southern Africa. Beyond the Vaal River, the Boers fought indigenous peoples (particularly the Sotho and the Griquas) in their path, stopping only when indigenous groups had been subordinated, and, given that total 'mastery' was rare, engaging in an ongoing series of bloody power struggles. This state of affairs was intensified following the formation of the two Boer Republics, the British Government's recognition of which missionaries deplored. In the 1870s and 1880s, Boers acquired more land in the most 'degraded' manner – essentially through treaties the 'natives' did not understand in exchange for their services as mercenaries. The Boer Republics increasingly victimised those of English origin who had come within their jurisdiction, as *uitlanders* ('foreigners'), to whom the Afrikaners refused voting rights. The British Government intervened to protect these 'victims', thus commencing the 1899–1901 war. After a surprisingly long campaign, the Afrikaners were crushed, and British control (constructed as peaceful) was finally established across what became the Union of South Africa.

This story became a familiar one in colonial discourse more widely, and it was often used to justify British colonial expansion. Missionaries were important in creating, disseminating and weaving this understanding into the British interpretation of colonial relations in southern Africa, and missionary magazines and periodicals were a forum where this narrative was forged.[46] The letters of individual missionaries, which recorded contemporary dilemmas with the Boers, were worked into a wider understanding of Boer violence. As each new episode of violence was recorded, it was located within a tradition of previous aggression and in turn was used as further evidence of the alleged pattern. In contemplating the establishment of the Transvaal, for example, missionaries drew on 'past events' which, they claimed, 'shew to a demonstration that between the natives and the Trans Vaal Boers there can be no peace, until the former . . . shall become the vassals of the latter'.[47] This interpretative framework tended to depoliticise each new war by marginalising its specific context. Instead, it was suggested that Boers were inherently, even racially, violent.

Whereas discourses of 'heathen' violence were used to construct all non-Christian people as distinct from Europeans, here violence was used specially to construct Boers as distinct from British settlers. In describing the Boers as 'a body of men of European extraction, and professing the Christian faith', missionaries both recognised the similarities they shared and distanced themselves from them.[48] Boer violence was portrayed as confirming the negative image already constructed of them, not as exceptional.[49] The incredibly violent acts some Boers engaged in, such as the beheading of Gasibonoe (the then paramount chief of the Tlhapping) by Boer 'braves' (the original vocabulary is significant), and the use of his decapitated head 'as a trophy', were not treated with the same sense of violated morality that atrocities committed by British settlers met.[50] The participation of Boer mercenaries in indigenous conflicts contributed to this effect.[51] Boer/African battles were often presented as having a 'tribal', not a 'colonial', quality, with Boer commandos constructed similarly to the Ndebele *impi*. Unlike violence inflicted by British settlers which, for the most part, was kept vague and thereby 'softened' in the missionary press, Boer violence, was (like 'heathen' violence) gruesomely detailed. Violence was used to suggest Boer 'degeneracy', and particularly a degenerate masculinity, as they became simply one of the 'tribes' against whom missionaries had to contend. Such a construction was used to ridicule further what missionaries read as a Boer insistence on racial superiority.

The alleged relationship between Boers and violence also had implications for the missionary understanding of European expansion in southern Africa. In comparison to that of 'other' colonialists, who, missionaries claimed, hurt 'vulnerable' Africans, British imperialism could be construed as peaceable and benign. For example, many missionaries deplored the formation of the Transvaal by claiming that 'so long as the Boers were on the same political footing as all other settlers in the colony, and were amenable to British law there was some guarantee that their aggressive schemes would be effectually restrained', but in their own colony, slavery would resurface and the Boers would be 'emboldened' to attack indigenous people.[52] Similarly, the missionary insistence that Boers were 'determined' that 'all the aborigines must become their vassals' was used to emphasise the allegedly anti-slavery stance of the British Empire.[53] In the 1860s, when the MP Edward Baines, speaking at the LMS's Anniversary Meeting, recalled the actions of John Philip, they celebrated him for 'delivering the Hottentots from the cruel bondage in which they were held by the Dutch Boers', not for chastising British settlers through the Aborigines Select Committee.[54] In doing so, a historical memory was constructed around Cape slavery that obscured the British participation in it.

Whilst the violence of 'whitemen' developed as a racialised discourse which established a division between 'black' and 'white' throughout the nineteenth century, 'Boer', 'British' and 'English' continued to operate as powerful identities. Discussions of violence were important in differentiating and defining relationships between these groups. One of the consequences of this was that the recording of violence, which appeared so troubling in colonial discourse, was fragmented.

Conquest and conflict: 'both black and white had a hand in this wanton destruction'

Thus far, I have been keen to focus on examples of small-scale colonial violence. This is partly because of its preponderance in missionary writing and partly because the historiography of violence and Empire has overly privileged catastrophic upheavals (the Indian Rebellion, for example), rather than the violence of everyday life.[55] Whilst understandable, focussing on large-scale 'eruptions' in imperial historiography has itself operated as a discourse of containment and detracted from the recognition that British (like German, Portuguese or Belgian) imperialism was a violent concern in itself.[56] Missionary writing demonstrates that violence was part of the everyday of colonial experience, informing the banal as well as the dramatic. Now, however, it is useful to focus on a moment of more turbulent colonial violence, the Ndebele War and Rebellion, to assess how violence operated to reconfigure difference from a different perspective.

Imperial historiography has often linked colonial conflict with the mid nineteenth-century 'hardening' of racial attitudes. The New Zealand Wars (1843–72), the Seventh and Eighth Cape Frontier Wars (1846–7, 1850–3), Indian Rebellion (1857–8) and the Morant Bay Uprising (1865) have all been linked with increasingly hostile attitudes towards indigenous people across the empire. Elkins and Anderson have similarly shown the speed at which attitudes to the Kikuyu shifted on the advent of MauMau, as 'overnight', the 'smiling servant' had become 'the murderous savage' enveloped in an 'atavistic' 'madness'.[57] The disorientating, frightening and disruptive effects of war have the power to melt existing racialisations, to consolidate them, or to produce new representations both of the 'self' and the 'other'. Violence also means the performance of difference. As Pnina Werbner explains, 'communities essentialised by the perpetrators of violent acts of aggression are not imagined situationally but defined as fixed, immoral and dangerous. In being demonised, they are reified.'[58] Some such shifts occurred around the Ndebele Rebellion.

In the 1890s, missionaries in Ndebeleland witnessed a series of violent upheavals. Over the previous decades, it had become widely believed that a second rand of gold lay beneath the Ndebeleland plateau, and the territories were much coveted by southern African colonies and European powers alike. In a series of very underhand treaties, the Ndebele King, Lobengula, was claimed to have signed away his rights to the land, principally to Rhodes's BSAC. LMS missionaries were implicated in 'translating' treaties supposedly legitimising the re-appropriation of land, most notably Reverend C. D. Helm (who it later transpired was in Rhodes' secret employ). In 1890, the BSAC, backed by the British Government, entered Mashonaland through Lobengula's territory, in a so-called 'pioneer' column of white settlers and established white access to land. A flood of traders, fortune-seekers and settlers followed them. So did more missionaries, many backed by Rhodes.[59] In 1893, Rhodes and his allies engineered a war in Ndebeleland and the BSAC invaded.[60] Fighting with assegai (spears) against guns, the Ndebele lost badly; Lobengula fled and died, and the monarchy was destroyed. The power of the Ndebele was broken and in 1895, the country became 'Rhodesia'.

The following year a rebellion broke out, known as the First Chimurenga (1896–1897).[61] It was facilitated by a temporary alliance between the 'Shona' and Ndebele and involved the killing of about 10 per cent of the European population and thousands of indigenous people.[62] Despite early African victories, the uprising was crushed by the colonisers who slaughtered thousands of civilians in acts of horrifically violent retribution. The 1893 war and the subsequent violence was deeply traumatic to Ndebele society resulting in the death of a unifying leader, the loss of land rights and the collapse of social institutions, such as the payment of bridewealth.[63] During the war and rebellion, LMS missionaries had to evacuate their stations, many of which were destroyed. Throughout the upheavals, missionaries wrote letters recording the violence both from close proximity to the struggle and, as they pieced together from rumours circulating, when in exile elsewhere in southern Africa.[64] As in previous conflicts, the missionary public in Britain would have followed the actions of 'their' missionaries through letters published in the *Chronicle*. But the disruption to the post caused by the war meant that the publication of their letters was disordered. As such, the political narrative of this episode of colonial resistance was disrupted and incoherent and the political significance of the rising obscured.

Missionaries often talked about the colonisation of Ndebeleland as a struggle between 'black' and 'white', but, once again, this Manichean division is misleading. Not only were the 'whitemen' discussed in Ndebeleland rather different from those lone 'traders' discussed above, but missionaries never lost sight of the fact that here they were dealing with the *Ndebele*, rather than another African group. As discussed in Chapter 5, missionaries had long represented the Ndebele as a peculiarly violent people and this directly affected the way in which *colonising* violence was represented. At least at first, white violence was not portrayed as having been unleashed upon 'helpless' 'natives', as it sometimes was elsewhere, and the Ndebele were denied the empathetic status of victimhood.

Helm claimed to 'rejoice greatly' over the occupation of Mashonaland (1890). He hoped 'that there will be no bloodshed' but that he believed the 'charge of the forces of the chartered company into Mashonaland' would be 'better for the Matebele themselves and immeasurably so for the Mashona'. 'The Matebele have for years been oppressing the Mashona', he continued, 'killing numbers and injuring the children in their country and making them as blood thirsty as they are themselves.'[65] The kind of violence Helm evoked was vampiric, inherent and racialised and was explicitly used to neutralise the impact of colonisation. Writing a few years later (1893), Helm continued to counter allegations of European violence *against* the Ndebele, that were raising concerns in the metropole, by reiterating aggressive images of the Ndebele.

> I hear Lord Rippon regrets the loss of life among the Matablele but what of the scores of Mashona men women and children who were slaughtered in cold blood by these very Matabele but a few days before. There is no fear of the white people exaggerating the cruelties practiced on the Mashona by the Matabele. I have many times heard the Matabele boast of their doings in this respect to helpless women and babies.[66]

Insisting on the Ndebele as *perpetrators* helped to deflect attention from the violence of colonisation.

As ever, missionaries racialised those they encountered from the perspective of their particular endeavour and the experience of their own colonial interactions. They responded to the war and rebellion in the 1890s through the lens of a history of frustrated engagement with the Ndebele. Sykes, Helm, Carnegie and Rees, amongst other Ndebeleland missionaries, had been long forced to recognise their powerlessness besides the Ndebele kings, to close their schools when demanded and to preach only when permission was granted. Their failure to make almost any converts at all had rendered the mission a source of embarrassment to their employers and great personal frustration to themselves. When, in the 1890s, the entire politics, governance and social fabric of Ndebeleland seemed on the brink of change, the LMS seemed prepared to accept political solutions, even violent ones, for the possibility of spiritual change it might have brought. Other colonists found it 'amusing to hear the missionaries talk... Regular fire-brands, they admit that the sword alone will Christianize the natives'.[67]

Despite feeling 'very sore at heart' given the violence sustained, LMS missionaries scarcely hid their delight at the destabilisation of Ndebele society and kingship such a war represented.[68] Mrs Rees saw in the destruction of the Ndebele monarchy a renewed potential for proselytisation. 'We rejoice to think that the power of the Matabele is broken', she wrote, 'Now we may have a chance of doing the work which we were sent out to do and those of our people who ever well disposed before the heathen power was broken, may now without fear throw down their arms and confess Christ publicly.'[69]

That missionaries had so readily aligned themselves with a violent coloniser did not, of course, go unnoticed by the Ndebele. Helm's role in the Rudd Concession (in his 'legitimate' and public role as interpreter) had generated friction with other missionaries who were implicated, through him, with the BSAC.[70] In 1889, David Carnegie indignantly reported having been attacked by some Ndebele men on his way home from preaching, having his pocket knife stolen and having been threatened with the words '"you – little white slave – if you come back here to preach again we will see to it that you don't escape without a thrashing"', an experience Carnegie found deeply humiliating.[71] The downfall of Lobengula brought a declaration of 'white' strength and a new discourse about the subordination of a people, of which missionaries were a part. In stark contrast to his earlier experiences, in 1894, Carnegie now wrote with some satisfaction that

> All [Ndebele] however admit they are now a conquered race and are not equal in strength to the white man. Now they are not allowed to go to and fro carrying shields, guns and spears... They address me now not as a slave but give me the title of my profession, teacher, or Inkosi or Baba. They are respectful in a way they never were before.[72]

Whilst in other writings, Carnegie may have distanced himself from such a blatant assertion of superiority and from the crushing violence, such a description is suggestive of an identification with the glory of that white victory.

In this context, missionaries did not only witness, critique and comment on racialised colonial violence but were performatively bound up in the political process of violent colonisation. From Britain, the LMS Directorate grew increasingly concerned about rumours of its missionaries 'sharing plunder and becoming participators in the robbery of the Matabele,' and ordered them to 'be sure to keep out of the every suspicion of connection with the gold hunters and land grabbers'.[73] In Ndebeleland itself, it seems such orders were hard to follow, particularly after BSAC rule had been established and missionaries had to negotiate with Rhodes over the fate of their missions.[74]

However, whilst in the eyes of others, missionaries had become increasingly implicated with 'whitemen', as the conflict progressed, the fractures between missionaries and other white groups reappeared. Not only did missionaries need to detach themselves from white perpetrators of violence in order to be trusted by potential indigenous converts, but the upheaval of colonisation itself made many aware that they too could suffer the consequences of colonial violence.[75] For most LMS missionaries, the war and rebellion meant two evacuations within several years. When they returned, it was to find their stations and homes destroyed or left with 'only the bare walls', as in the case of the Rees's house.[76] 'The natives looted everything in the way of clothing household linen and barter goods, also they smashed into small bits our beautiful American organ... For the rest of the damages we have to thank the white people', Reverend Rees wrote.[77] The Carnegies too came home to 'a homeless home' in 'a wrecked and ruined condition'.[78] 'Everything belonging to us was either broken, stolen or destroyed', David Carnegie lamented, his medicines, books and clothing were 'scattered about all over the house' and 'ruin, desolation and destruction were written on every door window and wall.'[79] Like his colleague, Carnegie did not only blame the Ndebele for destroying his home, but recognised that '[b]oth black and white had a hand in this awful wanton destruction'.[80] What did this open recognition of 'black' and 'white' involvement do to the representations of colonial violence discussed above? And how should Carnegie's implication that 'black' and 'white' were 'as bad as each other' be read in terms of the construction of difference?

'White violence' quickly became a recurrent and troubling discourse in missionary writing about the Ndebele War and Rebellion, extending the earlier depictions of gold-diggers and traders in southern Africa, discussed above. Given the power of violence as a means of racialisation, it is not surprising that shifting representations of violence were a powerful element in the construction of both coloniser and colonised. Bowen Rees significantly suggested a *metamorphosis* between the Ndebele and the 'whiteman', writing from Inyanti in April 1894 of the considerable change that Ndebeleland had recently experienced. 'It is true the Matabele Power has been broken', he wrote, 'but the devil has had reinforcements in the person of many a whiteman, whose deeds are too filthy to be recounted.'[81] The troubling implications of this transformation are evident in the reluctance with which the LMS in London incorporated its report into their published discourses. In the manuscript copy of Bowen Rees' letter, received in London, pencil editing marks cross out the word 'filthy' and replaced it with 'bad', an alteration made when this letter later appeared in the *Chronicle*. Whilst the editors of the *Chronicle* were prepared to inform the British public about white violence in southern Africa, even to suggest their actions were diabolical, the suggestion of sexual violence could not be publicly acknowledged. In 1896, when almost any news from Ndebeleland was welcomed into the *Chronicle,* the editors omitted Cullen Reed's report that 'the girls who had to come into contact with the white men had adopted the custom of burning sores on their arms and bodies to imitate a contagious disease in hopes of thereby avoiding evil.'[82]

But whilst the naming of the perpetrators of violence shifted, a metamorphosis did not occur in missionary attitudes to race as a marker of difference. 'Black' and 'white' were never represented as 'the same' in missionary discourse, not least because, although the relationship between 'whiteness', 'civilisation' and identity was certainly troubled when both 'white' and 'black' committed 'wanton destruction', there was no attempt to merge or abandon these racialised categories. They did not become, as Carnegie superficially suggested, interchangeable, not least because in responding to 'black' violence as 'to be expected' and 'white violence' as shocking, the dominant racialisation linking violence with otherness was re-encrusted.

'Whiteness' continued to be an ambivalent and unstable category in missionary thinking. The colonial violence inflicted during the Ndebele war and rebellion was overwhelmingly described as 'white'. As such, the aggressors were racialised through earlier representations of traders and gold-diggers, which managed to incorporate into a single label the diverse emigrants coming into Ndebeleland and Mashonaland from the Transvaal, British southern Africa, Britain, and elsewhere in Europe.[83] But, it was the recognition that some of this violence was being perpetrated by 'English' people which surfaced as a particularly troubling thread of this discourse, particularly given the growing unease missionaries felt about their *own* involvement in this colonising project. Cullen Reed went so far as to confess that 'the more I hear of the war and its causes and some of the subsequent dealings of the Company with the natives the more this feeling grows until I am almost ashamed of the name I have hitherto been proud to bear of Englishman.'[84] In the context of 1890s Ndebeleland, the shame Cullen Reed felt as an *Englishman,* as opposed to the general revulsion he felt at the violent actions of *whitemen,* needs to be considered carefully. Such identities were constituted differently across different colonial sites – how Englishness was articulated in Ndebeleland, in the context of a polyglot 'white' invasion, differed from what it meant in the context of intensified Afrikaner nationalism in the Cape, as well as from how Englishness was constituted in the metropole. Cullen Reed, who had only recently travelled to southern Africa from London, would have encountered different representations of this Englishness and contributed to its differentiated constitution across several spaces of empire. The transnational structure of the LMS meant the accumulation and rearticulation of these understandings back in Britain.

Conclusion

This chapter has traced missionary responses to and representations of several different manifestations of colonial violence. Some representations of colonial violence could coexist in missionary discourse alongside assertions that Europeans were, nevertheless, morally and culturally superior to those they encountered. But some encounters with violence were more rupturing and threatened to destabilise this framework. Different responses to colonial violence reflected the different imaginings of empire and identity across the missionary project, from India and southern Africa, from Bechuanaland to Ndebeleland, from 1840 to 1900, from writer to writer.

Missionaries wrote about colonial violence in southern Africa far more than their colleagues in India. This discrepancy can partly be attributed to differing geopolitical circumstances, but it also reflected imagined geographies. Whilst Africa was depicted through its dangerous darkness, India was a place where British colonial coercion was more thoroughly obscured from those back home. Although the violence of the Indian Rebellion is usually constructed as so shocking because it erupted in a territory largely considered 'passive', this interpretation marginalises the long frontier wars in the Punjab, and that it was the presence of the army, and constant threat of force, upon which this 'stability' was hinged. Missionaries in India operated in a militarised colonial state where the police and huge standing army were used both for external conquest and to suppress 'internal threats'.[85] In the aftermath of the rising, the coercive arm of the colonial state consolidated further. But besides its militarisation, India was presented as though governed by political and legal means (even by pageantry), rather than by coercion.[86] The devastating famines which, as Mike Davies argued, could have been avoided, inflicted starvation on a scale that must, surely, be considered 'violent', but these episodes were neutralised and represented as ecological, not colonial, in causation.[87] Recent work revealing torture in the police courts and inhumane conditions in the prisons has similarly exposed a side of British rule subdued in contemporary colonial discourses and historiographical understandings alike.[88] Even the suppression of the Rebellion, not least killing suspected mutineers by blowing them to pieces from the mouths of cannons, was offset by the endless production of images of murdered European women and children that were used to 'justify' the reprisals.[89] In missionary discourse, the coercive arm of the colonial state was very effectively hidden, if not necessarily intentionally, in both public and private writings. Missionaries, rarely, it seemed, came into contact with colonial violence in India, and where they did, it was depoliticised in their writings.[90]

Assessing how these variable responses to colonial violence grew from and fed back into the construction of difference is complicated. The missionary experience of all violence was racialised. Violence was never neutrally conceived but always perceived as inflicted by 'Europeans', 'Englishmen' or 'whitemen', by 'heathens', 'natives' or 'blacks'. At the same time, violence was a powerful racialising discourse in its own right and often othering of both victims and perpetrators of violence. Besides the claim that colonised peoples perpetrated a 'cruel', 'heathen' violence amongst themselves, it was also their victimhood to European violence that defined them as colonial others. In writing about the perpetrators of colonial violence, missionaries often conveyed a sense of shame, outrage or disappointment that grew from their identification with those who shared their skin-colour, language and nationality, in ways inconsistent with their claims elsewhere that people were defined through their spirituality. The perpetration of violence by those with a skin colour they shared troubled missionaries because that skin colour *mattered* as a signifier of identity. The evocation of violence in India and southern Africa also fed into depictions of race indirectly through the imagined spatial geography of empire which located violence as something that happened 'out there'.

Violence can both confirm and destabilise identity, and European violence overseas unsettled the missionary formation that violence was 'other'. But in missionary writings, the fundamental concept of colonial difference was reconfigured through violence rather than weakened by it. As with discourses of family or of sickness, the conjectures between colonising formations of violence are complicated, contradictory and unstable. The fluidity of colonial discourse meant that slippage always occurred between patterns of racialisation, which sought to identify and momentarily disentangle specific, ethnically defined groups, such as when the 'Ndebele', 'white traders', 'gentle Hindus' or 'British soldiers' and overarching homogenising discourses which juxtaposed colonisers against colonised. Discourses of difference were not only mutually constituted between metropole and colony, between colonial self and colonial others but also between a fragmented coloniser and multiple colonised peoples in ever-shifting contexts.

Conclusion: Thinking with Missionaries, Thinking about Difference

Writing in the *Chronicle* in July 1886, the Reverend W. Pierce reflected on a letter he had received from someone he described as 'a dusty-skinned man, born in the midst of heathenism, but now addressing us in the terms of Christian fellowship'. The letter had renewed Pierce's confidence in the 'universality of the kingdom of Christ', a vision with which many in the 1880s were becoming disillusioned. And it was not surprising, Pierce felt, that faith in the civilising project 'grows weak'. The extent of 'heathen' degradation, encountered here in India, signified a sense of otherness that could undermine the very foundations of the missionary enterprise. 'Can we, without entering the kingdom of moonshine', Pierce wondered, 'carry our theory of "a man and a brother" right the way through the human race?' The question was a topical one in the second half of the nineteenth century, when challenges to the universality of mankind were emerging from new discourses of race and when the language of cross-racial kinship, which Pierce was referencing, was becoming unpopular. Doubts concerning the limits of humanity, or in some formulations the relationship between race and species, pulled at the roots of the missionary project with growing strength from several directions. Defying these trends, Pierce responded firmly that the theory of a man and a brother could indeed be 'carried right through the human race' and that 'the missionary steps in' to debates about race 'with his profoundly significant facts'. Missionary work was special, he suggested, holding the power to prove that '[t]here are, in the most degraded types of savage life, uncrushed susceptibilities, responsive and still breathing possibilities of manhood and brotherhood'.[1]

The issues that Pierce reflected upon have, in a very different form, also puzzled historians assessing the contribution of missionary discourse to the evolution of racial thought within British imperial culture more broadly. Did missionaries believe that a limit could be drawn across humanity demarcating who was a 'man and brother' and who was not? Did missionaries step into debates about race to offer a distinctive position? And in what ways did their approaches to race intersect with the other discourses of difference to which they were committed?

As discussed in the Introduction, many historians have noticed a shift over the nineteenth century from the predominance of 'cultural' markers of 'race' to ones that are more 'biological'.[2] Tendencies towards polygenistic racial theorising; the demise of humanitarianism; indigenous resistance in India, southern Africa, the West Indies and New Zealand; and accelerating colonial expansion all reflected and contributed to a 'hardening' in racial thinking.

There is no doubt that changing registers of race altered the discursive web within which missionaries operated. As Andrew Porter notes, although missionaries in the early nineteenth century could be 'ridiculed' by their adversaries, both missionaries and most of their critics subscribed to an underlying 'belief in the fundamental unity of humanity'.[3] But when others came to believe that the differences between races were too great to be overcome, missionary thinking about race become potentially alienated from the mainstream.

From their late eighteenth and early nineteenth-century beginnings, missionary societies were committed to the concept of the 'family of man' and with it, human universality. Although this family was hierarchically organised, with non-European people positioned as (subordinate) *younger* brothers and sisters, or as children, missionaries used the image to demonstrate togetherness and likeness. Missionaries argued that there was no inherent difference between peoples – they all had the same genesis. In their thinking, there was nothing to stop cultural difference being swept away by their work or indigenous people being 'remade' in a European model. At least rhetorically, missionaries maintained these ideas throughout the nineteenth century. But, as popular attitudes towards race shifted away from these positions, such thinking could no longer be relied upon to be taken for granted, and missionaries were forced to adapt to the new ideas.

One way of interpreting the missionary response to the new racial discourses was that it was inconsistent, atomised and ultimately failed to construct a coherent rebuttal to harsher racial theorising. Missionaries did not counter, in any systematic way, new interpretations of race and the boundaries of mankind. Textual engagement with the 'hardening' of racial attitudes was sporadic and scanty. Articles such as 'Christian Missions in Relation to Nationality' or 'Christian Heathen or What?'

published in missionary periodicals revealed deep anxieties about the extent to which religious difference was also 'racial' but were unclear and, often indeed, divided in their stance.[4] Other articles such as 'The Parsees of India', 'The South African Races' or 'Some Phases of the South African Native Question' appeared to have been influenced by modes of racial thought often associated with non-missionary contemporaries, without explicitly acknowledging them.[5] What is most clear is that there was no one clear position taken by missionaries on the hardening of racial attitudes or a society 'line' on race.

To some extent, diverging missionary responses to racial thinking reflected the fragmented nature of what we might consider to be 'mainstream' discourses of difference across the Empire, with missionaries engaging with separate debates about race on particular colonial sites. In southern Africa, missionaries were negotiating the rapid colonisation of the interior and a volatile geopolitical system in which the idea of 'race war' could force racial thinking into particularly dichotomous lines. In India, the situation was otherwise. There, religion played a stronger role in the articulation of 'difference'. Furthermore, 'Caucasian' Hindus had fared rather better than Africans in the new racialised hierarchy. Discussions of race by missionaries in India frequently centred on the capacity of converts to succeed European missionaries, on the extent to which converts would still be 'Asiatic' and on how fully the cultural trappings of Indianness could or should be disentangled from new Christian identities.

In Britain, missionaries were more inclined to engage directly with debates about race, than their colleagues posted abroad. Writers such as Pierce met the strongest end of the new discourse, which posited 'race' as 'species' with ridicule. Missionaries were theoretically hostile to 'scientific' understandings of 'race' and professionally antagonistic to anthropological thought, which was where they located and sought to contain these ideas.[6] In the LMS's Anniversary Meeting of June 1867, J. Guinness Rogers ironically criticised the Anthropology Society. They were, he mocked, 'a learned philosophical society' whose members, 'accepting the notion that man is, after all, but a highly educated and nobly developed monkey, seem to be engaged in the very scientific though wearisome search, in quest of the missing link which is to connect these two different races and creatures together'.[7] It was not surprising, Rogers argued, that those 'gentlemen who are so fond of maintaining that the Negro belongs to an inferior race of beings have no love for Missionaries': it was missionaries that had 'demonstrated the great fact that the Negro has an intellect to think, has a heart to feel, has a soul to be saved'.[8] Rogers was, however, unusual, not so much in the direction of his thinking but in his willingness to articulate it this strongly. Even in Britain, few missionaries engaged extensively with shifts in racial theorising; and they did not theologise, to any significant extent, the meaning of race and the boundaries of mankind.

It was not just a matter of missionary discourse responding to a separate set of attitudes towards race outside their movement. 'Hardening' racial thought also had reverberations *inside* missionary thinking, not least because race had always been important to missionaries and formative to the shape of the missionary project. Race structured the social fabric of the missions, determined who could marry whom, who was given what job and demanded that white missionaries be treated differently from non-white converts. But as with the fragmented responses to racial theorising, the way in which the everyday situations missionaries created were shaped by racial difference was inconsistent across time and space, and racial structures within the missionary movement often took the form of unspoken rules, unarticulated by missionaries themselves.

Throughout the nineteenth century, missionaries tended to repeat their earlier commitments to the family of man. Whilst some anthropologists demanded that a line be drawn across the human race (to return to Pierce's phraseology), missionaries continued to insist that 'neither Jew nor Greek, neither Slave nor free' but all were one in the body of Christ. The language of kinship bound this family together; they were all brethren in Christ. One missionary argued that 'man, however degraded, is still man.'[9] The 'family of man', of 'mankind' of 'humankind' was fundamental to that project. And yet, although missionaries remained rhetorically committed to the 'family of man', throughout the century the meanings signified by that same language changed. Belonging to the family of man had never meant sameness; it was always hierarchically differentiated. But over the course of the nineteenth century, many of these divisions split further apart. Whilst subscribing to the idea of a common origin, many missionaries suggested that since Creation, human 'races' had become very separate. Writing in 1870s, John Mackenzie, an influential missionary in southern Africa, spoke candidly of the 'undenied superiority' of what he described as 'the Anglo-Saxon race'. When a 'European' encountered an Australian, or a New Zealander or an African, Mackenzie wrote 'it is as if a demi-god appeared to him.'[10] Both his confident articulation of Anglo-Saxon 'supremacy' and the force with which the thrust of his argument is made were far more characteristic of racial discourses in the second half of the nineteenth century than the first, demonstrating some permeation of more radical discourses of race into missionary thinking.

Other tensions also emerged between the conceptualisation of the human family as a universal unit and the growing conviction of the primacy of 'difference'. The Rev A. Hanney, engaging with the debate about the evangelistic utility of Christians indigenous to different fields, returned to ideas about commonality in a new way. 'It is true that God has made all the nations of the earth of one blood,' he reasoned, 'but it is also true that he made them of different types of mind.' Some had 'clear, hard, intellectual power', whilst there were some 'whose minds are almost altogether a thing of the imagination' and others whose minds were simply 'a coil of emotions'. These 'types of mind' and, as Hanney went on to make explicit, 'the races by whom those types of mind are represented', embodied difference, in missionary thinking, and difference that was far more wide-ranging than any simplistic understanding of 'racial' thought.[11]

In *Missionary Discourses*, I have argued that, alongside their proclamations about human universalism, missionaries structured their encounters through the marking of difference. Difference patterned accounts of everyday life, and shaped thinking about families, health and geopolitics. The book has established some of the lines around which difference was constituted and organised in missionary writing. Race, gender and religion were particularly important and formative ones. I have argued that the marking of difference was often structured around the body. Missionaries saw difference in the clothes, skin colour and posture of those they encountered. They strove to contain sex in institutionally sanctioned marriages and designated architectural spaces. Bodily intimacy could obscure difference or clarify it. Sickness could both reflect and create it. So too could violence. Concentrating on the sick, injured or violated bodies of Indians and Africans, missionaries not only implied their dependence on 'civilised' colonisers for help but reduced the 'other' to the somatic. Many of the insecurities missionaries harboured around their own bodies manifested themselves in concerns about their location in the colonial field, and the perceived vulnerability of this positioning. Race was 'seen' on the body and performed through day-to-day actions.

Difference was conceived hierarchically; the difference of others meant inferiority. Some forms of difference were, in missionary thinking, intolerable and frightening. Non-Christian beliefs were 'wrong', 'degraded' and 'heathen'. Unfamiliar practices of home-making, child-rearing, healing and warfare were considered unacceptable. Difference was seen as a fearful perversion of what was 'natural' but, crucially in missionary thinking, it was also understood as something that could be changed. Much missionary work was focussed on 'correcting', reforming and eradicating difference, an endeavour which encompassed destroying indigenous cultures and attempting to replace them with their own. Yet this endeavour, and the implicit suggestion that difference could be unfixed, dissolved or reduced was also potentially unsettling. It threatened to erode or unravel missionary identities which were themselves rooted in a privileged positioning on a spectrum of difference. Furthermore, the missionary desire to remove certain *forms* of difference did not mean that *all* difference was considered problematic or that it was not also understood to structure inequality in ways that were naturalised. Gender, age and sickness were equally hierarchical forms of difference, which, although they could also evoke fear, were fundamental to the missionary project.

There were other contradictions and complications. The constant slippage between biological and cultural registers of racial difference meant that while missionaries strove for cultural change, the body always operated as a signifier of difference that would outlast theological or cultural conversion. The missionary understanding that racial change would happen only very slowly appears to have complicated and undermined co-existent discourses of cultural reform. The construction of difference in missionary writing, then, was complex. Yet the constant intersections between the perception of difference both as something fearful that should be dissolved and as something ordered and naturalised helped provide difference with its discursive force.

Throughout, I have interrogated images of Indians and Africans alongside those of Europeans to demonstrate that difference was constituted through an ever-shifting interplay between colonisers and colonised. Although there was a strong tendency in missionary writing to construct colonial relationships oppositionally, categories of self and other were fundamentally unstable and even mutually permeable. Cross-cultural relationships threatened to unmask as intangible discrete lines of ethnic differentiation. When the Madras missionaries peered at Rachel's baby (Chapter 2), they noted that it was 'dark'; and trying to determine paternity on that basis, they grappled with the intangibility of the racial difference they believed should be visible. Anxiety about degeneration drew on the shifting nature of racial status. Violent and drunken behaviour could also undermine ethnic status, as in the case of the suicidal 'Sergeant A' (Chapter 6), who ran 'very lightly clothed and barefooted, wild and haggard'.[12] Criticisms of Europeans who behaved in ways that were considered 'fit for savages' drew on fears about the fluidity between 'us' and 'them' that posed race not as oppositional but as a spectrum upon which it was always possible to slide downwards. In exploring these entangled images of self and other, I contribute to the deconstruction of Orientalist discourses of the 'East' (or the 'Antipodes' in the African case) by placing them alongside an exploration of images of the 'West' latent in the same texts. In this way, I respond to the challenge of Edward Said and other postcolonial thinkers to explore the 'intertwined' histories of empire, unravelling some of the many fibres from which these entangled threads were twisted.[13]

Difference was not only fluid but also layered. 'Bechuana', for example, is quite a different label to that of 'the African' or 'Black'; likewise 'English' operated as a label alongside and across 'British', 'European' or 'white' and could itself be inter-cut by other labels such as 'trader' or 'drunkard'. The ability to change focus, to zoom in or step back, was an inherent part of the missionary construction of difference, and slippage between dichotomous and incremental registers could be rhetorically powerful. Missionary discourse was strongly attached to an archetypal 'heathen' – the 'heathen overseas' that, as Thorne argued, was used to throw into relief the 'heathen at home'. 'Heathen' sexuality was disordered; 'heathen' women were 'degraded'; and 'heathens' were 'barbarous'. 'Heathenism' itself was 'blind', 'uncivilised' and 'irrational'.

This 'heathen' was identified differently across different colonial sites. Representations of Indian women, increasingly located in the zenana, were depicted through a sexuality that was supposedly submissive in formulations that were utterly unlike those of African women, not least those matriarchs whom Livingstone encountered amongst the Balonda (Chapter 1). Both Africans and Indians were thought to be sick, but this sickness stood for injury in Africa and decay in India. Indians and Africans were both understood to be cruel but the visceral violence of African warfare was linked to 'tribalism', whilst the sadism evoked by missionaries to India was linked to religion. These differentiations were mapped onto wider thinking about empire – contributing to understandings of the 'East' as dominated by elaborate, yet problematic, 'civilisations' and Africa as 'savage'.

The layering of difference was articulated differently between metropole and colony. Missionaries in the field had more local knowledge and presented differentiated descriptions of ethnic groups, social classes, castes or 'tribes', more detailed than their Directors in the metropole were interested to record or, still less, the British public disposed to consume. In India, missionaries recorded encounters with women who were not subject to purdah, for example, as well as with those who were, and sometimes protested against the 'false impressions regarding the seclusion of Hindoo women' which they knew to be vastly exaggerated in Britain (Chapter 1).[14] Being located in different colonial spaces, or in the metropole as opposed to the periphery, also influenced how missionaries thought about themselves and their colleagues, not least because of the ruptures felt when moving between these spaces, discursive as well as physical. When abroad, missionaries often hinted at a gulf of misunderstanding between themselves and their employers in Britain. This was most strongly the case when experiencing anxiety. Samuel Mateer and his colleagues elsewhere felt utterly rejected when their employers reprimanded them for sick leave taken or complained about the expense of their treatment (Chapter 4). In Britain, the Directors of the society, always attentive to cost, were suspicious of demands made abroad that seemed excessive at home. The Ndebeleland missionaries felt similarly misunderstood by metropolitan Directors who warned them to keep out of negotiations with Rhodes which they felt unable to avoid (Chapter 6). Images of the Missionary Family circulated in missionary propaganda were so utterly unlike those idyllic images represented in the metropole that Elizabeth Price warned that her family in England would 'shout and shudder to think of my presuming to call [her cottage in Bechuanaland] a bonnie, snug home' (Chapter 2).[15]

Missionary discourse was polyvalent: fluid enough to change over time, flexible enough to negotiate contradictions and interruptions and open-ended enough to intercept and interact with other discourses. Missionary discourse was many-voiced. Missionaries spoke from different locations in time and space and from the perspective of people who were also defined through their gender, race, nationality and class. Certain core consistencies remained, yet, no matter how carefully composed the notes they should sing, harmony always risked becoming cacophony, and the conductors in London could not silence all discordant notes.

Difference structures inequality, and yet always does so according to the specificities of time and place. Expansionist imperialism was justified not only by those who wanted the more obvious rewards of power – wealth, political control or personal glory, and not only by those who were cruel, ruthless or sadistic. Colonial domination was also engaged in by those who sincerely believed they were 'doing the right thing', some of whom were missionaries. This is not to say that there were not overlaps, or that missionaries did not seek power and glory or have their own personal agendas. Imperialism was not only justified by overt racism but also by 'benevolent discrimination', much of which sought justification through discourses of the 'natural' body. Difference was a crucial discourse through which these formulations were configured. Analysing power dynamics structured around difference is therefore important to understanding colonialism historically.

But exploring difference is also of ongoing political importance. When working on this project, I have often been disturbed by its contemporary resonance. From the imperial roots of the 'War on Terror' to its current neo-colonial context; the location of 'terror' with the other; the mobilisation of burqa-clad women to signify 'degraded' Eastern 'victims'; to how leaders in both the UK and the US have drawn on values of liberty, and also God, to justify their actions, the motifs I have explored through missionary discourse seem frighteningly relevant today. As evident in the contemporary wave of Islamaphobia, race, culture and religion are constantly being realigned. The intersections between gender, class and nation that Islamaphobia draws upon point to the continued political imperative to interrogate and deconstruct the processes through which difference is understood as something frightening. The swing from multicultural to assimilationist policies in the United Kingdom threatens to reaffirm that difference is something problematic, something 'intolerant', something that signifies inferiority and something that should be dissolved. Such debates demonstrate the enduring legacies of the colonial discourses and the importance of unpicking their historical specificities.

Notes

Introduction: Difference and Discourse in the British Empire

1. R. Lovett (1899) *The History of the London Missionary Society, 1795–1895*, vols 1 and 2 (London: Oxford University Press), p. B1.
2. C. Binfield (1977) *So Down to Prayers: studies in English Nonconformity 1780–1920* (London: Dent).
3. Mr Bogue (August 1794) 'Appeal to the Evangelical Dissenters who Practice Infant Baptism', quoted in Lovett, *History*, vol. 1, p. B1.
4. Mr Burder (January 1795) 'Address', quoted in Lovett, *History*, vol. 1, p. B1.
5. A. Loomba (1998, repr. 2005) *Colonialism/Postcolonialism*, 2nd edn (London: Routledge), pp. 1–91.
6. F. Fanon (1961) *The Wretched of the Earth*, trans. C. Farrington (London: Penguin); F. Fanon (1952, repr. 2007) *Black Skin, White Masks*, New edn, trans. R. Philcox (New York: Grove Press).
7. Fanon, *Wretched*.
8. S. Hall (2000) 'Conclusion: the multi-cultural question' in Barnor Hesse, ed. *Un/Settled Multiculturalisms: diasporas, entanglements, transruptions* (London: Zed), p. 216.
9. H. Bhabha (1997) 'Of Mimicry and Man: the ambivalence of colonial discourse' in F. Cooper and A. L. Stoler, eds. *Tensions of Empire: colonial cultures in a bourgeois world* (London: California Press), pp. 152–63.
10. S. Hall (1997) 'The Spectacle of the Other' in S. Hall, ed. *Representation: cultural representations and signifying practices* (London: Sage), p. 235.
11. E. W. Said (1993) *Culture and Imperialism* (London: Knopf); E. Said (1979, repr. 1995) *Orientalism: western conceptions of the Orient*, 3rd edn (London: Penguin).
12. P. Chatterjee (1993) *The Nation and Its Fragments: colonial and postcolonial histories* (Princeton: Princeton University Press), pp. 18–33.
13. Ibid., p. 18.
14. Ibid., p. 20.
15. Porter (2004) *Missions versus Empire? British Protestant missionaries and overseas expansion, 1700–1914* (Manchester: Manchester University Press), p. 285.
16. A. Rattansi (2007) *Racism: a very short introduction* (Oxford: Oxford University Press).
17. Ibid., pp. 1–11.
18. Hall, 'Conclusion', p. 224.
19. R. Wheeler (2000) *The Complexion of Race: categories of difference in eighteenth-century British culture* (Pennsylvania: University of Pennsylvania Press).

20. C. Bolt (1971) *Victorian Attitudes to Race* (London: Macmillan); T. Holt (1992) *The Problem of Freedom: race, labor and politics in Jamaica and Britain 1832–1938* (Baltimore: Jonn Hopkins University Press); D. A. Lorimer (1978) *Colour, Class and the Victorians: english attitudes to the negro in the mid-nineteenth century* (Leicester: Leicester University Press); N. Stepan (1982) *The Idea of Race in Science: Great Britain 1800–1960* (London: Macmillan); G. Stocking, Junior (1991) *Victorian Anthropology* (New York: Macmillan).
21. S. van der Geest (1990) 'Anthropologists and Missionaries: brothers under the skin', *Man*, New Series, 25 (4), pp. 588–601.
22. R. Moffat (June 1840) *Missionary Magazine*, pp. 91–2.
23. C. Hall (2002) *Civilising Subjects: metropole and colony in the English imagination,1830–1867* (Cambridge: Polity Press).
24. See, for example, P. Levine, ed. (2004) *Gender and Empire* (Oxford: Oxford University Press); A. McClintock (1995) *Imperial Leather: race, gender and sexuality in the colonial contest* (London: Routledge); C. Midgley, ed. (1998) *Gender and Imperialism* (Manchester: Manchester University Press).
25. J. W. Scott (1986) 'Gender: a useful category of historical analysis', *The American Historical Review*, 91, pp. 1053–73.
26. C. Midgley (2006) 'Can Women Be Missionaries? Envisioning female agency in the early nineteenth-century British Empire', *The Journal of British Studies*, 45, pp. 335–58; R. A. Semple (2008) 'Missionary Manhood: professionalism, belief and masculinity in the nineteenth century British imperial field', *Journal of Imperial and Commonwealth Studies*, 36 (3), pp. 397–415; R. A. Semple (2003) *Missionary Women: gender, professionalism, and the Victorian idea of Christian mission* (Woodbridge: Boydell Press).
27. M. Taylor Huber and N. C. Lutkehaus, eds (1999) *Gendered Missions: women and men in missionary discourse and practice* (Ann Arbor: University of Michigan Press).
28. G. Spivak (1985) 'Can the Subaltern Speak? Speculations on widow sacrifice', *Wedge*, 7–8, pp. 120–30.
29. A. Johnston (2003) *Missionary Writing and Empire, 1880–1860* (Cambridge: Cambridge University Press).
30. McClintock, *Imperial Leather*, pp. 52–6; K. Malik (1996) *The Meaning of Race: race, history and culture in western society* (Basingstoke: Macmillan), pp. 92–100.
31. S. Thorne (1999) *Congregational Missions, and the Making of an Imperial Culture in 19th-Century England* (California: University of California Press), p. 82.
32. A. Quayson (2002) 'Looking Awry: tropes of disability in postcolonial writing' in D. T. Goldberg and A. Quayson, eds. *Relocating Postcolonialism* (Oxford: Blackwell), pp. 217–31; M. Sherry (2007) 'Postcolonizing Disability', *Wagadu*, 4, pp. 10–22.
33. Important exceptions include R. Edmond (2006) *Leprosy and Empire: a medical and cultural history* (Cambridge: Cambridge University Press); M. Vaughan (1991) *Curing Their Ills: colonial power and African illness* (Cambridge: Polity Press).
34. Hall, *Civilising Subjects*, p. 16.
35. J. de Groot, '"Sex" and "Race"; the construction of language and image in the nineteenth century' in C. Hall, ed. *Cultures of Empire: colonizers in*

Britain and the empire in the nineteenth and twentieth centuries (Manchester: Manchester University Press), pp. 37–61.

36. Fanon, *Wretched*, pp. 29–31.
37. Johnston, *Missionary Writing*, p. 5.
38. E. Kolsky (2005) 'Codification and the Rule of Colonial Difference: criminal procedure in British India', *Law and History Review*, 25, pp. 631–85.
39. Hall, *Civilising Subjects*, p. 15. See also, Hall, ed., *Cultures of Empire*.
40. B. Stanley (1990) *The Bible and the Flag: protestant missions and British imperialism in the nineteenth and twentieth centuries* (Leicester: Apollo); Porter, *Religion versus Empire*.
41. F. Cooper and A. L. Stoler (1997) 'Between Metropole and Colony: rethinking a research agenda' in F. Cooper and A. L. Stoler, eds. *Tensions of Empire: colonial cultures in a bourgeois world* (London: California Press), pp. 1–59.
42. A. L. Stoler (2002) *Carnal Knowledge and Imperial Power: race and the intimate in colonial rule* (California: University of California Press), p. 42.
43. A. L. Stoler (1989) 'Rethinking Colonial Categories: European communities and the boundaries of rule', *Comparative Studies in Society and History*, 31 (1), pp. 134–61; Stoler, *Carnal Knowledge*.
44. Ibid., p. 49; A. L. Stoler (1989) 'Making Empire Respectable: the politics of race and sexual morality in 20th-century colonial cultures', *American Ethnologist*, 16 (4), p. 647.
45. M. A. Render (2001) '"Sentiments of a Private Nature": a comment on Ann Laura Stoler's "Tense and Tender Ties"', *Journal of American History*, 88, pp. 882–7.
46. C. Hall (2006) 'Commentary' in A. L. Stoler, ed. *Haunted by Empire: geographies of intimacy in North American history* (Durham: Duke University Press), pp. 452–68; T. Ballantyne and A. Burton, eds (2008) *Moving Subjects: gender, mobility, and intimacy in an age of global empire* (Chicago: Illinois University Press).
47. A. Porter (2005) 'An Overview, 1700–1914' in N. Etherington, ed. *Missions and Empire* (Oxford: Oxford University Press), pp. 64–86.
48. For general studies see, for example: J. Cox (2008) *The British Missionary Enterprise Since 1700* (Oxford: Routledge); A. Twells (2009) *The Heathen at Home and Overseas: the middle class and the civilising mission, Sheffield 1790–1843* (Basingstoke: Macmillan); N. Etherington, ed. (2005) *Missions and Empire* (Oxford: Oxford University Press); Porter, *Religion versus Empire*. For southern Africa see: J. L. Comaroff and J. Comaroff (1991) *Of Revelation and Revolution*, vol. 1, *Christianity, colonialism, and consciousness in South Africa* (Chicago: University of Chicago Press); E. Elbourne (2002) *Blood Ground: colonialism, missions, and the contest for Christianity in the Cape Colony and Britain, 1799–1853* (Montreal: McGill-Queen's University Press); R. Price (2008) *Making Empire: colonial encounters and the creation of imperial rule in nineteenth-century Africa* (Cambridge: Cambridge University Press). For India see: Jeffrey Cox (2002) *Imperial Fault Lines: Christianity and colonial power in India, 1818–1940* (California: Stanford University Press); A. Shourie (1994) *Missionaries in India: continuities, changes, dilemmas* (New Delhi: ASA Publications).
49. Porter, *Religion versus Empire*, pp. 39–63.
50. Cox, *The British Missionary*, p. 100.

51. F. K. Prochaska (1978) 'Little Vessels: children in the nineteenth-century English missionary movement', *The Journal of Imperial and Commonwealth History*, 6 (2), pp. 103–19.
52. Hall, *Civilising Subjects*, pp. 292–4.
53. Porter, *Religion versus Empire*, p. 190.
54. Thorne, *Congregational Missions.*
55. P. D. Curtin, ed. (1972) *Africa & the West: intellectual responses to European culture* (Madison: University of Wisconsin Press).
56. P. Brantlinger (1988) *Rule of Darkness: British literature and imperialism, 1830–1914* (Ithaca: Cornell University Press), p. 173.
57. Title Piece (February 1857) 'Livingstone's Journey Across Southern Africa', *Missionary Magazine.*
58. C. Crais (1992) *White Supremacy and Black Resistance in Pre-Industrial South Africa: the making of the colonial order in the Eastern Cape, 1770–1865* (Cambridge: Cambridge University Press); A. Lester (2001) *Imperial Networks: creating identities in nineteenth-century South Africa and Britain* (London: Routledge); T. Keegan, *Colonial South Africa and the Origins of the Racial Order* (London: Leicester University Press); R. Ross (1983) *Cape of Torments: slavery and resistance in South Africa* (London: Routledge & Keegan Paul).
59. Johnston, *Missionary Writing*, pp. 16–17. Elbourne, *Blood Ground*, pp. 90–92; Comaroff and Comaroff, *Of Revelation*, vol. 1, pp. 84–5. For more on the social background of Protestant missionaries generally see Cox, *The British Missionary*, pp. 93–113.
60. Comaroff and Comaroff, *Of Revelation*, vol. 1, p. 84.
61. D. I. Stuart (1994) ' "Of Savages and Heroes"; discourses of race, nation and gender in the evangelical missions to Southern Africa in the early nineteenth century' (Institute of Commonwealth Studies: unpublished PhD thesis); Elbourne, *Blood Ground*, pp. 197–233.
62. Elbourne, *Blood Ground*; Lester, *Imperial Networks.*
63. Z. Laidlaw (2005) *Colonial Connections 1815–45: patronage, the information revolution and colonial government* (Manchester: Manchester University Press).
64. Andrew Bank, amongst others, convincingly argues that the decline of humanitarianism occurred in the Cape before it did elsewhere. A. Bank (1999) 'Losing Faith in the Civilizing Mission: the premature decline of humanitarian liberalism at the Cape, 1840–60' in M. Daunton and R. Halpern, eds. *Empire and Others: British encounters with indigenous peoples, 1600–1850* (London: UCL Press), pp. 364–83.
65. Elbourne, *Blood Ground*; Lester, *Imperial Networks.*
66. Lovett, *History*, vol. 1, pp. 572–4.
67. T. R. H. Davenport and C. Saunders (2000) *South Africa: a modern history*, 5th edn (Basingstoke: Macmillan), pp. 36–49; N. Etherington (2001) *The Great Treks: the transformation of South Africa, 1815–1854* (London: Longman).
68. Ibid., pp. 80–6.
69. Ibid., pp. 129–92.
70. P. Delius (1983) *The Land Belongs To Us: the Pedi polity, the Boers and the British in the nineteenth-century Transvaal* (Johannesburg: Raven Press); K. Shillington (1985) *The Colonisation of the Southern Tswana, 1870–1900*

(Braamfontein: Ravan Press); J. Guy (1979) *The Destruction of the Zulu Kingdom: the civil war in Zululand, 1879–1884* (London: Longman); S. Samkange (1968) *Origins of Rhodesia* (London: Heinemann).

71. P. Landau (1995) *The Realm of the Word: language, gender and Christianity in a southern African kingdom* (Portsmouth: Heinemann), pp. 5–7. As Landau suggests, the relationship between these shifting labels and 'identity' is difficult to determine and was undergoing considerable change in the mid nineteenth century.
72. Landau, *The Realm*. For LMS accounts of this period see: C. H. Lyall, ed. (1895) *Twenty Years in Khama's Country: and pioneering among the Batauana of Lake Ngami. Told in the letters of J. D. Hepburn* (London: Hodder and Stoughton).
73. D. Carnegie (July 1890) *Chronicle*, p. 256.
74. A. Sillery (1971) *John Mackenzie of Bechuanaland 1835–1899: a study in humanitarian imperialism* (Cape Town: Balkema), pp. 52–3; W. D. Mackenzie (1902) *John Mackenzie: South African missionary and statesman* (London: Hodder and Stroughton).
75. T. O. Ranger (1967) *Revolt in Southern Rhodesia, 1896–7: a study in African resistance* (London: Heinemann); Samkange, *Origins of Rhodesia*; J. Alexander (2006) *The Unsettled Land: state-making & the politics of land in Zimbabwe, 1893–2003* (Oxford: James Currey), p. 20.
76. Ranger, *Revolt*.
77. N. Bhebe (1979) *Christianity and Traditional Religion in Western Zimbabwe, 1859–1923* (London: Longman).
78. G. Cuthbertson, A. Grundlingh, and M. Suttie, eds (2002) *Writing a Wider War: rethinking gender, race and identity in the South African War 1899–1902* (Athens: Ohio University Press).
79. B. Metcalf and T. Metcalf (2006) *A Concise History of Modern India* (Cambridge: Cambridge University Press), pp. 61–3.
80. E. Storrow (1859) *India and Christian Missions* (London: John Snow), p. 1; C. A. Bayly (1996) *Empire and Information: intelligence gathering and social communication in India, 1780–1870* (Cambridge: Cambridge University Press).
81. I. Copland (2006) 'Christianity as an Arm of Empire: the ambiguous case of India under the company, c. 1813–1858', *Historical Journal*, 49 (4), pp. 1025–54.
82. Stanley, *The Bible*, pp. 98–100.
83. Johnston, *Missionary Writing*, p. 65.
84. Although in many ways it always remained very much distinct, the South India Mission could also include Ceylon. My study, however, is restricted to mainland India.
85. Metcalf and Metcalf, *A Concise History of Modern*, p. 80.
86. See, for example, A. F. Lacroix (1851) *Voyage du Missionnaire A.F. Lacroix au Temple de Jogonnath* (Neuchatel: Henri Wolfrath).
87. E. Kent (2004) *Converting Women: gender and Protestant Christianity in colonial South India* (Oxford: Oxford University Press), p. 43.
88. LMS (annual) *Report of the Native Female School Society in Connection with the London Missionary Society*; BMS (1858) *History of Native Female Education in Calcutta*; LMS (1855) *Bhowanipore Boarding School: report* (London: LMS).

89. Hall, *Civilising Subjects*, pp. 370–1.
90. R. Guha (1983) *Elementary Aspects of Peasant Insurgency in Colonial India* (Delhi: Oxford University Press).
91. J. Kennedy (1884) *Life and Work in Benares and Kumaon, 1839–1877* (London: T. Fisher Unwin), pp. 174–205.
92. Editor (November 1857) *Missionary Magazine*, p. 242.
93. T. Metcalf (1964) *The Aftermath of Revolt, India, 1857–1870* (London: Princeton University Press).
94. B. Cohn (1987) 'Representing Authority in Victorian India' in B. Cohn, ed. *An Anthropologist among the Historians and Other Essays* (Oxford: Oxford University Press), pp. 632–82.
95. R. Moore (1999) 'Imperial India, 1858–1914' in A. Porter ed. *Oxford History of the British Empire*, vol. 3: *the nineteenth century* (Oxford: Oxford University Press), p. 424.
96. See, for example, Storrow, *India and Christian Missions*, pp. 95–105; Kennedy, *Life and Work*, pp. 75–6.
97. Kent, *Converting Women*, pp. 97–8. For the LMS response to the Rebellion, see *Annual Report of the London Missionary Society*, 1858; Editor (August 1858) *Missionary Magazine*, p. 177.
98. Editor (February 1860) *Missionary Magazine*, pp. 32–5.
99. Ibid., p. 33.
100. LMS (1895) *Annual Report of the London Missionary Society*.
101. M. Davis (2001) *Late Victorian Holocausts: El Niño famines and the making of the third world* (London: Verso).
102. Ibid., p. 7.
103. Directors (October 1877) *Chronicle*, p. 214.
104. Lovett, *History*, vol. 2, p. 52. See also, E. Storrow (1888) *Protestant Missions in Pagan Lands: a manual of facts and principles relating to foreign missions throughout the world* (London: John Snow). For a more detailed discussion of the differences between the Indian and southern African missions, see E. Cleall (2009) 'Thinking with Missionaries: discourses of differences in India and southern Africa, c. 1840–1895' (University College London: unpublished PhD thesis), pp. 77–82.
105. Cox, *Imperial Fault Lines*; Thorne, *Congregational Missions*.
106. E. Cleall (June 2009) 'Missionary Masculinities and War: the LMS in Southern Africa, c. 1860–1899', *South African Historical Journal*, 61 (2), pp. 232–52.
107. See, for example, Laidlaw, *Colonial Connections*; D. Lambert and A. Lester, eds (2006) *Colonial Lives Across the British Empire: imperial careering in the long nineteenth century* (Cambridge: Cambridge University Press); A. Lester (2006) 'Imperial Circuits and Networks: geographies of the British Empire', *History Compass*, 4 (1), pp. 124–41; R. Phillips (2006) *Sex, Politics and Empire: a postcolonial geography* (Manchester: Manchester University Press).
108. A. Coombes (1994) *Reinventing Africa: museums, material culture and popular imagination* (New Haven: Yale University Press), pp. 187–214; E. Cleall (2005) 'The Missionary Contribution to Imperial Display: missionary exhibitions, 1869–1939' (University of Sheffield: unpublished MA thesis).
109. Johnston, *Missionary Writing*, p. 32.
110. Thorne, *Congregational Missions*, pp. 5, 16.

111. For more on the utility of missionary periodicals as an historical source see T. Barringer (2004) 'What Mrs Jellyby Might Have Read: missionary periodicals: a neglected source', *Victorian Periodical Review*, 37 (4), pp. 46–72.
112. Directors (January 1860) *Missionary Magazine*, p. 2.
113. Johnston, *Missionary Writing*, p. 197.

Part I Families and Households: Difference and Domesticity

1. S. Gilman (1985) *Difference and Pathology: stereotypes of sexuality, race and madness* (Ithaca: Cornell), p. 81.
2. J. Morgan (2005) 'Male Travellers, Female Bodies, and the Gendering of Racial Ideology, 1500–1770' in T. Ballantyne and A. Burton, eds. *Bodies in Contact: rethinking colonial encounters in world history* (Durham: Duke University Press), pp. 54–67.
3. E. W. Said (1995) *Orientalism: western conceptions of the orient*, 1st published 1979 (London: Penguin), p. 190.
4. For a direct comparison of the sexualisation and commoditisation of African and Indian women in early modern colonial literature see N. Bhattacharya (1998) *Reading the Splendid Body: gender and consumerism in eighteenth-century British writing on India* (Newark: University of Delaware Press), pp. 23–35.
5. M. Sinha (1995) *Colonial Masculinity: the 'Manly Englishman' and the 'Effeminate Bengali' in the late nineteenth century* (Manchester: Manchester University Press).
6. K. Wilson (2004) 'Empire, Gender and Modernity in the Eighteenth Century' in P. Levine, ed. *Gender and Empire, the Oxford History of the British Empire Companion Series* (Oxford: Oxford University Press), pp. 14–45; C. Hall (2004) 'Of Gender and Empire: reflections on the nineteenth century' in P. Levine, ed. *Gender and Empire, the Oxford History of the British Empire Companion Series* (Oxford: Oxford University Press), pp. 46–77.
7. J. Mill (1817) *A History of India*, vol. 1 (London: Baldwin, Cradock and Joy), p. 293.
8. Ibid., pp. 293–4.
9. Editor (February 1860) *Missionary Magazine*, p. 40.
10. Lata Mani argues that 'a specifically colonial discourse on *sati* produc[ed] troubling consequences for how 'the women question' was to be posed thereafter. L. Mani (2003) 'Multiple Mediations: feminist scholarship in the age of multinational reception' in C. McCann, ed. *Feminist Theory Reader: local and global perspectives* (London: Routledge), p. 374. See also L. Mani (1998) *Contentious Traditions: the debate on sati in colonial India* (Berkeley: University of California Press).
11. T. Hunt (2002) 'Introduction: the colonial gaze' in T. Hunt and M. Lessard, eds. *Women and the Colonial Gaze* (Basingstoke: Palgrave), p. 1; R. W. Herndon, 'Women as Symbols of Disorder in Early Rhode Island' in T. Hunt and M. Lessard, eds. *Women and the Colonial Gaze* (Basingstoke: Palgrave), pp. 79–91.
12. Mill, *History*, p. 309.
13. For discussions of masculinity in the mid-nineteenth century see, for example, N. Jayasena (2007) *Contested Masculinities: crises in colonial male identity*

from Joseph Conrad to Satyajit Ray (London: Routledge); M. Roper and J. Tosh, eds (1991) *Manful Assertions: masculinities in Britain since 1800* (London: Routledge); R. W. Connell (1995) *Masculinities* (Cambridge: Cambridge University Press); H. Sussman (1995) *Victorian Masculinities: manhood and masculine poetics in early Victorian literature and art* (Cambridge: Cambridge University Press); J. Tosh (1999) *A Man's Place: masculinity and the middle-class home in Victorian England* (New Haven: Yale University Press); J. Tosh (2005) *Manliness and Masculinities in Nineteenth-Century Britain: essays on gender, family, and empire* (Harlow: Longman).

14. Hall, 'Of Gender and Empire', p. 51.
15. L. Davidoff and C. Hall (2002) *Family Fortunes: men and women of the English middle class: 1780–1850*, 2nd edn (Basingstoke: Routledge).
16. L. Davidoff, M. Doolittle, and J. Fink (1999) *The Family Story: blood, contract and intimacy, 1830–1960* (London: Longman).

1 Representing Homes: Gender and Sexuality in Missionary Writing

1. Editor (July 1850) *Missionary Magazine*, p. 117.
2. C. Whyte (January 1901) *Chronicle*, p. 44. Whilst they addressed British audiences, 'English' is the hegemonic cultural formation to explain this domestic identity and was used by English, Scots and Welsh missionaries alike.
3. A. Burton (2000) 'Women and "Domestic" Imperial Culture: the case of Victorian Britain' in M. J. Boxer and J. H. Quataert, eds. *Connecting Spheres: European women in a globalizing world, 1500 to the present* (Oxford: Oxford University Press), p. 180.
4. W. C. Bentall (August 1907) *Chronicle*, p. 154.
5. A. Fletcher (March 1844) *Missionary Chronicle*, p. 39; J. Read (May 1841) *Missionary Chronicle*, p. 76.
6. Mr Thomson (February 1874) *Chronicle*, p. 25.
7. C. Hall (2002) *Civilising Subjects: metropole and colony in the English imagination, 1830–1867* (Cambridge: Polity Press), pp. 91–2, 96.
8. Editor (October 1883) *Chronicle*, p. 341.
9. Ibid., p. 341.
10. D. Langmore (1989) 'The Object Lesson of a Civilised, Christian Home' in M. Jolly and M. Macintyre, eds. *Family and Gender in the Pacific: domestic contradictions and the colonial impact* (Cambridge: Cambridge University Press), pp. 84–94.
11. Anon. (February 1880) *Chronicle*, p. 24.
12. Other contributors to this domestic ideal also remain hidden in these writings, such as indigenous servants. This will be discussed in Chapter 2.
13. W. M. Stratham (June 1877) *Chronicle*, p. 127.
14. Ibid., pp. 127–8.
15. Anon. (February 1880) *Chronicle*, p. 24.
16. Editor (April 1896) *Chronicle*, p. 85.
17. Anon. (February 1880) *Chronicle*, p. 24.
18. L. Davidoff and C. Hall (2002) *Family Fortunes: men and women of the English middle class: 1780–1850*, 2nd edn (Basingstoke: Routledge).

19. E. Beuttner (2004) *Empire Families: Britons and late imperial India* (Oxford: Oxford University Press).
20. E. Barclay (October 1897) *Chronicle*, p. 230.
21. P. Grimshaw (2004) 'Faith, Missionary Life, and the Family' in P. Levine, ed. *Gender and Empire, the Oxford History of the British Empire Companion Series* (Oxford: Oxford University Press), pp. 271–2.
22. There are interesting comparisons to be made here between concerns that missionaries and other philanthropists had about working-class living arrangements in Britain. Part of the discursive work performed by missionaries abroad was to marginalise these parallels, instead subsuming lived conditions in the metropole within their Evangelical ideal. See, for example, S. Koven (2004) *Slumming: sexual and social politics in Victorian London* (Princeton: Princeton University Press).
23. Mr Passmore (September 1842) *Missionary Magazine*, p. 130.
24. Editor (July 1842) *Missionary Magazine*, p. 107.
25. Ibid., p. 107.
26. It is possible that their reactions were deliberately exaggerated for the British readership. Lata Mani has discussed how horrified representations of *sati* were much more extreme when written for a British audience than they were when produced in India – a different voice was adopted. L. Mani, (1998) *Contentious Traditions: the debate on sati in colonial India* (Berkeley: University of California Press), p. 111.
27. See, for example, A. J. Wookey (August 1884) *Chronicle*, p. 261.
28. R. Moffat (April 1856) *Missionary Magazine*, p. 69.
29. J. Mackenzie (1871) *Ten Years North of the Orange River: a story of everyday life and work among the South African tribes, from 1859 to 1869* (Edinburgh: Edmonston & Douglas), p. 303.
30. R. Moffat (February 1856) *Missionary Magazine*, p. 25.
31. See, for example, R. Moffat (1842) *Missionary Labours and Scenes in Southern Africa* (London: John Snow), p. 151.
32. A. J. Wookey (August 1884) *Chronicle*, p. 261.
33. R. Birt (October 1841) *Missionary Magazine*, p. 163.
34. Ibid.
35. Ibid.
36. D. Livingstone (January 1857) *Missionary Magazine*, p. 14.
37. Ibid.
38. D. Livingstone (January 1857) *Missionary Magazine*, p. 14; D. Livingstone (February 1857) *Missionary Magazine*, p. 33.
39. D. Livingstone (February 1857) *Missionary Magazine*, p. 34.
40. Ibid.
41. Ibid.
42. Editor (February 1857) *Missionary Magazine*, p. 33.
43. E. Holub (1884) quoted in J. Mackenzie (April 1884) *Chronicle*, pp. 113–4. Mackenzie's *Ten Years* itself demonstrates this use of architecture to reinforce assumptions about people, race and language. See the appendix, 'The Races of South Africa', Mackenzie, *Ten Years*, pp. 483–508.
44. Editor summarising J. Mackenzie (April 1884) *Chronicle*, p. 113.
45. Ibid., p. 133.
46. Ibid., p. 144.

47. Dr Wyckoff (September 1907) *Chronicle*, p. 179.
48. C. Hall (2004) 'Of Gender and Empire: reflections on the nineteenth century' in P. Levine, ed. *Gender and Empire: the Oxford History of the British Empire Companion Series* (Oxford: Oxford University Press), pp. 52–5.
49. A. Major (2006) *Pious Flames: European encounters with sati 1500–1830* (Oxford: Oxford University Press).
50. For the age of consent controversy, see also, M. Sinha (1995) *Colonial Masculinity: the 'Manly Englishman' and the 'Effeminate Bengali' in the late nineteenth century* (Manchester: Manchester University Press), pp. 138–80; H. Bannerji (1998) 'Age of Consent and Hegemonic Social Reform' in C. Midgely, ed. *Gender and Imperialism* (Manchester: Manchester University Press), pp. 21–45.
51. M. Lacroix (1862) *Brief Memorials of Mrs Mullens, by her Sister* (London: James Nisbet); E. R. Pitman (1897) *Heroines of the Mission Field: biographical sketches of female missionaries who have laboured in various lands among the heathen* (London: Cassell), pp. 81–6.
52. Editor (June 1864) *Missionary Chronicle*, pp. 178–9.
53. See, for example: LMS (n.d.) *Six Zenana Recitations for Little Girls* (London: LMS); LMS (n.d.) *Boys and Girls From Other Lands; a missionary cantata* (London: LMS.); M. E. Leslie (1862) *The Dawn of Light: a story of the zenana mission*, with an introduction by Reverend E. Storrow (London: John Snow); Lacroix, *Brief Memorials*; Pitman, *Heroines*, pp. 21–42; M. E. Weitbrecht (1875) *The Women of India and Christian Work in the Zenana* (London: James Nisbet).
54. E. Cleall (2005) 'The Missionary Contribution to Imperial Display: missionary exhibitions 1869–1939' (University of Sheffield: unpublished MA thesis).
55. J. P. Ashton (February 1888) *Chronicle*, p. 65.
56. See, for example, C. Campbell (March 1865) *Missionary Magazine*, p. 60.
57. E. Kent (2004) *Converting Women: gender and Protestant Christianity in colonial South India* (Oxford: Oxford University Press), p. 18.
58. A. Johnston (2003) *Missionary Writing and Empire, 1880–1860* (Cambridge: Cambridge University Press), p. 69.
59. Ibid., p. 72.
60. H. Mullens (December 1861) *Missionary Magazine*, p. 331.
61. H. Mullens (August 1861) *Missionary Magazine*, p. 230.
62. Mrs Sewell (April 1863) *Missionary Magazine*, pp. 87–9.
63. Ibid.
64. Ibid.
65. Ibid.
66. Editor (June 1863) *Missionary Magazine*, p. 88.
67. LMS, *Boys and Girls*, p. 13.
68. Johnston, *Missionary Writings*, pp. 88–9.
69. C. Valentine (March 1875) *Chronicle*, p. 62.
70. A. Burton (1996) 'Contesting the Zenana: the mission to make "Lady Doctors for India" 1874–1885', *The Journal of British Studies*, 35 (3), pp. 368–97; S. S. Maughan (2000) 'Civic Culture, Women's Foreign Missions, and the British Imperial Imagination, 1860–1914' in F. Trentmann, ed. *Paradoxes of Civil Society: new perspectives on modern German and British history* (Oxford: Berghahn); Janaki Nair (2000) 'Uncovering the *zenana*: visitations of Indian womanhood in Englishwomen's writings, 1813–1940' in C. Hall, ed. *Cultures*

of Empire, A Reader: colonisers in Britain and the Empire in the nineteenth and twentieth centuries (Manchester: Manchester University Press), pp. 224–45.

71. See, for example, LMS, *Six Zenana Recitations*; LMS, 'India: Hindu Girl', *Boys and Girls*, pp. 112–13; M. E. Haskard (1890) *Zenana Work: the opportunity among women in India* (London: LMS).
72. '"Z" for Zenana', from LMS (n.d.) *A Missionary Alphabet: for recitation at missionary entertainments* (London: LMS).
73. B. Cassin (June 1881) *Chronicle*, p. 150.
74. Ibid. Technically marriage at the age of nine was illegal at this point following the 1860 Age of Consent Act. Marriage below the then legal age of 10 undoubtedly continued to occur, but the fuzziness around actual ages here is typical.
75. E. Barclay (October 1897) *Chronicle*, p. 230.
76. Bannerji, 'Age of Consent', pp. 21–45.
77. See, for example, E. Stevens (February 1896) *Chronicle*, p. 40; A. B. Webster (July 1898) *Chronicle*, p. 168.
78. E. Barclay (October 1897) *Chronicle*, p. 230.
79. W. Robinson (March 1890) *Chronicle*, p. 74.
80. A. Spicer (June 1883) *Chronicle*, p. 221.
81. W. Sykes (April 1881) *Chronicle*, p. 79.
82. Nair, 'Uncovering the *Zenana*', p. 235.
83. Ibid., p. 221.
84. The international attention focussed on the zenana was noted with some envy by the southern African LMS missionaries, who were also anxious to raise the state of women. P. Landau (1995) *The Realm of the Word: language, gender and Christianity in a southern African kingdom* (Portsmouth: Heinemann), p. 101.
85. Editor (February 1860) *Missionary Magazine*, p. 40.

2 Re-Making Homes: Ambiguous Encounters and Domestic Transgressions

1. A. L. Stoler, 'Intimidations of Empire: predicaments of the tactile and unseen' in A. L. Stoler, ed. *Haunted by Empire: geographies of intimacy in North American history* (Durham: Duke University Press), p. 24.
2. A. J. Wookey (September 1884) *Chronicle*, p. 303.
3. W. Thompson (November 1881) *Chronicle*, p. 260.
4. R. Ross (1995) 'The Social and Political Theology of Western Cape Missions' in H. Bredekamp and R. Ross, eds. *Missions and Christianity in South African History* (Johannesburg: Witwatersrand University Press), p. 101.
5. P. Scully (1997) *Liberating the Family?: gender and British slave emancipation in the rural Western Cape, South Africa, 1823–1853* (Oxford: James Currey), pp. 75–80, 136–40.
6. Ibid., pp. 82–3, 109–33.
7. J. L. Comaroff and J. Comaroff (1991) *Of Revelation and Revolution*, vol. 1, *Christianity, colonialism, and consciousness in South Africa* (Chicago and London: University of Chicago Press), vol. 2, p. 298.

8. A. Spicer (June 1883) *Chronicle*, p. 220. Although there had been an experimental boarding school for the children of Xhosa chiefs in Cape Town, this did not become a widespread policy in southern Africa.
9. Numerous (not infrequently inconsistent) examples of statistics of schools and students are available, but to take the 'very reliable' Statistical Tables of Protestant Missions in India for 1881, as an example, it seems there were 1,120 girls' day-schools, with 40,897 scholars, 155 boarding schools with 6,379 boarders, and 2,845 orphanages. E. Storrow (January 1887) *Chronicle*, p. 11.
10. J. Russell (August 1856) *Missionary Magazine*, p. 166.
11. Dr Wyckoff (September 1907) *Chronicle*, p. 179.
12. Storrow, *Protestant Missions*, pp. 36–8.
13. For a typical fictional example, see, M. E. Leslie (1868) *The Dawn of Light: a story of the Zenana mission*, with an introduction by Rev. E. Storrow (London: John Snow).
14. See, for example, Engraving (July 1871) *Chronicle*, p. 143.
15. See, for example, A. W. Forde (January 1857) *Missionary Magazine*, p. 2.
16. T. D. Philip (April 1881) *Chronicle*, p. 77. A. J. Wookey (September 1884) *Chronicle*, p. 303.
17. W. Forde (January 1857) *Missionary Magazine*, p. 5.
18. M. Budden (July 1895) *Chronicle*, p. 181.
19. G. Hall (March 1857) *Missionary Magazine*, p. 63. As so often in missionary writing, the structure of this narrative softens some of the emotional impact of a universalising discourse through the infantilising (and possibly feminisation) of the father and by the culmination of the story in the renunciation of caste (and its suggestions of self-interest).
20. J. Mackenzie (1858) quoted in Comaroff and Comaroff, *Of Revelation*, vol. 2, p. 274.
21. T. D. Phillip (August 18656) *Missionary Magazine*, p. 175.
22. F. Baylis (November 1859) *Missionary Magazine*, p. 266.
23. Ibid., pp. 266–7.
24. U. Long (1950) 'Introduction' in E. L. Price, ed. (1950) *The Journals of Elizabeth Lees Price: written in Bechuanaland, Southern Africa, 1854–1883 with an epilogue 1889–1900*, with Una Long (London: Edmond Arnold), pp. 28–32.
25. Ibid., p. 32.
26. Ibid., pp. 110–11.
27. H. Bhabha (1997) 'Of Mimicry and Man: the ambivalence of colonial discourse' in F. Cooper and A. L. Stoler, eds. *Tensions of Empire: colonial cultures in a bourgeois world* (London: California Press), p. 153.
28. Long, 'Introduction', p. 29.
29. Ibid., p. 30.
30. T. E. Slater (January 1894) *Chronicle*, p. 23.
31. P. Chatterjee (1993) *The Nation and Its Fragments: colonial and postcolonial histories* (Princeton: Princeton University Press), p. 18.
32. A. Porter (2004) *Religion versus Empire? British Protestant missionaries and overseas expansion, 1700–1914* (Manchester: Manchester University Press), pp. 256–8.
33. Ibid., p. 257.

34. E. Barclay (October 1897) *Chronicle*, p. 230.
35. Jane Haggis discusses the continued use of boarding schools for the children of Christians in Travancore. J. Haggis (1991) 'Professional Ladies and Working Wives: female missionaries in the London Missionary Society and its South Travancore District, South India in the 19th century' (University of Manchester: unpublished PhD thesis), pp. 281–329.
36. Stoler quoted in K. H. Skeie (1999) 'Building God's Kingdom: the importance of the house to nineteenth-century Norwegian missionaries in Madagascar' in K. Middleton, ed. *Ancestors, Power and History in Madagascar* (Lyden: Brill), p. 96.
37. M. Procida (2002) *Married to the Empire: gender, politics and imperialism in India, 1883–1947* (Manchester: Manchester University Press), p. 61.
38. M. Weitbrecht (1853) *Female Missionaries in India: letters from a missionary wife abroad, to a friend in England* (London: James Nisbet), p. 55.
39. C. Mullens (1862) 'Home Life' in J. Mullens, ed. *Brief Memories of the Rev. Alphonse François Lacroix: missionary of the London Missionary Society in Calcutta* (London: James Nisbet), p. 349.
40. Ibid., p. 357.
41. See, for example, the Anglo-Indian families discussed by E. Beuttner (2004) *Empire Families: Britons and late imperial India* (Oxford: Oxford University Press), and Dutch-Indonesian families discussed by A. L. Stoler (2002) *Carnal Knowledge and Imperial Power: race and the intimate in colonial rule* (California: University of California Press).
42. Much missionary correspondence was spent detailing such arrangements. See, for example, Johnston's arrangements for his three children. Mr Johnston (21 January 1858) Nundial, CWM/LMS/South India/Tamil/Incoming Correspondence/B12/F1/JA.
43. J. Mullens (January 1880) *Chronicle*, p. 16.
44. Stoler, *Carnal Knowledge*.
45. Ibid., p. 16.
46. Editor (February 1881) *Chronicle*, p. 37.
47. Price, ed., *Journals*, p. 105.
48. For the civilising role of women in Britain, see L. Davidoff and C. Hall (2002) *Family Fortunes: men and women of the English middle class: 1780–1850*, 2nd edn (Basingstoke: Routledge).
49. Price, ed., *Journals*, pp. 215–16
50. Skeie, 'Building God's Kingdom', p. 96.
51. Price, ed., *The Journals*, p. 104.
52. Haggis, 'Professional Ladies', pp. 242–3.
53. Ibid., p. 279.
54. Clinton (1959) *"These vessels . . . ": the story of Inyati 1859–1959* (Bulawayo: Stuart Manning), p. 38.
55. Elizabeth Hepburn's account of how utterly devastating this removal was – to dismantle the church and house her husband had built by hand and see the places where she had raised her children abandoned – is suggestive of how 'homelike' (her word) Shoshong had become. Such feelings of 'home' must always be placed alongside other readings of home more influenced by national identity and domestic comfort. C. H. Lyall, ed. (1895) *Twenty years in Khama's Country: and, pioneering among the Batauana of Lake*

Ngami, told in the letters of J. D. Hepburn (London: Hodder and Stoughton), pp. 304–322.

56. Haggis, 'Professional Ladies', pp. 244, 279.
57. Price, ed., *Journals*, pp. 215–6.
58. Ibid., p. 98
59. Ibid. p. 137.
60. Weitbrecht, *Female Missionaries*, p. 57.
61. For the colonial contact zone, see M. L. Pratt (1992) *Imperial Eyes: travel writing and transculturation* (London: Routledge).
62. Mission stations, like the houses of clergymen in Britain, were also often semi-public spaces, with professional as well as private uses. In this section, however, I am referring to missionary homes as 'private'. Although established mission stations could also serve public functions (e.g. as a room for teaching or dispensing medicine), areas of the home were always private (e.g. bedrooms) or private at certain times of day (e.g. evenings). For those missionaries whose only home was a 'wagon', this was always a private space.
63. Price, ed., *Journals*, p. 406.
64. J. Hepburn (February 1878) *Chronicle*, p. 34.
65. R. Birt (October 1841) *Missionary Magazine*, p. 163.
66. Mrs A. Coles to the Ladies at Carr's Lane (9 May 1850) Bellary, CWM/LMS/South India/Canarese/Incoming Correspondence/B7b/F5/JA.
67. Ibid.
68. Ibid.
69. Ibid.
70. S. Ahmed (2007) 'A Phenomenology of Whiteness', *Feminist Theory*, 8 (2), pp. 149–68; S. Ahmed (2006) *Queer Phenomenology: orientations, objects, others* (Durham: Duke University Press).
71. Coles to the Ladies at Carr's Lane (9 May 1850).
72. J. B. Coles (11 September 1850) Bellary, CWM/LMS/South India/Canarese/Incoming Correspondence/B7b/F5/JA.
73. When John Moffat and Thomas M. Thomas asked King Mzilikazi for servants in their mission in Ndebeleland, Mzilikazi sent them an 8-year-old girl, and a boy of 5 or 6, and a girl of 7 and boy of 4, respectively. As Iris Clinton writes 'these children were a responsibility rather than a help. Yet they could not ask the King to take them back, as they were told that if they refused his gift, the children would be left out in the forest to die.' Clinton, *These Vessels*, p. 38.
74. Weitbrecht, *Female Missionaries*, p. 67.
75. For the elaborate patterns of servant-keeping in Anglo-India see: Beuttner, *Empire Families*; F. Dussart (2005) 'The Servant/Employer Relationship in Nineteenth-Century England and India' (University of London: unpublished PhD dissertation); Procida, *Married*.
76. A. L. Stoler (1995) *Race and the Education of Desire: Foucault's History of Sexuality and the colonial order of things* (London: Duke University Press), pp. 137–64.
77. F. Brockway (August 1895) *Chronicle*, pp. 212–14.
78. Many indeed were not – although missionaries in India preferred to employ Indian Christians, they were difficult to come by. Weitbrecht, *Female Missionaries*, p. 67.

79. Davidoff and Hall, *Family Fortunes.*
80. Dussart, 'The Servant/Employer'; Procida, *Married.*
81. Dussart, 'The Servant/Employer', p. 266.
82. Price, ed., *Journals*, p. 101.
83. Weitbrecht, *Female Missionaries*, p. 68.
84. P. Levine (2004) 'Sexuality, Gender, and Empire' in P. Levine, ed. *Gender and Empire: the Oxford history of the British Empire companion series* (Oxford: Oxford University Press), p. 122.
85. E. J. Manktelow (2010) 'Missionary Families and the Formation of the Missionary Enterprise: the London Missionary Society and the Family 1795–1875' (Kings College London: unpublished PhD thesis), pp. 34–77.
86. See also Haggis, 'Professional Ladies'.
87. Thomas Haweis (1794), cited in Manktelow, 'Missionary Families', p. 36–7.
88. Manktelow, 'Missionary Families', p. 36–7.
89. E. Elbourne (2002) *Blood Ground: colonialism, missions, and the contest for Christianity in the Cape Colony and Britain, 1799–1853* (Montreal: McGill-Queen's University Press); D. I. Stuart (1994) '"Of Savages and Heroes"; discourses of race, nation and gender in the evangelical missions to Southern Africa in the early nineteenth century' (Institute of Commonwealth Studies: unpublished PhD thesis).
90. Elbourne, *Blood Ground*, p. 232.
91. Often such matters only appear in the London correspondence as an absolute last resort and when there is clearly a long history of the 'affair' being well known and widely discussed.
92. W. Porter to A. Tidman (11 October 1851) Madras. CWM/LMS/South India/Tamil/Incoming Correspondence/B10/F5/JB.
93. 'Minutes for the Madras Eastern Committee', Adis, Lechler, Porter, Hey et al., Madras (5 May 1852) CWM/LMS/South India/Tamil/Incoming Corespondence/B10/F5/JB.
94. Ibid.
95. Mr Cox, of the same mission, met with the same career fate after his own marriage to an Indian woman in 1861. Haggis, 'Professional Ladies', p. 44.
96. J. Kennedy (April 1888) *Chronicle*, p. 183. Written in response to 'Islam and Christianity in India', first published in *The Contemporary Review* (February 1888).
97. Mr Ashton (1860) quoted in R. Lovett (1899) *The History of the London Missionary Society, 1795–1895*, vols 1 and 2 (London: Oxford University Press), p. 58.
98. G. Hall (26 January 1857) Madras, CWM/LMS/South India/Tamil/Incoming Correspondence/B11/F5/JA.
99. Ibid.
100. Unlike the pay discrepancies of 'native' Indians, however, this inequality was often contested by East Indian missionaries, who were usually confident (if not always successful) in their dealings with metropolitan Britain. Nimmo himself contests his pay some months before this case emerges.

    J. E. Nimmo (29 March 1856) Tripassore, CWM/LMS/South India/Tamil/Incoming Correspondence/B11/F4/JB.
101. Many thanks to Val Anderson for talking me through this. For more on the ambiguous status of 'East Indians' and 'Eurasians', see L. Bear (2007) *Lines*

of a Nation. Indian railway workers: bureaucracy and the intimate historical self (New York: Columbia University Press), pp. 191–226; C. J. Hawes (1996) *Poor Relations: the making of a Eurasian community in British India, 1773–1833* (Richmond: Curzon).

102. Hall was devastated by the libel claims and alleged that his health was broken on account of a year of anxiety concerning Nimmo's affairs. G. Hall (17 June 1857) Madras, CWM/LMS/South India/Tamil/Incoming Correspondence/B11/F5/JB.
103. G. Hall (10 October 1857) Madras, CWM/LMS/South India/Tamil/Incoming Correspondence/B11/F5/JD.
104. Ibid.
105. G. Hall (20 May 1857) Madras CWM/LMS/South India/Tamil/B11/F5/JB.
106. Hall, Kubler, Campbell, Sewell and Gordon from 'Investigation of Mr Paul', G. Hall (Secretary) (20 May 1857) Madras, CWM/LMS/South India/Tamil/Incoming Correspondence/B11/F5/JB.
107. Gordon, in Ibid.
108. Campbell, in Ibid.
109. Hall et al., in Ibid.

Part II Sickness and the Embodiment of Difference

1. W. E. Richards (February 1889) *Chronicle*, p. 37.
2. S. Thorne (2006) 'Religion and Empire at Home' in C. Hall and S. O. Rose, eds. *At Home with the Empire: metropolitan culture and the imperial world* (Cambridge: Cambridge University Press), p. 150.
3. J. Reed (December 1840) *Missionary Magazine*; Mr De. Rodt (January 1841) *Missionary Magazine*, p.12.
4. My use of the word 'sickness' is intended to bridge both 'disease' (as an epidemiological phenomenon or biological experience) and 'illness' (as the social experience of it). I take a socially constructivist approach to sickness, believing that disease is culturally constructed and devoid of any externally measurable 'truth', but mediate this through a conviction that the effects of disease (including death) are very 'real'.
5. R. Edmond (2006) *Leprosy and Empire: a medical and cultural history* (Cambridge: Cambridge University Press), p. 12.
6. M. Vaughan (1991) *Curing Their Ills: colonial power and African illness* (Cambridge: Polity Press), p. 12.
7. H. Lane (1993) *The Mask of Benevolence: disabling the deaf community* (New York: Knopf).
8. A. Quayson (2002) 'Looking Awry: tropes of disability in postcolonial writing' in D. T. Goldberg and A. Quayson, eds. *Relocating Postcolonialism* (Oxford: Blackwell).
9. M. Sherry (2007) 'Postcolonizing Disability', *Wagadu*, 4, pp. 10–22.
10. D. Arnold (1993) *Colonizing the Body: state medicine and epidemic disease in nineteenth-century India* (Berkeley: University of California Press). See also D. Arnold, ed. (1988) *Imperial Medicine and Indigenous Societies* (Manchester: Manchester University Press); A. Kumar (1998) *Medicine and the Raj: British medical policy in India 1835–1911* (New Deli and London: AltaMira Press);

R. MacLeod, and M. Lewis, eds (1988) *Disease, Medicine, and Empire: perspectives on western medicine and the experience of European expansion* (London and New York: Routledge).

11. For work on medical missions see, for example, C. Good, Junior (2004) *The Steamer Parish: the rise and fall of missionary medicine on an African frontier* (Chicago: University of Chicago Press); D. Hardiman, ed. (2006) *Healing Bodies, Saving Souls: medical missions in Asia and Africa* (Amsterdam: Rodopi); D. Hardiman (2008) *Missionaries and Their Medicine: a Christian modernity for tribal India* (Manchester: Manchester University Press); M. Hokkanen (2007) *Medicine and Scottish Missionaries in the Northern Malawi Region, 1875–1930: quests for health in a colonial society* (Lewiston: Edwin Mellen Press).
12. A. Bashford (2004) *Imperial Hygiene: a critical history of colonialism, nationalism and public health* (Basingstoke: Macmillan); L. Magner (1992) *A History of Medicine* (New York: Dekker); R. Porter (2006) 'Medical Science' in R. Porter, ed. *The Cambridge History of Medicine* (Cambridge: Cambridge University Press), pp. 152–4.
13. Magner, *A History of Medicine*, p. 321.
14. An important exception is Hokkanen, *Medicine and Scottish Missionaries*.

3 Pathologising Heathenism: Discourses of Sickness and the Rise of Medical Missions

1. M. Vaughan (1991) *Curing Their Ills: colonial power and African illness* (Cambridge: Polity Press), p. 57.
2. J. Cox (April 1861) *Missionary Magazine*, p. 80; J. Cox (February 1861) *Missionary Magazine*, p. 41; J. Cox (June 1861) *Missionary Magazine*, p. 158.
3. I. Hacker (February 1889) *Chronicle* pp. 43–4.
4. J. Sewell (19 August 1841) Bangalore, CWM/LMS/South India/Canarese/Incoming Correspondence/B5a/F2/J3.
5. S. Gilman (1998) *Disease and Representation: images from madness to AIDS* (Ithaca: Cornell).
6. S. Sontag (1991) *Illness as Metaphor and AIDS and Its Metaphors* (London: Penguin), p. 67.
7. Ibid., p. 60.
8. M. Poovey (1995) *Making a Social Body: British cultural formation, 1830–1864* (Chicago: University of Chicago Press), pp. 56–64.
9. A. Bashford (2004) *Imperial Hygiene: a critical history of colonialism, nationalism and public health* (Basingstoke: Palgrave). A. Bashford and C. Hooker, eds (2001) *Contagion: historical and cultural studies* (London: Routledge).
10. D. Arnold (1993) *Colonizing the Body: state medicine and epidemic disease in nineteenth-century India* (Berkeley: University of California Press), pp. 159–200.
11. P. Setel (1991) '"A Good Moral Tone": Victorian ideals of health and the judgements of persons in nineteenth-century travel and mission accounts from East Africa', *Working Papers in African Studies, African Studies Center, Boston University*, 150, p. 6.
12. Poovey, *Making a Social Body*.

13. M. Harrison (1994) *Public Health in British India: Anglo-Indian preventive medicine 1859–1914* (Cambridge: Cambridge University Press).
14. P. Curtin (1961) 'The White Man's Grave: image and reality, 1780–1850', *Journal of British Studies*, 1, pp. 94–110.
15. A. L. Stoler (1995) *Race and the Education of Desire: Foucault's History of Sexuality and the colonial order of things* (London: Duke University Press).
16. Amongst many others see: Gen 19.4–11; Acts 13.6–13, Job 5.12–14, Ps 69.23, Seph 1.17, Zech 12.4, Zec 14.12, Wis 2.21, Wisd. 19.17. References from J. Hull (2001) *In the Beginning There was Darkness* (Canterbury: SCM Press), pp. 59–66.
17. Isa 59.9–10, in Ibid., p. 97.
18. Mr Nimmo (May 1840) *Missionary Magazine*, pp. 68–70.
19. See, for example, E. Taylor (September 1909) *Chronicle*, p. 167.
20. J. Mullens (September 1862) *Missionary Magazine*, p. 261.
21. E. L. Price, ed. (1950) *The Journals of Elizabeth Lees Price: written in Bechuanaland, Southern Africa, 1854–1883 with an epilogue 1889–1900*, with Una Long (London: Edmond Arnold), p. 82.
22. See, for example, G. McCallum (March 1891) *Chronicle*, p. 78.
23. Price, ed., *Journals*, p. 82.
24. J. R. Bacon (December 1887) *Chronicle*, p. 516.
25. M. Philips (August 1877) *Chronicle*, p. 172.
26. Anon. (October 1905) *Chronicle*, p. 289.
27. For cases of blindness in the zenanas see, for example, Mrs Sewell (April 1863) *Missionary Magazine*, p. 87. See also 'Extracts from Mrs Sewell's Journal of Zenana Visitation in Bangalore' (5 September–18 November 1862). CWM/LMS/South India/Journals/B5.
28. Mrs Mullens (February 1860) *Missionary Magazine*, p. 41.
29. B. Cassin (June 1881) *Chronicle*, p. 150.
30. Examples of disabled characters in Victorian fiction associated with 'disorder' include, the 'woman in the attic' in *Jane Eyre* and Long John Silver in Robert Louis Stevenson's *Treasure Island*. Others, were portrayed sentimentally (such as 'Tiny Tim'), or as particularly virtuous people, such as Mrs Craik's 'Olive'. M. S. Holmes (2007) 'Victorian Fictions of Interdependency: Gaskell, Craik, and Yonge', *Journal of Literary Disability*, 2 (1), pp. 29–41.
31. See, for example, in Africa, R. Price (April 1868) *Missionary Magazine*, p. 75. See, for example, in India, J. Mullens (February 1851) *Missionary Magazine*, p. 26.
32. G. McCallum (March 1891) *Chronicle*, p. 78.
33. G. M. Bulloch (February 1890) *Chronicle*, pp. 47–50.
34. Vaughan, *Curing Their Ills*, pp. 77–100.
35. See, for example, R. Price (December 1868) *Chronicle*, p. 75.
36. K. Heasman (1964) 'The Medical Mission and the Care of the Sick Poor in Nineteenth-Century England', *The Historical Journal*, 7, p. 40.
37. G. Cousins, ed. (1908) *Handbooks for our Medical Missions of the Society* (London: LMS), p. 7.
38. D. Hardiman (2006) 'Introduction' in D. Hardiman, ed. *Healing Bodies, Saving Souls: medical missions in Asia and Africa* (Amsterdam: Rodopi), pp. 5–59.

39. P. C. Williams (1982) 'Healing and Evangelism: the place of medicine in later Victorian Protestant missionary thinking' in W. J. Shiels, ed. *The Church and Healing* (Oxford: Basil Blackwells), pp. 271–85.
40. Vaughan, *Curing Their Ills*, pp. 58–9. C. M. Good, Junior (2004) *The Steamer Parish: the rise and fall of missionary medicine on an African frontier* (Chicago: University of Chicago Press), p. 8.
41. J. Paul (1977) 'Medicine and Imperialism in Morocco', *MERIP* (Middle East Research Information Project) *Reports*, 60, p. 4; R. Fitzgerald (1996) 'A "Peculiar and Exceptional Measure": the call for women medical missionaries for India in the later nineteenth century' in R. A. Bickers and R. Seton, eds. *Missionary Encounters: sources and issues* (Surrey: Curzon Press), pp. 174–97.
42. Ibid., pp. 2–5.
43. Unusually, the mission actually had older roots, with some medicial activity made in the 1830s. By 1861, however, when Dr Lowe arrived at Travancore, this activity had completely ceased, and the mission was started anew. Many LMS books ignore these early roots altogether. See, for example, Cousins, *Medical Missions*.
44. LMS (1895) *Annual Report of the London Missionary Society*, p. 212.
45. J. Lowe (June 1870) *Chronicle*, pp. 132–3.
46. See, for example, G. A. Turner (23 July 1870) 'Compound Fracture Treated with Carbolic Acid; and tetanus treated with calabar bean', *The Lancet*, 96, pp. 11–15.
47. J. Lowe (February 1867) *Chronicle*, p. 27.
48. Ibid., p. 28.
49. Cousins, *Medical Missions*; I. H. Hacker (1887) *Memoirs of T.S. Thomson: medical missionary at Neyoor, Travancore, south India* (London: Religious Tract Society), pp. 60–79.
50. C. S. Valentine, 'Female Medical Agency in Upper India', cited in, Valentine (March 1875) *Chronicle*, p. 62. See also Fitzgerald, 'A "Peculiar and Exceptional Measure"', pp. 174–97. Women were also become more involved in colonial medicine elsewhere. A. Burton (1996) 'Contesting the Zenana: the mission to make "Lady Doctors for India" 1874–1885', *The Journal of British Studies*, 35 (3), pp. 368–97.
51. Although a hospital was developed at Molepolole in the early twentieth century.
52. W. Dower (March 1871) *Chronicle*, p. 56.
53. Ibid., p. 54.
54. W. Sykes (December 1870), p. 256.
55. For work in central southern Africa by other societies, see Good, *The Steamer Parish* and M. Hokkanen (2007) *Medicine and Scottish Missionaries in the Northern Malawi Region, 1875–1930: quests for health in a colonial society* (Lewiston: Edwin Mellen Press).
56. R. Moffat (January 1858) *Missionary Magazine*, p. 204.
57. J. L. Comaroff and J. Comaroff (1991) *Of Revelation and Revolution*, vol. 1, *Christianity, colonialism, and consciousness in South Africa* (Chicago and London: University of Chicago Press), vol. 2, pp. 330–45; Hardiman, 'Introduction', p. 37; Dr Davidson (April 1864) *Missionary Magazine*, p. 78.
58. W. Sykes (September 1868) *Missionary Magazine*, p. 194.

59. W. Sykes (April 1881) *Chronicle*, p. 83; W. Sykes (November 1885) *Chronicle*, p. 341.
60. J. Lowe (1886) *Medical Missions: their place and power* (London: T. Fisher Unwin), p. 153.
61. Williams, 'Healing and Evangelism', pp. 271–5.
62. Ibid., p. 278.
63. E. L. Joyce (n.d. [c. 1900]) *The Work of Healing* (London: LMS).
64. See special 'Medical Number' of *Chronicle*: [various] (February 1906) *Chronicle*, p. 25. Paul, 'Medicine and Imperialism', p. 4.
65. Joyce, *The Work of Healing*, pp. 6–7; J. Kennedy (March 1884) *Chronicle*, p. 79.
66. S. Fry (March 1890) *Chronicle*, p. 89; Kennedy (March 1884) *Chronicle*, p. 79.
67. G. Francis-Dehqani (2002) 'Medical Missions and the History of Feminism: Emmeline Stuart of the CMS Persia Mission' in S. Morgan, ed. *Women Religion and Feminism in Britain, 1750–1900* (Basingstoke: Palgrave), p. 198.
68. LMS (n.d. [c.1900]) *The Finger of God: pictures of medical missions* (London: LMS), p. 11.
69. T. S. Thomson (December 1873) *Chronicle*, p. 256.
70. Lowe, *Medical Missions*, p. 16.
71. Ibid.
72. B. Stanley, ed. (2001) *Christian Missions and the Enlightenment* (Richmond: Curzon).
73. A. Porterfield (2005) *Healing in the History of Christianity* (Oxford: Oxford University Press), pp. 3–4.
74. Good, *The Steamer Parish*, p. 8; Vaughan, *Curing Their Ills*, pp. 58–9. Neither did other British Protestant and Anglo-Catholic Missionary Societies.
75. T. O. Ranger (1982) 'Medical Science and Pentecost: the dilemma of Anglicanism in Africa' in W. J. Shiels, ed. *The Church and Healing* (Oxford: Basil Blackwell), pp. 333, 335.
76. Ibid.
77. For non-missionary examples, see Burton, 'Contesting the Zenana'.
78. S. C. Williams (1999) *Religious Belief and Popular Culture in Southwark, c. 1880–1939* (Oxford: Oxford University Press), pp. 63–9.
79. W. C. Bentall (February 1906) *Chronicle*, p. 40.
80. W. C. Bentall (August 1907) *Chronicle*, pp. 154–5.
81. Vaughan, *Curing Their Ills*, p. 67.
82. A. Bashford (1998) *Purity and Pollution: gender, embodiment and Victorian medicine* (Basingstoke: Macmillan); K. Swenson (2005) *Medical Women and Victorian Fiction* (Columbia and London: University of Missouri Press).
83. W. Burns Thomson (1895) *Reminiscences of Medical Missionary Work* (London: Hodder and Stroughton); LMS, *Medical Missions at Home and Abroad*. See also Heasman, 'The Medical Mission', p. 232.
84. A. Fells (December 1895) *Chronicle*, p. 337.
85. Alice Hawker (May 1900) *Chronicle*, p. 103.
86. Ibid., p. 103.
87. W. Sykes (April 1881) *Chronicle*, p. 83; W. Sykes (November 1885) *Chronicle*, p. 341.
88. Miss Macdonnell (an interview with), *Chronicle*, May 1900, p. 109.
89. Fells (December 1894) *Chronicle*, p. 336.

90. Bashford, *Purity*, p. 16. See also M. Pelling (2001) 'The Meaning of Contagion: reproduction, medicine and metaphor' in Bashford and Hooker, eds. *Contagion*, pp. 15–39.
91. A. Fells (December 1895) *Chronicle*, pp. 336–7.
92. J. Lowe (June 1870) *Chronicle*, p. 132.
93. See for the division into European and 'native' hospitals in Almorah, for example, G.M.B. (January 1893) *Chronicle*, p. 4.
94. 'Extract from Dr. Lowe's Last Report' (1866) reproduced in (February 1867) *Chronicle*, p. 25.
95. Anon. [An Evangelist], *Chronicle*, November 1875, p. 223.
96. Vaughan, *Curing Their Ills*, p. 73.
97. R. Ashton (July 1901) *Chronicle*, p. 66.
98. A. Hawker (May 1900) *Chronicle*, p. 103.
99. Vaughan, *Curing Their Ills*, pp. 58–61.
100. W. Sykes (September 1868) *Chronicle*, p. 194.
101. W. E. Richards (February 1889) *Chronicle*, p. 37.

4 Illness on the Mission Station: Sickness and the Presentation of the 'Self'

1. E. Storrow(1888) *Protestant Missions in Pagan Lands: a manual of facts and principles relating to foreign missions throughout the world* (London: John Snow), p. 138.
2. Markku Hokkanen's study of the Livingstonia mission in northern Malawi is a striking exception to this, including accounts of missionary encounters with 'blackwater' and other 'tropical' diseases. M. Hokkanen (2007) *Medicine and Scottish Missionaries in the Northern Malawi Region, 1875–1930: quests for health in a colonial society* (Lewiston: Edwin Mellen Press), pp. 212–30.
3. A. Porter (2004) *Religion versus Empire? British Protestant missionaries and overseas expansion, 1700–1914* (Manchester: Manchester University Press), p. 57. R. Lovett (1899) *The History of the London Missionary Society, 1795–1895*, vols 1 and 2 (London: Oxford University Press), pp. 477–80.
4. R. Brewin (1889) *Among the Palms: or stories of Sierra Leone and its missions* (London: Andrew Crombie).
5. Lovett, *History*, vol. 1, p. 649.
6. Ibid., pp. 640–70.
7. E. Crisp (10 June 1841) Bangalore, CWM/LMS/South India/Canarese/Incoming Correspondence/B5a/F2/J2.
8. G. Endfield and D. Nash (2005) '"Happy is the Bride the Rain Falls On": climate, health and "the woman question" in nineteenth-century missionary documentation', *Transactions of the Institute of British Geographers*, 30, p. 374.
9. CWM/LMS/Home/Candidates' Papers/1796-1899/B1-28. Medical matters also preoccupied the examiners committee. See also: CWM/LMS/Home/Candidates' Examination Committee/B6-11.
10. R. Seton (1996) '"Open Doors for Female Labourers": women candidates of the London Missionary Society, 1875–1914' in R. Bickers and R. Seton, eds. *Missionary Encounters: sources and issues* (Surrey: Curzon), pp. 63–4.

11. Candidates Examination Committee Minutes (October 1863), quoted in Endfield and Nash, '"Happy is the Bride"', p. 373.
12. Endfield and Nash, '"Happy is the Bride"', p. 381.
13. M. P. Ashley (2001) 'It's Only Teething... A report of the myths and modern approaches to teething', *British Dental Journal*, 191 (1), pp. 4–8.
14. L. N. Magner (1992) *A History of Medicine* (New York: Dekker), p. 279.
15. B. Haley (1978) *The Healthy Body and Victorian Culture* (Cambridge: Harvard University Press).
16. R. Porter (2006) 'Medical Science' in R. Porter, ed. *The Cambridge History of Medicine* (Cambridge: Cambridge University Press), pp. 152–4. Magner, *A History of Medicine*, p. 321.
17. Usually, they only chose to engage with European medicine, but missionaries in both India and southern Africa do sometimes resort to indigenous remedies. For a discussion of this in the African case, see N. Etherington (1987) 'Missionary Doctors and African Healers in Mid-Victorian South Africa', *South African Historical Journal*, 19, pp. 77–93.
18. In some ways, this was a different manifestation of a more common colonial discourse: Europeans 'thought', 'natives' 'felt'. This is not, however, to undermine the importance of 'soul' in other missionary discourses of the self.
19. P. M. Logan (1997) *Nerves and Narratives: a cultural history of hysteria in 19th-century British prose* (Berkeley: University of California Press).
20. J. Lowe to Mullens (19 May 1868) Nagercoil, CWM/LMS/Travancore/Incoming Correspondence/B7/F3/JC and J. Lowe to Duthie (3 January 1867) Neyoor, CWM/LMS/Travancore/Incoming Correspondence/B7/F3/JC.
21. J. Sewell (23 April 1841) Bangalore, CWM/LMS/South India/Canarese/Incoming Correspondence/B5a/F2/J2.
22. K. O. Kupperman (1984) 'Fear of Hot Climates in the Anglo-American Colonial Experience', *The William and Mary Quarterly*, 3rd Ser., 42 (2), pp. 213.
23. M. Harrison (1999) *Climates and Constitutions: health, race, environment and British imperialism in India 1600–1850* (Oxford: Oxford University Press), p. 10.
24. Ibid.
25. K. Kiple and C. O. Kriemhild (1996) 'Race, War and Tropical Medicine in the Eighteenth-Century Caribbean' in D. Arnold, ed. *Warm Climates and Western Medicines* (Amsterdam: Rodopi), pp. 65–80.
26. M. Bell (1993) '"The Pestilence that Walketh in Darkness": imperial health, gender and images of South Africa c. 1880–1910', *Transactions of the Institute of British Geography*, 18, pp. 335, 332.
27. J. S. Moffat to Tidman (17 July 1866) Kuruman, CWM/LMS/South Africa/Bechuanaland/Incoming Correspondence/B34/F1/JB.
28. Williamson to Mullens (9 May 1867) Dysselsdorp, CWM/LMS/South Africa/Bechuanaland/Incoming Corresondence/B34/F4/JA.
29. M. Wallace (1827) quoted in Endfield and Nash, '"Happy is the Bride"', p. 375.
30. John Thompson (1855) CWM/LMS/Home/Candidates' Papers/1796-1899/B16.

31. Both Indians and Africans were expected, however, to have a severe reaction to the British climate. Tragic stories of model converts paraded on missionary deputations in Britain succumbing to chills and phenomena in the British climate are distressingly common.
32. Such as eating less meat, for example. E. M. Collingham (2001) *Imperial Bodies: the physical experiences of the Raj, c. 1800–1947* (Cambridge: Polity Press), pp. 26–7.
33. M. Harrison (1996) '"The Tender Frame of Man": disease, climate, and racial difference in India and the West Indies, 1760–1860', *Bulletin of the History of Medicine*, 70, pp. 68–93.
34. Ibid., p. 91; Harrison, *Climates and Constitutions*; W. Anderson (2002) *The Cultivation of Whiteness: science, health and racial destiny in Australia* (Melbourne: Melbourne University Press).
35. W. Anderson (1996) 'Race and Acclimatization in Colonial Medicine: disease, race, and Empire', *Bulletin of the History of Medicine*, 70, pp. 62–7. Stoler has similarly explored the ways in which such thinking could cast 'degeneration' in both physical and moral tones. A. L. Stoler (1995) *Race and the Education of Desire: Foucault's History of Sexuality and the colonial order of things* (London: Duke University Press) and A. L. Stoler (2002) *Carnal Knowledge and Imperial Power: race and the intimate in colonial rule* (Berkeley: University of California Press).
36. J. Lowe (9 May 1862) Neyoor, CWM/LMS/South India/Travancore/Incoming Correspondence/B6/F1/JB; J. Duthie to members of the TDC (12 March 1866) Nagercoil, CWM/LMS/Travancore/Incoming Correspondence/B6/F5/JB; J. Duthie (19 November 1866) Nagercoil, CWM/LMS/Travancore/Incoming Correspondence/B6/F3/JB; J. Lowe (24 May 1862) Neyoor, CWM/LMS/Travancore/Incoming Correspondence/B6/F1/JB.
37. See, for example, James Emlyn anticipated he would be unable 'to stand the climate of England' after 25 years in India. J. Emlyn to TDC (23 January 1893) Nagercoil, CWM/LMS/Travancore/Incoming Correspondence/B15/F1/JA.
38. Mary Curzon quoted in Bell, '"The Pestilence"', p. 329.
39. See, for example, the condition of Mrs Mabbs. Ross et al. (September 1866) CWM/LMS/Travancore/Incoming Correspondence/B6/F5/JB.
40. Bell, '"The Pestilence"', pp. 327–41.
41. Unlike the 'private' performance of family life, sickness was performed away from African/Indian eyes. With the probable exception of servants, Europeans suffering seems to have been largely hidden from indigenous people: they were treated in the privacy of their station.
42. J. Lowe, Medical Certificate (9 May 1862) Neyoor, CWM/LMS/Travancore/Incoming Correspondence/B6/F1/JB.
43. Emily Lewis (25 June 1862) Madras, CWM/LMS/Travancore/Incoming Correspondence/B6/F1/JB.
44. J. Duthie, et al., to Travancore District Committee, Nagercoil (May 1862) CWM/LMS/Travancore/Incoming Correspondence/B6/F1/JB.
45. Emily Lewis (25 June 1862).
46. G. Becker quoted in S. Kilshaw (2004) '"004. Friendly Fire": the construction of Gulf War Syndrome narratives', *Anthropology and Medicine*, 11 (2), p. 151.

47. Kilshaw, '"004. Friendly Fire"', p. 149.
48. S. Mateer to J. Duthie (12 March 1866) Nagercoil, CWM/LMS/Travancore/Incoming Correspondence/B6/F5/JB.
49. That illness could affect the lucid participation in prayer was a key concern. See, for example, Rev. Taylor on the death of Brother Reid. J. Taylor (20 January 1842) Bellary, CWM/LMS/South India/Canarese/Incoming Correspondence/B5a/F1/JA.
50. P. Jalland (1996) *Death in the Victorian Family* (Oxford: Oxford University Press); J. Whaley, ed. (1981) *Mirrors of Mortality: studies in the social history of death* (London: Europa); M. Wheeler (1990) *Death and the Future Life in Victorian Literature and Theology* (Cambridge: Cambridge University Press).
51. J. Brown to Tidman (11 August 1866) Kuruman, CWM/LMS/South Africa/Bechuanaland/Incoming Correspondence/B34/F1/JB.
52. See the discussion of Lowe's work in *Chronicle* (February 1867), p. 29. J. Lowe (1886) *Medical Missions: their place and power* (London: T. Fisher Unwin).
53. R. Price (2008) *Making Empire: colonial encounters and the creation of imperial rule in nineteenth-century Africa* (Cambridge: Cambridge University Press), pp. 74–5.
54. E. Crisp (10 June 1841) Bangalore, CWM/LMS/South India/Canarese/Incoming Correspondence/B5a/F2/J2.
55. Dr Birch (9 July 1841) Madras, CWM/LMS/South India/Canarese/Incoming Correspondence/B5a/F2/J2.
56. Ibid.
57. Ibid.
58. Ibid.
59. Ibid.
60. J. Sewell (19 August 1841) Bangalore, CWM/LMS/South India/Canarese/Incoming Correspondence/B5a/F2/J3.
61. Ibid.
62. Directors (June 1861) *Missionary Magazine*, pp. 161–70. For representations of the Mokololo Expedition in the wider British press, see, for example, 'The Makololo Mission' (25 May 1861) *Examiner*.
63. Dr Ross, Medical Certificate for Mrs Mabbs (26 September 1866), enclosed in Mr Mateer to Secretary, Trevandrum (10 December 1867) CWM/LMS/South India/Canarese/Incoming Correspondence/B7/F2/JB.
64. C. W. Murray (20 January 1866) Hackney (via Cape Town), CWM/LMS/South Africa/Bechuanaland/Incoming Correspondence/B34/F1/JC.
65. Ibid.
66. J. Duthie (12 March 1866) Nagercoil, CWM/LMS/Travancore/Incoming Correspondence/B6/F5/JB.
67. S. Mateer to TDC (January 1868) CWM/LMS/Travancore/Incoming Correspondence/B7/F1/JB.
68. J. Lowe (24 January 1868) Neyoor, CWM/LMS/Travancore/Incoming Correspondence/B7/F1/JB.
69. Ibid.
70. Editor (January 1905) *Chronicle*, p. 15.
71. Editor (December 1870) *Chronicle*, pp. 249–50.
72. Ibid.

Part III Violence and Racialisation

1. See, for example, D. Spurr (1993) *The Rhetoric of Empire: colonial discourse in journalism, travel-writing and imperial administration* (Durham: Duke University Press), pp. 1–13; F. Fanon (1961) *The Wretched of the Earth*, trans. C. Farrington (London: Penguin); A. Coombes (1994) *Reinventing Africa: museums, material culture and popular imagination in late Victorian and Edwardian England* (London and New Haven: Yale University Press); F. Driver, ed. (2001) *Geography Militant: cultures of exploration and empire* (Oxford: Blackwell); A. Maxwell (1999) *Colonial Photography and Exhibitions: representations of the 'native' and the making of European identities* (London: Leicester University Press); M. L. Pratt (1992) *Imperial Eyes: travel writing and transculturation* (London: Routledge); J. Ryan (1997) *Picturing Empire: photography and the visualization of the British Empire* (London: Riktean).
2. R. Stanfield (2009) 'Violence and the Intimacy of Imperial Ethnography: the endeavour in the Pacific' in T. Ballantyne and A. Burton, eds. *Moving Subjects: gender, mobility, and intimacy in an age of global Empire* (Urbana: University of Illionois Press), p. 31.
3. Fanon, *Wretched*.
4. For discussions of the role of the witness or viewer of violence, see, for example, S. Sontag (2003) *Regarding the Pain of Others* (London: Hamish Hamilton); K. Oliver (2001) *Witnessing: beyond recognition* (Minneapolis: University of Mennesota Press).
5. Even here, colonial warfare is often discussed in terms of its diplomatic results and is dislocated from the experience of violence itself.
6. Transatlantic Slavery and the Indian Rebellion have, in different ways, been seen as violent aberrations from a general trend. So far, studies that deal with colonial warfare as explicitly violent seem to have focussed on wars associated with decolonisation, rather than of conquest. See, for example, Fanon, *Wretched*; D. Anderson (2005) *Histories of the Hanged. Britain's dirty war in Kenya and the end of empire* (London: Weidenfeld and Nicholson); C. Elkins (2005) *Britain's Gulag: the brutal end of empire in Kenya* (London: Jonathon Cape).
7. See, for example, C. Anderson, *Legible Bodies: race, criminality and colonialism in South Asia* (Oxford: Berg); C. Anderson (2000) *Convicts in the Indian Ocean: transportation from South Asia to Mauritius, 1815–53* (Basingstoke: Macmillan); F. Dikötter and I. Brown (2007) *Cultures of Confinement: a history of the prison in Africa, Asia and Latin America* (Ithaca: Cornell University Press); S. Pierce and A. Rao, eds (2002) *Discipline and the Other Body: correction, corporeality, colonialism* (London: Duke University Press).
8. See P. Hinchliffe (1984) 'The Blantyre Scandal: Scottish missionaries and colonialism', *Journal of Theology for Southern Africa*, 46, pp. 29–38.
9. E. Scarry (1985) *The Body in Pain: the making and unmaking of the world* (Oxford: Oxford University Press), pp. 3, 60–157.
10. C. Leys (1965) 'Violence in Africa', *Transition*, 21, p. 17; Scarry, *The Body*, pp. 66–7.
11. E. A. Stanko (2003) 'Introduction: conceptualising the meanings of violence' in E. Stanko, ed. *The Meanings of Violence* (London: Routledge), p. 11.

12. For discussions of the specific difficulties in defining violence cross-culturally see, for example, G. Aijmer and J. Abbink (2000) *Meanings of Violence: a cross cultural perspective* (Oxford: Berg).
13. L. Franey makes a strong case for the verbal being a way in which women were recognised to use violence. Franey contends that in their travel writings Victorian women wrote about exercising power through language that they described as 'producing somatic effects equal to, if not greater than, the negative somatic effects of physical violence,' claiming words as 'tangible objects', 'weapons' capable of 'wounding' and causing 'physical pain'. L. Franey (2003) *Victorian Travel Writing and Imperial Violence: British writing on Africa, 1855–1902* (Basingstoke: Palgrave), p. 8.
14. A. Lester (2001) *Imperial Networks: creating identities in nineteenth-century South Africa and Britain* (London: Routledge); Z. Laidlaw (2005) *Colonial Connections 1815–45: patronage, the information revolution and colonial government* (Manchester: Manchester University Press).

5 Violence and the Construction of the Other

1. W. Morton (April 1846) *Missionary Magazine*, p. 51.
2. Mr Edwards (February 1848) *Missionary Magazine*, pp. 26–7.
3. P. Brantlinger (1988) *Rule of Darkness: British literature and imperialism, 1830–1914* (Ithaca: Cornell University Press), p. 179.
4. C. C. Eldridge (1996) *The Imperial Experience from Carlyle to Forster* (Basingstoke: Macmillan), p. 67.
5. C. Bolt (1971) *Victorian Attitudes to Race* (London: Routledge), p. 122.
6. See, for example, D. Livingstone (1857) *Missionary Travels and Researches in South Africa: including a sketch of sixteen years' residence in the interior of Africa, and a journey from the Cape of Good Hope to Loanda, on the west coast, thence across the continent, down the river Zambesi, to the eastern ocean* (London: John Murrey); C. H. Lyall, ed. (1895) *Twenty years in Khama's Country: and, pioneering among the Batauana of Lake Ngami, told in the letters of J. D. Hepburn* (London: Hodder and Stoughton); J. Mackenzie (1883) *Day-Dawn in Dark Places: a story of wanderings and work in Bechwanaland* (London: Cassell); J. Mackenzie (1871) *Ten years North of the Orange River: a story of everyday life and work among the South African tribes, from 1859 to 1869* (Edinburgh: Edmonston and Douglas). Nineteenth-century biographies of these 'heroes' do similar discursive work. See, for example, H. G Adams (1868) *The Life and Adventures of Dr. Livingston [sic] in the Interior of South Africa: comprising a description of the regions which he traversed, an account of missionary pioneers, and chapters on cotton cultivation, slavery, wild animals, etc.* (London: James Blackwood); A. Manning (1875) *Heroes of the Desert: the story of the lives and labours of Moffat and Livingstone* (London: T. Nelson & Sons); W. Williams (1884) *Life and Labours of Robert Moffat, D.D., Missionary in South Africa: with additional chapters on Christian missions in Africa and throughout the world* (London: Walter Scott).
7. R. Moffat (September 1858) *Missionary Magazine*, p. 203.
8. W. Sykes (December 1870) *Chronicle*, p. 255.
9. See, for example, J. G. Rogers (June 1865) *Missionary Magazine*, p. 176.

10. J. Mackenzie (November 1863) *Missionary Magazine*, p. 316.
11. My comments here are specific to the missionary periodical genre. Graphic descriptions of violent crime against British people did exist in the mainstream British press. See, for example, J. Archer and Jo Jones (2003) 'Headlines from History: violence in the press, 1850–1914' in E. A. Stanko, ed. (2003) *The Meanings of Violence* (London: Routledge), pp. 17–32. In Britain, class rather than ethnicity, demarcated whose injuries could be viewed, and whose merited discretion.
12. R. Moffat (January 1856) *Missionary Magazine*, p. 5.
13. Ibid., p. 5.
14. R. Moffat (April 1856) *Missionary Magazine*, p. 70.
15. J. Mackenzie (June 1863) *Missionary Magazine*, p. 311.
16. Editor (February 1889) *Chronicle*, p. 45.
17. For pictures of exhibitions of the Ndebele consisting *only* of weapons see, for example, Engraving (December 1893) *Chronicle*, p. 307. In the aftermath of the colonisation of Ndebeleland, Ndebele weaponry was exhibited in Britain. These trophies embodied both the linking of the Ndebele with violence and their colonial disenfranchisement. The heavy concentration of weaponry in visual representations of southern Africans was not, however, limited to the Ndebele. See, for example, Engraving, 'Some of Khama's Warriors' (May 1884) *Chronicle*.
18. B. Shephard (1986) 'Showbiz Imperialism: the case of Peter Lobengula' in J. MacKenzie, ed. *Imperialism and Popular Culture* (Manchester: 1986), p. 95.
19. C. Bolt, quoted in Ibid., p. 96. See also H. Streets (2004) *Martial Races: the military, race and masculinity in British imperial culture 1857–1914* (Manchester: Manchester University Press).
20. J. Cockin (January 1880) *Chronicle*, p. 15.
21. R. Moffat (April 1856) *Missionary Magazine*, p. 70.
22. Ibid., p. 27.
23. R. Moffat (January 1856) *Missionary Magazine*, p. 5.
24. Mr Thompson (February 1874) *Chronicle*, p. 28.
25. The way in which King Khama's Ngwato Kingdom was represented presents a striking contrast to that of the Ndebele. The rule of King Khama, a Christian, was found to be 'kind and just'. Violence, and the increasingly authoritarian nature of Khama's rule, was kept out of the missionary press. A. J. Wookey (March 1890) *Chronicle*, p. 72; Anon. (October 1888) *Chronicle*, p. 466.
26. J. D. Hepburn (March 1882) *Chronicle*, p. 75. C. Hall (2002) *Civilising Subjects: metropole and colony in the English imagination, 1830–1867* (Cambridge: Polity Press).
27. T. W. Laqueur (1989) 'Bodies, Details, and the Humanitarian Narrative' in L. Hunt, ed. *The New Cultural History* (Berkeley: University of California Press), p. 177.
28. As discussed in S. Sontag (2003) *Regarding the Pain of Others* (London: Hamish Hamilton).
29. Mackenzie, *Ten Years*, pp. 283–4. The account was also reproduced by the *Missionary Magazine*: J. Mackenzie (November 1863) *Missionary Magazine*, pp. 309–10.
30. E. Cleall (2009) 'Missionary Masculinities and War: the LMS in Southern Africa, c. 1860–1899', *South African Historical Journal*, 61 (2), pp. 245–7.

31. Whilst the power actually exercised by chiefs varied greatly between southern African societies, it was often perceived as absolute, and missionaries seem to have ignored, or misunderstood the complex divisions of power, through chiefly advisers and homesteads in favour of autocratic models. For the divisions of power in different southern African polities see, for example, J. Guy (1979) *The Destruction of the Zulu Kingdom: the civil war in Zululand, 1879–1884* (London: Longman); K. Shillington (1985) *The Colonisation of the Southern Tswana, 1870–1900* (Braamfontein: Ravan Press); J. B. Peires (1981) *The House of Phalo: a history of the Xhosa people in the days of their Independence* (Johannesburg: Raven Press); C. Saunders, ed. (1998) *Black Leaders in Southern African History* (London: Heinemann). The construction of the chief as having absolute power was particularly important in the way in which missionaries constructed the Zulu. See, for example, C. Hamilton (1998) *Terrific Majesty: the powers of Shaka Zulu and the limits of historical imagination* (Cambridge: Harvard University Press); J. Guy (1996) 'Shaka KaSenzargakhona – a reassessment', *Journal of Natal and Zulu History*, 16, pp. 1–29. Significantly, autocratic power exercised by Christians was rarely seen as problematic as in depictions of the 'kind and just' (though very autocratic) King Khama, but if 'heathen', that power signified 'despotism'. A. J. Wookey (March 1890) *Chronicle*, p. 72; Anon. (October 1888) *Chronicle*, p. 466.
32. Mr Edwards (February 1848) *Missionary Magazine*, pp. 26–7.
33. Ibid.
34. Richard Price makes a similar point recording an encounter between Maqoma, an important Xhosa Chief, and Richard Calderwood, an LMS missionary, over an alleged infanticide. Price argues that Calderwood's response to the alleged infanticide and ensuing argument pushed him into 'a period of emotional turmoil, perhaps real clinical depression' and contributed to his transition into, as Price puts it, 'a modern racist'. Whilst I may question Price's terminology, I similarly see this event, and others like it, as a formative experience which could indeed have the power to shift racial thinking and challenge Calderwood's own identity. However, whilst Price dismisses the impact of the infanticide itself, claiming 'it was not the horror of such cultural practices' that so upset Calderwood, as the fact he was intellectually overpowered by Maqoma in the ensuring arguments, I would attach greater significance to the fact that it was a violent incident, or at least the report of one, around which Calderwood's narratives was hinged. Real or imagined, that incidents of violence were used to articulate missionary anxieties about other power dynamics displaced from their wider experiences, is, I believe, significant. R. Price (2008) *Making Empire: colonial encounters and the creation of imperial rule in nineteenth-century Africa* (Cambridge: Cambridge University Press), pp. 112–14.
35. Editor (February 1848) *Missionary Magazine*, p. 26.
36. R. Inden (1986) 'Orientalist Constructions of India', *Modern Asian Studies*, 20 (3), pp. 401–46.
37. See, for example, W. Beynon (November 1857) *Missionary Magazine*, p. 244. For the most part in missionary writing, 'Hindoos' were seen as 'mere dupes'.
38. See, for example, H. C. Mullens (1857) *Faith and Victory: a story of progress of Christianity in Bengal* (London: James Nisbet).

39. I. H. Hacker (July 1880) 'A Shrine of Idols', p. 212.
40. J. J. Kripal and R. F. McDermott (2003) 'Introducing Kālī Studies' in J. J. Kripal and R. F. McDermott, eds. *Encountering Kālī: in the margins, at the center, in the west* (Berkeley: University of California Press); A. Hiltebeitel and K. M. Eindl (2000) *Is the Goddess a Feminist: the politics of a South Asian goddess* (Sheffield: Sheffield Academic Press).
41. H. B. Urban (2003) ' "India's Darkest Heart", Kālī in the colonial imagination' in Kripal and McDermott, eds. *Encountering Kālī*, pp. 169–95.
42. A. F. Lacroix (April 1852) *Missionary Magazine*, p. 63.
43. H. Hacker (July 1890) *Chronicle*, p. 213.
44. Ibid., p. 213.
45. Accounts of Hindu festivals are too regular a feature in the LMS periodicals to cite but for a striking example see A. F. Lacroix (1851) *Voyage du Missionnaire, A.F. Lacroix au Temple de Jogonnath* (Neuchatel: Henri Wolfrath).
46. See, also Mr Drew (August 1847) *Missionary Magazine*, p. 129. Lacroix also described the worship of the goddess Kali where 'devotees [had] thrown themselves on thorns and knives' – A. F. Lacroix (April 1852) *Missionary Magazine*, p. 63.
47. Although defining activities towards a person's own self as *violence* is problematic, in missionary writing self-inflicted physical pain is certainly *constructed* as 'violent'.
48. G. O. Oddie (1986) 'Hook-Swinging and Popular Religion in South India during the Nineteenth Century', *Indian Economic Social History Review*, 23, pp. 93–106.
49. E. Fooks (April 1893) *Chronicle*, p. 137.
50. Ibid.
51. N. Dirks (2001) *Castes of Mind: colonialism and the making of modern India* (Princeton: Princeton University Press), pp. 154–72.
52. E. Fooks (April 1893) *Chronicle*, p. 137.
53. Dirks, *Castes of Mind*, pp. 151–64.
54. Ibid.
55. *Calcutta Christian Advocate* quoted in LMS (January 1843) *Missionary Magazine*, p. 7.
56. Ibid.
57. Ibid.
58. G. Spivak (1985) 'Can the Subaltern Speak? Speculations on widow sacrifice', *Wedge*, 7–8, pp. 120–30.
59. N. Paxton (1992) 'Rape in British Novels About the Indian Uprising of 1857', *Victorian Studies*, 36, p. 7.
60. Mrs Porter (March 1845) *Missionary Magazine*, p. 34.
61. See, for example, Editor (May 1844) *Missionary Magazine*, pp. 68–9; Editor (November 1845) *Missionary Magazine*, p. 164; Wilkins (January 1894) *Chronicle*, p. 8.
62. Mrs Porter (March 1845) *Missionary Magazine*, p. 34.
63. Ibid.
64. Ibid.
65. 'Heathenism' was consistently used in missionary accounts to assert the victimhood of Indian woman who killed their children and therefore demonstrates the way in which the phenomenon was understood in colonial

thinking. However, it is also important to remember that alterative discourses, many of which were similarly sympathetic to the mother, were mobilised elsewhere to explain the 'unnatural' phenomenon of infanticide. In Britain, gender, class, age and insanity were axis through which infanticide could be explained. D. J. R. Grey (2008) 'Discourses of Infanticide in England. 1880–1922' (University of Roehampton: unpublished PhD thesis).
66. See D. Arnold (1993) *Colonizing the Body: state medicine and epidemic disease in nineteenth-century India* (Berkeley: University of California Press), pp. 116–58.
67. W. O. Simpson (June 1881) *Chronicle*, p. 152.
68. Ibid.
69. Rev. Goffin (December 1886) *Chronicle*, p. 499.
70. C. Mead (August 1844) *Missionary Magazine*, pp. 117–18.
71. For similar trends elsewhere, see A. Coombes (1994) *Reinventing Africa: museums, material culture and popular imagination in late Victorian and Edwardian England* (London and New Haven: Yale University Press), p. 177.
72. D. W. Savage (1997) 'Missionaries and the Development of a Colonial Ideology of Female Education in India', *Gender and History*, 9 (2), pp. 201–21.
73. E. Porter (July 1848) *Missionary Magazine*, p. 100.
74. Editor (November 1845) *Missionary Magazine*, p. 164.
75. Ibid.
76. Editor (May 1844) *Missionary Magazine*, pp. 68–9.
77. *The Calcutta Christian Advocate* (n.d.) reproduced in LMS, (January 1843) *Missionary Magazine*, p. 7.
78. *The Friend of India*, quoted in, *Missionary Magazine*, October 1850, pp. 180–1.
79. Ibid., p. 181.
80. J. Mackenzie (1887) *Austral Africa: losing it or ruling it*, vol. 2 (London: Sampson Low), p. 503
81. Mackenzie, *Austral Africa*, vol. 1, p. 133.
82. J. Mackenzie (1884) *Bechuanaland and our Progress Northward: a lecture* (Cape Town: Murray and St. Leger), p. 4.
83. Brantlinger, *Rule of Darkness*, p. 195.
84. R. Moffat (April 1853) *Missionary Magazine*, p. 65.
85. W. Beinart (1992) 'Political and Collective Violence in Southern African Historiography', *Journal of Southern Africa Studies*, 18 (3), p. 455. For changes in population due to pressures of European colonialism see, for example, E. Eldredge (1993) *A South African Kingdom: the pursuit of security in nineteenth-century Lesotho* (Cambridge: Cambridge University Press), p. 40. T. R. H. Davenport and C. Saunders (2000) *South Africa: a modern history*, 5th edn (Basingstoke: Macmillan), pp. 129–94; Shillington, *The Colonisation*; Guy, *The Destruction*.
86. W. Sykes (July 1869) *Chronicle*, p. 153.
87. Ibid.

6 Colonial Violence: Whiteness, Violence and Civilisation

1. E. White (June 1883) *Chronicle*, p. 201.
2. Ibid.

3. Michael Paris notes, after 1850 there was 'rarely a year' when British troops were not engaged in military action. M. Paris (2000) *Warrior Nation: images of war in British popular culture, 1850–2000* (London: Reaktion), p. 8. See also, I. Beckett (2003) *The Victorians at War* (London: Hambledon and London); E. Spiers (1992) *The Late Victorian Army* (Manchester: Manchester University Press); B. Vandervort (1998) *Wars of Imperial Conquest in Africa, 1830–1914* (London: UCL).
4. F. Fanon (1961) *The Wretched of the Earth*, trans. C. Farrington (London: Penguin), p. 31.
5. J. McCulloch (2004) 'Empire and Violence, 1900–1939' in P. Levine, ed. *Gender and Empire, the Oxford History of the British Empire Companion Series* (Oxford: Oxford University Press); J. de Moor and H. L. Wesseling, eds (1989) *Imperialism and War: essays on colonial wars in Asia and Africa* (Leiden: Universitaire pers Leiden).
6. C. Hall (2002) *Civilising Subjects: metropole and colony in the English imagination, 1830–1867* (Cambridge: Polity Press).
7. Z. Laidlaw (2005) *Colonial Connections 1815–45: patronage, the information revolution and colonial government* (Manchester: Manchester University Press); A. Lester (2001) *Imperial Networks: creating identities in nineteenth-century South Africa and Britain* (London: Routledge). For similar thinking later in the century see the thinking of Thomas Hodgkin: Z. Laidlaw (2007) 'Heathens, Slaves and Aborigines: Thomas Hodgkin's critique of missions and anti-slavery', *History Workshop Journal*, 64, pp. 133–62.
8. A. Porter (2004) *Religion versus Empire? British Protestant missionaries and overseas expansion, 1700–1914* (Manchester: Manchester University Press); J. G. Greenlee and C. M. Johnston (1999) *Good Citizens: British missionaries and imperial states, 1870–1918* (Montreal: McGill-Queens University Press).
9. C. Bolt (1971) *Victorian Attitudes to Race* (London: Routledge); Hall, *Civilising Subjects*; T. Holt (1992) *The Problem of Freedom: race, labor and politics in Jamaica and Britain, 1832–1938* (Baltimore: John Hopkins University Press).
10. In making this argument, I draw on Carolyn Strange's article 'The "Shock" of Torture' about the reaction of the western media to the revelations of torture at Abu Ghraib, a response she argued was framed entirely through a lexicon of 'shock' and being 'appalled'. Such a response, she argued, performed a potent justificatory role in the coalition's war on terror and mission of democratisation. 'Only countries as civilized and culturally refined as Britain and the US could have felt shame so keenly.' Through emphasising Anglo-American 'shame' at the 'episode', and blaming it on a 'few bad apples' its impact was contained, and torture reiterated as something that happens 'out there'. C. Strange (2006) 'The "Shock" of Torture: a historiographical challenge', *History Workshop Journal*, 61, p. 137.
11. W. M. Hinkley (September 1893) *Chronicle*, p. 244.
12. Ibid.
13. W. M. Hinkley (January 1894) *Chronicle*, p. 17.
14. Ibid.
15. Ibid.
16. W. M. Hinkley (September 1893) *Chronicle*, p. 244.
17. John MacKenzie claims that there was a 'transformation' of images of the military in popular culture between 1800 and 1900, with the identification

of the military as 'heroic defenders' during the 1850s, a tradition of Christian militarism in the 1860s and institutional reform in the 1870s. J. MacKenzie (1992) 'Introduction: popular imperialism and the military' in J. M. MacKenzie, ed. *Popular Imperialism and the Military 1850–1950* (Manchester: Manchester University Press), pp. 1–24. For the C.D. legislation and subsequent agitation see P. Levine (2003) *Prostitution, Race, and Politics: policing venereal disease in the British Empire* (New York: Routledge). For the heroic images of the 'Christian Soldier' emergent in this period see G. Dawson (1994) *Soldier Heroes: British adventure, empire and the imaginings of masculinities* (London and New York: Routledge).

18. G. M. Bulloch (January 1886) *Chronicle*, pp. 17–19.
19. Ibid., pp. 17–20. There are also clear links here between the mission 'overseas' and the 'mission at home'. In Britain, the working class were particularly identified as needing missionary work. See S. Thorne (1999) *Congregational Missions, and the Making of an Imperial Culture in 19th-Century England* (California: California University Press).
20. See, for example, F. Brockway (August 1895) *Chronicle*, p. 212.
21. G. M. Bulloch (January 1886) *Chronicle*, p. 18.
22. Dawson, *Soldier Heroes*.
23. McCulloch, 'Empire and Violence', pp. 229–32.
24. R. Moffat, et al. (July 1866) *Chronicle*, pp. 212–13.
25. Ibid., p. 213.
26. Issues of imitation also occurred in terms of debates around missionary strategy. The Wesleyan missionary Michael Elliot, for example, strikingly wrote of the ' "apishness" ' of the African by which he claimed to mean the 'servile *imitation* of the European'. M. J. Elliott (1885) *The Race for the Heart of Africa: missionary observations from within and without* (Durham: Consett).
27. Editor (July 1866) *Chronicle*, p. 213.
28. Ibid.
29. J.O.W. (November 1882) *Chronicle*, pp. 368–70.
30. J.O.W. (December 1882) *Chronicle*, p. 386.
31. For more on the link between degeneration, insanity and a tropical location see W. Anderson (2002) *The Cultivation of Whiteness: science, health and racial destiny in Australia* (Melbourne: Melbourne University Press), pp. 73–95, 165–191. As Anderson notes, alcohol, as well as climate, was sometimes seen as the 'curse' of Europeans overseas. Anderson, *The Cultivation of Whiteness*, p. 112.
32. For a careful mapping of the shifting politics of whiteness see: M. Lake and H. Reynolds (2008) *Drawing the Global Colour Line: white men's countries and the international challenge of racial equality* (Cambridge: Cambridge University Press).
33. R. Dyer (1997) *White* (London: Routledge), p. xiv.
34. S. Ahmed (2007) 'A Phenomenology of Whiteness', *Feminist Theory*, 8 (2), pp. 149–68.
35. M. Wray (2006) *Not Quite White: white trash and the boundaries of whiteness* (Durham: Duke University Press), p. 3.
36. A. L. Stoler (1995) *Race and the Education of Desire: Foucault's History of Sexuality and the colonial order of things* (London: Duke University Press), p. 100.

37. R. Moffat (June 1866) *Chronicle*, p. 162.
38. Concerns about drinking that had first developed in Britain inevitably acquired new inflections as they were exported to the colonies. Earlier in the century, the question of drink had been raised during the Aborigines Select Committee, when humanitarians had expressed concerns that indigenous peoples were being exposed to a 'European vice'. In the case of Nelson and other contemporary examples, drink is constructed as though possessing agency and was also used to *explain* the brutalised and violent behaviour of Europeans towards indigenous peoples.
39. R. Moffat (July 1866) *Chronicle*, p. 213.
40. R. Moffat (June 1866) *Chronicle*, p. 162.
41. G. Stocking, Junior (1991) *Victorian Anthropology* (New York: Macmillan); S. Van der Geest (1990) 'Missionaries and Anthropologists: brothers under the skin', *Man*, New Series 25 (4), pp. 588–601.
42. For the formation of (white) ethnic identities in late eighteenth and early nineteenth-century Cape see R. Ross (1999) *Status and Respectability in the Cape Colony, 1750–1870* (Cambridge: Cambridge University Press).
43. A. Burton (2000) '"States of Injury": Josephine Butler on slavery, citizenship and the Boer War' in L. Mayhall, P. Levine, and I. C. Fletcher, eds. *Women's Suffrage in the British Empire: citizenship, nation and race* (London: Routledge), pp. 24–5.
44. In turn, the hostility of the Boers to the British became central to the story of Afrikaner nationalism. For a different perspective see, M. Streak (1974) *The Afrikaner as Viewed by the English, 1795–1854* (Cape Town: C. Struik).
45. Editor (March 1859) *Missionary Magazine*, p. 48.
46. For other missionary writings in which such a story appears, see, for example, J. Sibree (1895) *South Africa: outlines of foreign missions* (London: LMS), in LMS (1895) *Outlines of Foreign Missions* (London: LMS), p. 22.
47. Robert Moffat (April 1856) *Missionary Magazine*, p. 75.
48. Editor (February 1853) *Missionary Magazine*, p. 32.
49. W. Ashton (November 1869) *Chronicle*, pp. 245–8.
50. Ibid.
51. John Mackenzie wrote and spoke extensively on this theme. See, for example, his Anniversary Speech of 1883. J. Mackenzie (June 1883) *Chronicle*, pp. 205–9.
52. Editor et al (February 1853) *Chronicle*, p. 32; Editor (March 1859) *Missionary Magazine*, p. 48.
53. R. Moffat (April 1856) *Missionary Magazine*, pp. 75–6.
54. E. Baines (June 1861) *Chronicle*, p. 152.
55. For a related discussion on the relationship between violence committed by individuals and the colonial state, see, McCulloch, 'Empire and Violence', pp. 220–2.
56. See, for example, N. Ferguson (2004) *Empire: how Britain made the modern world* (London: Penguin).
57. D. Anderson (2005) *Histories of the Hanged. Britain's dirty war in Kenya and the end of empire* (London: Weidenfeld and Nicholson), pp. 1–2; C. Elkins (2005) *Britain's Gulag: the brutal end of empire in Kenya* (London: Jonathan Cape), pp. 46–50.

58. P. Werbner (1997) 'Essentialising Essentialism, Essentialising Silence: ambivalence and multiplicity in the constructions of racism and ethnicity' in P. Werbner and T. Modood, eds. *Debating Cultural Hybridity: multi-cultural identities and the politics of anti-racism* (London: Zed), p. 228.
59. T. O. Ranger (1967) *Revolt in Southern Rhodesia, 1896–7: a study in African resistance* (London: Heinemann); Samkange, *Origins of Rhodesia*; S. Samkange (1985) *The Origin of African Nationalism in Zimbabwe* (Harare: Harare Publishing House).
60. J. Alexander (2006) *The Unsettled Land: state-making & the politics of land in Zimbabwe, 1893–2003* (Oxford: James Currey), p. 18.
61. McCulloch, 'Empire and Violence', p. 221.
62. Ibid.
63. Alexander, *The Unsettled*, p. 18.
64. See Ranger, *Revolt.*
65. C. D. Helm (11 August 1890) Kimberley, CWM/LMS/South Africa/Matabeleland/Incoming Correspondence/B2a/F4/JA
66. C. D. Helm (28 August 1893) Phalapye, CWM/LMS/South Africa/Matabeleland/Incoming Correspondence/B2b/F5/JA.
67. Lendy quoted in, Terrance Ranger, *Revolt*, p. 38.
68. B. Rees (20 November 1893) Kuruman, CWM/LMS/South Africa/Matabeleland/Incoming Correspondence/B2b/F5/JA.
69. Mrs Rees (13 April 1894) Inyati, CWM/LMS/South Africa/Matabeleland/Incoming Correspondence/B2b/F5/JB.
70. N. Bhebe (1979) *Christianity and Traditional Religion in Western Zimbabwe, 1859–1923* (London: Longman), pp. 83–4.
71. D. Carnegie (26 March 1889) quoted in Bhebe, *Christianity*, pp. 84–5.
72. D. Carnegie (6 April 1894) Hope Fountain, CWM/LMS/South Africa/Matabeleland/Incoming Corresopndence/B2b/F5/JB.
73. G. C. Reed (December 5) 1895, quoted in Bhebe, *Christianity*, p. 84.
74. See, for example, the battle over the Hope Fountain Mission. G. Cullen Reed, Hope Fountain (31 October 1895) CWM/LMS/South Africa/Matabeleland/Incoming Corresopndence/B2/F5/JD.
75. This was by no means the first time that this had happened. Missionaries experienced similar upheavals and destruction during the Cape Frontier Wars as well as elsewhere in the Empire.
76. B. Rees (31 January 1894) Natowani, CWM/LMS/South Africa/Matabeleland/Incoming Correspondence/B2b/F5/JB.
77. B. Rees (27 April 1894) Inyati, CWM/LMS/South Africa/Matabeleland/Incoming Correspondence/B2b/F5/JB.
78. D. Carnegie (6 April 1894) Hope Fountain, CWM/LMS/South Africa/Matabeleland/Incoming Correspondence/B2b/F5/JB.
79. Ibid.
80. Ibid.
81. B. Rees (27 April 1894).
82. G. Cullen Reed (14–21 September 1896) Hope Fountain, CWM/LMS/South Africa/Matabeleland/Incoming Correspondence/B2b/F6/JA.
83. For the diversity of new immigrants, see Alexander, *The Unsettled*, p. 19.
84. G. Cullen Reed (5 December 1895) Bulilima, CWM/LMS/South Africa/Matabeleland/B2b/F5/JD.

85. P. Robb (2002) *A History of India* (Basingstoke: Palgrave), pp. 125–6.
86. To some extent this has been replicated in the historiography. See, for example, D. Cannadine (2002) *Ornamentalism, How the British Saw Their Empire* (London: Allen Lane).
87. M. Davis (2001) *Late Victorian Holocausts: El Niño famines and the making of the third world* (London: Verso).
88. A. Rao (2006) 'Problems of Violence, States of Terror: torture in colonial India' in S. Pierce and A. Rao, eds. *Discipline and the Other Body: correction, corporeality, colonialism* (London: Duke University Press), pp. 115–51; E. Kolsky (2009) *Colonial Justice in British India: white violence and the rule of law* (Cambridge: Cambridge University Press). E. Kolsky (2007) 'Crime and Punishment on the Tea Plantations of Colonial India' in M. D. Dubber and L. Farmer, eds. *Modern Histories of Crime and Punishment* (Stanford: Stanford University Press), pp. 272–99.
89. Certainly the British reprisals were justified in missionary writing, as the missionary to Calcutta, Edward Storrow wrote, 'history will record that we erred in not punishing sufficiently, rather than in punishing too much.' E. Storrow (1859) *India and Christian Missions* (London: John Snow), p. 98.
90. The exception to this is the Indian Rebellion which, owing to the extensive historiographical attention it has already received, I have not explored here. See, for example: C. A. Bayly (1988) *Indian Society and the Making of the British Empire* (Cambridge: Cambridge University Press); G. Chakravarty (2005) *The Indian Rebellion and the British Imagination* (Cambridge: Cambridge University Press); Dawson, *Soldier Heroes*; R. Guha (1983) *Elementary Aspects of Peasant Insurgency in Colonial India* (Delhi: Oxford University Press); T. Metcalf (1964) *The Aftermath of Revolt, India, 1857–1870* (London: Princeton University Press); N. L. Paxton (1999) *Writing Under the Raj: gender, race and rape in the British colonial imagination, 1830–1947* (New Brunswick: Rutgers University Press).

Conclusion: Thinking with Missionaries; Thinking about Difference

1. W. Pierce (July 1886) *Chronicle*, p. 264.
2. C. Bolt (1971) *Victorian Attitudes to Race* (London: Routledge); Hall, *Civilising Subjects*; C. Hall (2002) *Civilising Subjects: metropole and colony in the English imagination, 1830–1867* (Cambridge: Polity Press); T. Holt (1992) *The Problem of Freedom: race, labor and politics in Jamaica and Britain, 1832–1938* (Baltimore: John Hopkins University Press).
3. Porter, *Religion versus Empire*, p. 283.
4. J. Mullens (November 1867) *Chronicle*, pp. 216–220; Rev. Dr Simon (May 2888) *Chronicle*, pp. 199–203.
5. J. S. Taylore (December 1856), pp. 252–55; (February 1876), *Chronicle*; W. C. Willoughby (July 1900) *Chronicle*, pp. 164–8.
6. S. Van der Geest (1990) 'Missionaries and Anthropologists: brothers under the skin', *Man*, New Series 25 (4), pp. 588–601.
7. J. Guinness Rogers (June 1865) *Missionary Magazine*, p. 176.
8. Ibid.

9. Speaker (May 1867) *Chronicle,* p. 82.
10. J. Mackenzie (June 1870) *Chronicle,* p. 127.
11. A. Hanney (June 1867) *Chronicle,* p. 113.
12. J.O.W. (December 1882) *Chronicle,* p. 386.
13. E. W. Said (1993) *Culture and Imperialism* (London: Knopf).
14. C. Campbell (March 1865) *Missionary Magazine,* p. 60.
15. E. L. Price (1950) *The Journals of Elizabeth Lees Price. Written in Bechuanaland, Southern Africa, 1854–1883 with an epilogue 1889–1900,* with an introduction and annotations by Una Long (London: Edward Arnold), p. 98.

Bibliography

Archive material and manuscripts

Archive of the Council of World Mission (formerly LMS), School of Oriental and African Studies, London [CWM/LMS]

HOME

Annual Reports (1840–1895)

The Report of the Directors to the Forty-Fifth General Meeting of the Missionary Society, Usually Called the London Missionary Society (1840).

The Report of the Directors to the Forty-Sixth General Meeting of the Missionary Society, Usually Called the London Missionary Society (1841).

. . . annually until . . .

The Centenary Report of the London Missionary Society (1895).
Candidates' Papers (1896–1899) Boxes 1–28.
Candidates' Examination Committee Boxes 6–11.
LMS Register of Missionaries.

INDIA

North India, Bengal, Incoming Correspondence (1839–1895)
Boxes 6–17.
North India, United Provinces, Incoming Correspondence (1836–1897)
Boxes 2–15b.
South India, Canarese, Incoming Correspondence (1836–1897)
Boxes 4–19.
South India, Tamil, Incoming Correspondence (1841–1895)
Boxes 8b–19.
South India, Telegu, Incoming Correspondence (1835–1899)
Boxes 2–8.
South India, Travancore, Incoming Correspondence (1839–1893)
Boxes 3–16.

AFRICA

South Africa, Incoming Correspondence (1840–1895)
Boxes 17–52.
South Africa, Matabeleland, Incoming Correspondence (1835–1899)
Boxes 1–3.

Cory Library, Grahamstown South Africa [CL]

MS., Letters and journals, Elizabeth Price.

Periodicals

Chronicle of the London Missionary Society
Edinburgh Medical Missionary Society Quarterly Paper
Ends of the Earth
Examiner
India's Women: the magazine of the Church of England Zenana Missionary Society
Juvenile Missionary Magazine
Lancet
Medical Missions at Home and Abroad
Missionary Magazine and Chronicle
Missionary Quarterly Sketches
News of Female Missions in connection with the LMS
Our Indian Sisters: a quarterly magazine of the Ladies' Zenana Mission in connection with the Baptist Missionary Society
Quarterly News of Woman's Work
Quarterly Zenana Record
The Cape Times
The Female Indian Evangelist
The Juvenile, a Magazine for the Young
The Juvenile Missionary Magazine of the LMS

Books and pamphlets published before 1900

Adams, H. G. (1868) *The Life and Adventures of Dr. Livingston [sic] in the Interior of South Africa: comprising a description of the regions which he traversed, an account of missionary pioneers, and chapters on cotton cultivation, slavery, wild animals, etc.* (London: James Blackwood).

BMS. (1858) *History of Native Female Education in Calcutta* (Calcutta: Baptist Missionary Press).

Brewin, R. (1889) *Among the Palms: or stories of Sierra Leone and its missions* (London: Andrew Crombie).

Brightwell, C. L. (1874) *Dr Vanderkemp: the friend of the Hottentot* (London: LMS).

Buyers, W. (1840) *Letters on India, with special reference to the spread of Christianity* (London: John Snow).

Carlyle, J. E. (1878) *South Africa and its Mission Fields* (London: James Nisbet).

Cousins, G., ed. (1908) *Handbooks to Our Mission Fields: medical missions of the society* (London: LMS).

Cullen, A. H. (1900) *John Kenneth Mackenzie: medical man and missionary* (London: LMS).

Elliott, M. J. (1885) *The Race for the Heart of Africa: missionary observations from within and without* (Durham: Consett).

Hacker, I. H. (1887) *Memoirs of T.S. Thomson, medical missionary at Neyoor, Travancore, South India* (London: Religious Tract Society).

Haskard, M. E. (1890) *Zenana Work: the opportunity among women in India* (London: LMS).
Hepburn, E. (1928) *Jottings, by Khama's friend, Mrs. J.D. Hepburn* (London: Simpkin, Marshall, Hamilton, Kent & Co).
Joyce, E. L. (n.d. [c.1900]) *The Work of Healing* (London: LMS).
Kennedy, J. (1884) *Life and Work in Benares and Kumaon, 1839–1877* (London: T. Fisher Unwin).
Lacroix, A. F. (1846) *Extracts from the Journal of a Missionary Itinerancy in Bengal . . . in December 1845 and January 1846* (Glasgow: Bell and Bain).
Lacroix, A. F. (1851) *Voyage du Missionnaire, A.F. Lacroix au Temple de Jogonnath* (Neuchatel: Henri Wolfrath).
Lacroix, M. (1862) *Brief Memorials of Mrs Mullens, by her Sister* (London: James Nisbert).
Leslie, M. E. (1868) *The Dawn of Light: a story of the Zenana mission*, with an introduction by Rev. E. Storrow (London: John Snow).
Livingstone, D. (1857) *Missionary Travels and Researches in South Africa: including a sketch of sixteen years' residence in the interior of Africa, and a journey from the Cape of Good Hope to Loanda, on the west coast, thence across the continent, down the river Zambesi, to the eastern ocean* (London: John Murrey).
LMS. (n.d.) *A Missionary Alphabet: for recitation at missionary entertainments* (London: LMS).
LMS. (n.d.) *Boys and Girls of Other Lands; a missionary cantata* (London: LMS).
LMS. (n.d.) *Six Zenana Recitations for Little Girls* (London: LMS).
LMS. (n.d. [c.1900]) *The Finger of God: pictures of medical missions* (London: LMS).
LMS. (1812) *Memoir of the Rev. J. T. Van Der Kemp, late missionary in South Africa* (London: LMS).
LMS. (1855) *Bhowanipore Boarding School: report* (London: LMS).
LMS. (1871) *A Life's Labours in South Africa: the story of the life-work of Robert Moffat, apostle to the Bechuana tribes* (London: LMS).
LMS. (1873) *The Handbook of Christian missions: a world of information, of facts, incidents, sketches and anecdotes, relating to the Christian missions of all denominations, in all ages and countries* (London: Elliot Stock).
LMS. (1895) *Outlines of Foreign Missions* (London: LMS).
Lovett, R. (1899) *The History of the London Missionary Society, 1795–1895*, vols 1 and 2 (London: Oxford University Press).
Lowe, J. (1886) *Medical Missions: their place and power* (London: T. Fisher Unwin).
Lyall, C. H., ed. (1895) *Twenty years in Khama's Country: and, pioneering among the Batauana of Lake Ngami, told in the letters of J. D. Hepburn* (London: Hodder and Stoughton).
Mackenzie, J. (1871) *Ten years North of the Orange River: a story of everyday life and work among the South African tribes, from 1859 to 1869* (Edinburgh: Edmonston and Douglas).
Mackenzie, J. (1883) *Day-Dawn in Dark Places: a story of wanderings and work in Bechwanaland* (London: Cassell).
Mackenzie, J. (1884) *Bechuanaland and Our Progress Northward: a lecture* (Cape Town: Murray and St. Leger).
Mackenzie, J. (1884) *Bechuanaland: its lessons to the Cape Colony and to South Africa* (Cape Town: Murray & St Leger).

Mackenzie, J. (1887) *Austral Africa: losing it or ruling it*, vols 1 and 2 (London: Sampson Low).
Mackenzie, J. (1888a) *Austral Africa: extension of British influence in trans-colonial territories, proceedings at a meeting of the London Chamber of Commerce, assembled on the 14th May 1888* (London: King & Son).
Mackenzie, J. (1888b) *The London Missionary Society in South Africa: a retrospective sketch* (London: LMS).
Manning, A. (1875) *Heroes of the Desert: the story of the lives and labours of Moffat and Livingstone* (London: T. Nelson & Sons).
Mateer, S. (1883) *Native Life in Travancore* (London: W. H, Allen).
Mateer, S. (1886) *The Gospel in South India: or the religious life, experience, and character of the Hindu Christians* (London: Religious Tract Society).
Mill, J. (1817) *A History of India*, vol. 1 (London: Baldwin, Cardock and Joy).
Moffat, J. S. (1885) *The Lives of Robert & Mary Moffat* (London: T. Fisher Unwin).
Moffat, R. (1842) *Missionary Labours and Scenes in Southern Africa* (London: John Snow).
Moffat, R. (1855) *Visit to Moselekatse, King of the Matabele, communicated to the London Missionary Society with a map* (London: Clowes and Sons).
Moffat, R. (1859) *The Boers of the Transvaal Republic, and the mission station at Kuruman* (Cape Town: [n.p.]).
Mullens, H. C. (1857) *Faith and Victory: a story of progress of Christianity in Bengal* (London: James Nisbet).
Mullens, J ([1858]) *The Results of Missionary Labour in India* ([Calcutta]: [*Calcutta Review*]).
Mullens, J. (1860) *The Religious Aspects of Hindu Philosophy Stated and Discussed: a prize essay* (London: Smith, Elder & Co.).
Mullens, J. (1862) *Brief Memories of the Rev. Alphonse François Lacroix, missionary of the London Missionary Society in Calcutta* (London: James Nisbet).
Mullens, J. (1863) *A Brief Review of Ten Years' Missionary Labour in India Between 1852 and 1861: prepared from local reports and original letters* (London: James Nisbet).
Mullens, J. (1869) *London and Calcutta Compared in their Heathenism, their Privileges, and their Prospects: showing the great claims of foreign missions upon the Christian church* (London: James Nisbet).
Mullens, J. (1884) *Missions in South India Visited and Described* (London: W. H. Dalton).
Pitman, E. R. (1897) *Heroines of the Mission Field: biographical sketches of female missionaries who have laboured in various lands among the heathen* (London: Cassell).
Porter, M. K. Mrs (1885) *Short Records of the Missionary Work of the Rev. Edward Porter of the London Missionary Society in Vizagapatam and Cuddapah, India, from 1835 to 1868: with a brief memoir, compiled by his widow* (London: Morgan and Scott).
Price, E. L. (1950) *The Journals of Elizabeth Lees Price. Written in Bechuanaland, Southern Africa, 1854–1883 with an epilogue 1889–1900*, with an introduction and annotations by Una Long (London: Edward Arnold).
Sibree, J. (1895) *South Africa: outlines of foreign missions* (London: LMS).
Storrow, E. (1859) *India and Christian Missions* (London: John Snow).

Storrow, E. (1888) *Protestant Missions in Pagan Lands: a manual of facts and principles relating to foreign missions throughout the world* (London: John Snow).
Storrow, E. (1895) *India: outlines of foreign missions* (London: LMS).
Thompson, W. B. (1883) *The Claims of the Cape Colony and Its Missions. Congregational Union of South Africa, being prepared as the address of the chairman, at its annual meeting to be held in Cape Town, 1883* (Cape Town: Saul Solomon).
Thomson, W. B. (1895) *Reminiscences of Medical Missionary Work* (London: Hodder and Stoughton).
Weitbrecht, M. (1853) *Female Missionaries In India: letters from a missionary wife abroad to a friend in England* (London: James Nisbet).
Weitbrecht, M. E. (1875) *The Women of India and Christian Work in the Zenana* (London: James Nisbet).
Williams, W. (1884) *Life and Labours of Robert Moffat, D.D., Missionary in South Africa: with additional chapters on Christian missions in Africa and throughout the world* (London: Walter Scott).

Books published after 1900

Ahmed, S. (2006) *Queer Phenomenology: orientations, objects, others* (Durham: Duke University Press).
Aijmer, G. and Abbink, J., eds (2000) *Meanings of Violence: a cross cultural perspective* (Oxford: Berg).
Alexander, J. (2006) *The Unsettled Land: state-making & the politics of land in Zimbabwe, 1893–2003* (Oxford: James Currey).
Anderson, C. (2000) *Convicts in the Indian Ocean: transportation from South Asia to Mauritius, 1815–53* (Basingstoke: Macmillan).
Anderson, C. (2004) *Legible Bodies: race, criminality and colonialism in South Asia* (Oxford: Berg).
Anderson, D. (2005) *Histories of the Hanged. Britain's dirty war in Kenya and the end of empire* (London: Weidenfeld and Nicholson).
Anderson, W. (2002) *The Cultivation of Whiteness: science, health and racial destiny in Australia* (Melbourne: Melbourne University Press).
Arendt, H. (1970) *On Violence* (London: Allen Lane).
Arnold, D. (1993) *Colonizing the Body: state medicine and epidemic disease in nineteenth-century India* (Berkeley: University of California Press).
Arnold, D., ed. (1988) *Imperial Medicine and Indigenous Societies* (Manchester: Manchester University Press).
Arnold, D., ed. (1996) *Warm Climates and Western Medicine 1500–1900* (Amsterdam: Rodopi).
Ashcroft, B., Griffiths, G. and Tiffin, H., eds (2006) *The Postcolonial Studies Reader*, 2nd edn (London: Routledge).
Ballantyne, T. (2002) *Orientalism and Race: Aryanism in the British Empire* (Basingstoke: Palgrave).
Ballantyne, T. and Burton, A., eds (2005) *Bodies in Contact: rethinking colonial encounters in world history* (Durham: Duke University Press).
Ballantyne, T. and Burton, A., eds (2008) *Moving Subjects: gender, mobility, and intimacy in an age of global empire* (Illinois: University of Illinois Press).

Bashford, A. (1998) *Purity and Pollution: gender, embodiment and Victorian medicine* (Basingstoke: Macmillian).
Bashford, A. (2004) *Imperial Hygiene: a critical history of colonialism, nationalism and public health* (Basingstoke: Palgrave).
Bashford, A. and Hooker, C., eds (2001) *Contagion: historical and cultural studies* (London: Routledge).
Bayly, C. A. (1988) *Indian Society and the Making of the British Empire* (Cambridge: Cambridge University Press).
Bayly, C. A. (1996) *Empire and Information: intelligence gathering and social communication in India, 1780–1870* (Cambridge: Cambridge University Press).
Bear, L. (2007) *Lines of a Nation. Indian railway workers, bureaucracy and the intimate historical self* (New York: Columbia University Press).
Bebbington, D. W. (1989) *Evangelicalism in Modern Britain: a history from the 1730s to the 1890s* (London: Unwin).
Beckett, I. (2003) *The Victorians at War* (London: Hambledon and London).
Beuttner, E. (2004) *Empire Families: Britons and late imperial India* (Oxford: Oxford University Press).
Bhattacharya, N. (1998) *Reading the Splendid Body: gender and consumerism in eighteenth-century British writing on India* (Newark: University of Delaware Press).
Bhebe, N. (1979) *Christianity and Traditional Religion in Western Zimbabwe, 1859–1923* (London: Longman).
Bickers, R. and Seton, R., eds (1996) *Missionary Encounters: sources and issues* (Surrey: Curzon Press).
Binfield, C. (1977) *So Down to Prayers: studies in English Nonconformity 1780–1920* (London: Dent).
Blom, I., Hagemann, K. and Hall, C., eds (2000) *Gendered Nations: nationalisms and gender order in the long nineteenth century* (Oxford and New York: Berg).
Bolt, C. (1971) *Victorian Attitudes to Race* (London: Routledge).
Bourke, J. (1996) *Dismembering the Male: men's bodies, Britain and the Great War* (London: Reaktion).
Bourke, J. (1999) *An Intimate History of Killing* (London: Granta).
Bowie, F., Kirkwood, D. and Ardener, S., eds (1993) *Women and Missions: past and present anthropological and historical perceptions* (Oxford: Berg).
Boxer, M. and Quataert, J. H., eds (2000) *Connecting Spheres: European women in a globalizing world, 1500 to the present* (Oxford: Oxford University Press).
Brantlinger, P. (1988) *Rule of Darkness: British literature and imperialism, 1830–1914* (Ithaca: Cornell University Press).
Bredekamp, H. and Ross, R., eds (1995) *Missions and Christianity in South African History* (Johannesburg: Witwatersrand University Press).
Bridge, C., and Fedorowich, K. (2003) *The British World: diaspora, culture, and identity* (London: Portland).
Burton, A. (1994) *Burdens of History: British feminists, Indian women, and imperial culture, 1865–1915* (Chapel Hill: University of North Carolina Press).
Burton, A. (1998) *At the Heart of the Empire: Indians and the colonial encounter in late-Victorian Britain* (Berkeley: University of California Press).
Bush, B. (1999) *Imperialism, Race and Resistance: Africa and Britain, 1919–1945* (London: Routledge).
Butler, J. (1993) *Bodies that Matter: on the discursive limits of 'sex'* (London: Routledge).

Cannadine, D. (2002) *Ornamentalism: how the British saw their empire* (London: Allen Lane).

Chakravarty, G. (2005) *The Indian Rebellion and the British Imagination* (Cambridge: Cambridge University Press).

Chatterjee, P. (1993) *The Nation and Its Fragments: colonial and postcolonial histories* (Princeton: Princeton University Press).

Clinton, I. (1959) *"These vessels ...": the story of Inyati 1859–1959* (Bulawayo: Stuart Manning).

Codell, J. F., ed. (2003) *Imperial Co-Histories: national identities and the British and colonial press.* (Madison: Fairleigh Dickinson University Press).

Cohn, B. (1987) *An Anthropologist among the Historians, and Other Essays* (Oxford: Oxford University Press).

Cohn, B. (1997) *Colonialism and Its Forms of Knowledge* (Oxford: Oxford University Press).

Collingham, E. M. (2001) *Imperial Bodies: the physical experiences of the Raj, c. 1800–1947* (Cambridge: Polity Press).

Collini, S., Whatmore, R. and Young, B., eds (2000) *History, Religion and Culture: British intellectual history 1750–1850* (Cambridge: Cambridge University Press).

Comaroff, J. L. and Comaroff, J. (1991) *Of Revelation and Revolution*, vol. 1, *Christianity, colonialism, and consciousness in South Africa* (Chicago and London: University of Chicago Press).

Comaroff, J. L. and Comaroff, J. (1997) *Of Revelation and Revolution*, vol. 2, *the dialectics of modernity on a South African Frontier* (Chicago and London: University of Chicago Press).

Connell, R. W. (1995) *Masculinities* (Cambridge: Cambridge University Press).

Coombes, A. (1994) *Reinventing Africa: museums, material culture and popular imagination in late Victorian and Edwardian England* (London and New Haven: Yale University Press).

Cooper, F. and Stoler, A. L., eds (1997) *Tensions of Empire, colonial cultures in a bourgeois world* (London: California Press).

Corker, M. and Shakespeare, T., eds (2002) *Disability/Postmodernity: embodying disability theory* (London: Continuum).

Cox, J. (2002) *Imperial Fault Lines: Christianity and colonial power in India, 1818–1940* (California: Stanford University Press).

Cox, J. (2008) *The British Missionary Enterprise Since 1700* (Oxford: Routledge).

Cracknell, K. (1995) *Justice, Courtesy and Love: theologians and missionaries encountering world religions 1846–1914* (London: Epworth).

Crais, C. C. (1992) *White Supremacy and Black Resistance in Pre-Industrial South Africa: the making of the colonial order in the Eastern Cape, 1770–1865* (Cambridge: Cambridge University Press).

Curtin, P. D., ed. (1972) *Africa & The West: intellectual responses to European culture* (Madison: University of Wisconsin Press).

Curtin, P. D. (1989) *Death by Migration: Europe's encounter with the tropical world in the nineteenth century* (Cambridge: Cambridge University Press).

Cutherbertson, G., Grundlingh, A. and Suttie, M., eds (2002) *Writing a Wider War: rethinking gender, race and identity in the South African War 1899–1902* (Athens: Ohio University Press).

Daunton, M. and Halpern, R., eds (1999) *Empire and Others: British encounters with indigenous peoples, 1600–1850* (London: UCL Press).

Davenport, T. R. H. and Saunders, C. (2000) *South Africa: a modern history*, 5th edn (Basingstoke: Macmillan).

Davidoff, L., Doolittle, M. and Fink, J. (1999) *The Family Story: blood, contract and intimacy, 1830–1960* (London: Longman).

Davidoff, L. and Hall, C. (2002) *Family Fortunes: men and women of the English middle class: 1780–1850*, 2nd edn (Basingstoke: Routledge).

Davis, M. (2001) *Late Victorian Holocausts: El Niño famines and the making of the third world* (London: Verso).

Dawson, G. (1994) *Soldier Heroes: British adventure, empire and the imaginings of masculinities* (London and New York: Routledge).

D'Cruze, S., ed. (2000) *Everyday Violence in Britain, 1850–1950: gender and class* (Essex: Pearson).

Delius, P. (1984) *The Land Belongs to Us: the Pedi Polity, the Boers and the British in nineteenth-century Transvaal* (Johannesburg: Raven Press).

Dikötter, F. and Brown, I. (2007) *Cultures of Confinement: a history of the prison in Africa, Asia and Latin America* (Ithaca: Cornell University Press).

Dirks, N. B. (2001) *Castes of Mind: colonialism and the making of modern India* (Princeton: Princeton University Press).

Donald, J. and Rattansi, A., eds (1992) *'Race', Culture and Difference* (London: Sage).

Driver, F., ed. (2001) *Geography Militant: cultures of exploration and empire* (Oxford: Blackwell).

Dubber, M. D and Farmer, L., eds (2007) *Modern Histories of Crime and Punishment* (Stanford: Stanford University Press).

Dyer, R. (1997) *White* (London: Routledge).

Edmond, R. (2006) *Leprosy and Empire: a medical and cultural history* (Cambridge: Cambridge University Press).

Eiesland, N. (1994) *The Disabled God: toward a liberatory theology of disability* (Nashville: Abingdon Press).

Elbourne, E. (2002) *Blood Ground: colonialism, missions, and the contest for Christianity in the Cape Colony and Britain, 1799–1853* (Montreal: McGill-Queen's University Press).

Eldredge, E. A. (1993) *A South African Kingdom: the pursuit of security in nineteenth-century Lesotho* (Cambridge: Cambridge University Press).

Eldridge, C. C. (1984) *British Imperialism in the Nineteenth Century* (London: Macmillan).

Eldridge, C. C. (1996) *The Imperial Experience from Carlyle to Forster* (Basingstoke: Macmillian).

Elkins, C. (2005) *Britain's Gulag: the brutal end of empire in Kenya* (London: Jonathan Cape).

Etherington, N. (2001) *The Great Treks: the transformation of South Africa, 1815–1854* (London: Longman).

Etherington, N., ed. (2005) *Missions and Empire: The Oxford History of the British Empire Companion Series* (Oxford: Oxford University Press).

Fanon, F. (1952, repr. 2007) *Black Skin, White Masks*, trans. R. Philcox (New York: Grove Press).

Fanon, F. (1961) *The Wretched of the Earth*, trans. C. Farrington (London: Penguin).

Ferguson, N. (2004) *Empire: how Britain made the modern world* (London: Penguin).

Foucault, M. (1998) *The History of Sexuality*, vol. 1, *the will to knowledge*, trans. R. Hurley, 1st published 1976 (London: Penguin)

Foucault, M. (2001) *Madness and Civilisation: a history of insanity in the Age of Reason*, trans. R. Howard, 1st published 1961 (London: Routledge).

Franey, L. E. (2003) *Victorian Travel Writing and Imperial Violence: British writing on Africa, 1855–1902* (Basingstoke: Palgrave).

Fry, M. (2000) *The Scottish Empire* (Edinburgh: Birlinn).

Frykenberg, R. E., ed. (2003) *Christians and Missionaries in India: cross cultural communication since 1500* (London: Curzon).

Gelfand, M. (1984) *Christian Doctor and Nurse: the history of medical missions in South Africa 1899–1976*, with the assistance of material collected by the late R.D. Aitken and the late G.W. Gale (Stanton: Marrian Hill Mission Press).

Geller, P. L. and Stockett, M. K., eds (2006) *Feminist Anthropology: past, present, and future* (Philadelphia: University of Pennsylvania Press).

Gikandi, S. (1996) *Maps of Englishness: writing identity in the culture of colonialism* (New York: Columbia University Press).

Gilbert, A. D. (1976) *Religion and Society in Industrial England: church, chapel and social change 1740–1914* (London: Longman).

Gilman, S. (1985) *Difference and Pathology: stereotypes of sexuality, race and madness* (Ithaca: Cornell).

Gilman, S. (1998) *Disease and Representation: images from madness to AIDS* (Ithaca: Cornell).

Gleadle, K., ed. (2000) *Women in British Politics, 1780–1860: the power of the petticoat* (Basingstoke: Macmillan).

Goldberg, D. T. and Quayson, A., eds (2002) *Relocating Postcolonialism* (Oxford: Blackwell).

Goldstein, J. S. (2002) *War and Gender: how gender shapes the war system and vice versa* (Cambridge: Cambridge University Press).

Good, C. M., Jnr. (2004) *The Steamer Parish: the rise and fall of missionary medicine on an African frontier* (Chicago: University of Chicago Press).

Goodhall, N. (1954) *A History of the London Missionary Society 1895–1945* (London: Oxford University Press).

Grant, K. (2005) *A Civilised Savagery: Britain and the new slaveries in Africa, 1884–1926* (London: Routledge).

Grant, K., Levine, P. and Trentmann, F., eds (2007) *Beyond Sovereignty: Britain, empire and transnationalism, c.1880–1950* (Basingstoke: Palgrave).

Greenlee, J. G. and Johnston, C. M. (1999) *Good Citizens: British missionaries and imperial states, 1870–1918* (Montreal: McGill-Queens University Press).

Gruchy, J. D., ed. (1999) *The London Missionary Society in Southern Africa: historical essays in celebration of the bicentenary of the LMS in Southern Africa, 1799–1999* (Cape Town: David Phillip).

Guha, R. (1983) *Elementary Aspects of Peasant Insurgency in Colonial India* (Delhi: Oxford University Press).

Gupta, T. D., ed. (2007) *Race and Racialization: essential readings* (Toronto: Canadian Scholars' Press).

Guy, J. (1979) *The Destruction of the Zulu Kingdom, the civil war in Zululand, 1879–1884* (London: Longman).

Hagemann, K. and Schüler-Springorum, S., eds (2002) *Home/Front: the military, war and gender in twentieth-century Germany* (Oxford: Berg).

Haley, B. (1978) *The Healthy Body and Victorian Culture* (Cambridge: Harvard University Press).

Hall, C. (1992) *White, Male and Middle Class: explorations in feminism and history* (Cambridge: Routledge).

Hall, C., ed. (2000) *Cultures of Empire, A Reader: colonisers in Britain and the Empire in the nineteenth and twentieth centuries* (Manchester: Manchester University Press).

Hall, C. (2002) *Civilising Subjects: metropole and colony in the English imagination, 1830–1867* (Cambridge: Polity Press).

Hall, C. and Rose, S. O., eds (2006) *At Home with the Empire: metropolitan culture and the imperial world* (Cambridge: Cambridge University Press).

Hall, S., ed. (1997) *Representation: cultural representations and signifying practices* (London: Sage).

Hall, S. and Gieben, B., eds (1992) *Formations of Modernity* (Cambridge: Polity Press).

Hamilton, C. (1998) *Terrific Majesty: the powers of Shaka Zulu and the limits of historical imagination* (Cambridge: Harvard University Press).

Hardiman, D., ed. (2006) *Healing Bodies, Saving Souls: medical missions in Asia and Africa* (Amsterdam: Rodopi).

Hardiman, D. (2008) *Missionaries and their Medicine: a Christian modernity for tribal India* (Manchester: Manchester University Press).

Harrison, M. (1994) *Public Health in British India: Anglo-Indian preventive medicine 1859–1914* (Cambridge: Cambridge University Press).

Harrison, M. (1999) *Climates and Constitutions: health, race, environment and British imperialism in India 1600–1850* (Oxford: Oxford University Press).

Hawes, C. J. (1996) *Poor Relations: the making of a Eurasian community in British India, 1773–1833* (Richmond: Curzon).

Hays, J. N. (1998) *The Burdens of Disease: epidemics and human response in western history* (New Brunswick: Rutgers University Press).

Headrick, D. R. (1988) *The Tentacles of Progress, technology transfer in the Age of Imperialism, 1850–1940* (New York: Oxford University Press).

Hesse, B., ed. (2000) *Un/settled Multiculturalisms: diasporas, entanglements, transruptions* (London: Zed).

Hiltebeitel, A. and Eindl, K. M. (2000) *Is the Goddess a Feminist: the politics of a South Asian goddess* (Sheffield: Sheffield Academic Press).

Hilton, B. (1988) *The Age of Atonement: the influence of evangelicalism on social and economic thought, 1795–1865* (Oxford: Clarendon).

Hokkanen, M. (2007) *Medicine and Scottish Missionaries in the Northern Malawi Region, 1875–1930: quests for health in a colonial society* (Lewiston: Edwin Mellen Press).

Holt, T. (1992) *The Problem of Freedom: race, labor and politics in Jamaica and Britain, 1832–1938* (Baltimore: John Hopkins University Press).

Huber, M. T. and Lutkehaus, N. C., eds (1999) *Gendered Missions: women and men in missionary discourse and practice* (Ann Arbor: University of Michigan Press).

Hudson, R. P. (1983) *Disease and Its Control: the shaping of modern thought* (Connecticut: Greenwood Press).

Hull, J. M. (2001) *In the Beginning There was Darkness* (Canterbury: SCM Press).

Hunt, L., ed. (1989) *The New Cultural History* (Berkeley: University of California Press).

Hunt, T. and Lessard, M., eds (2002) *Women and the Colonial Gaze* (Basingstoke: Palgrave).
Jalland, P. (1996) *Death in the Victorian Family* (Oxford: Oxford University Press).
Jayasena, N. (2007) *Contested Masculinities: crises in colonial male identity from Joseph Conrad to Satyajit Ray* (London: Routledge).
Jeffery, K., ed. (1996) *"An Irish Empire"? Aspects of Ireland and the British Empire* (Manchester: Manchester University Press)
Jeffs, E. H. (1934) *The Doctor Abroad: the story of medical missions of the London Missionary Society* (London: The Livingstone Press).
Johnston, A. (2003) *Missionary Writing and Empire, 1880–1860* (Cambridge: Cambridge University Press).
Jolly, M. and Macintyre, M., eds (1989) *Family and Gender in the Pacific: domestic contradictions and the colonial impact* (Cambridge: Cambridge University Press).
Keegan, T. (1996) *Colonial South Africa and the Origins of the Racial Order* (London: Leicester University Press).
Kent, E. (2004) *Converting Women: gender and Protestant Christianity in colonial South India* (Oxford: Oxford University Press).
Kiernan, V. G. (1969) *The Lords of Human Kind. European attitudes to the outside world in the imperial age* (New York: Columbia University Press).
Kolsky, E. (2009) *Colonial Justice in British India: white violence and the rule of law* (Cambridge: Cambridge University Press).
Koven, S. (2004) *Slumming: sexual and social politics in Victorian London* (Princeton: Princeton University Press).
Krebs, P. M. (1999) *Gender, Race, and the Writing of Empire: public discourse and the Boer War* (Cambridge: Cambridge University Press).
Kripal, J. J. and McDermott, R. F., eds (2003) *Encountering Kālī: in the margins, at the center, in the west* (Berkeley: University of California Press).
Kumar, A. (1998) *Medicine and the Raj: British medical policy in India 1835–1911* (New Delhi and London: AltaMira Press).
Kuper, A. (1973) *Anthropologists and Anthropology, the British School 1922–1972* (London: Pica Press).
Kuper, A. (1982) *Wives for Cattle: bridewealth and marriage in southern Africa* (London: Routledge).
Laidlaw, Z. (2005) *Colonial Connections 1815–45: patronage, the information revolution and colonial government* (Manchester: Manchester University Press).
Lake, M. and Reynolds, H. (2008) *Drawing the Global Colour Line: white men's countries and the international challenge of racial equality* (Cambridge: Cambridge University Press).
Lambert, D. and Lester, A., eds (2006) *Colonial Lives Across the British Empire: imperial careering in the long nineteenth century* (Cambridge: Cambridge University Press).
Landau, P. (1995) *The Realm of the Word: language, gender and Christianity in a southern African kingdom* (Portsmouth: Heinemann).
Lane, H. (1993) *The Mask of Benevolence: disabling the deaf community* (New York: Knopf).
Langmore, D. (1989) *Missionary Lives. Papua, 1874–1914* (Honolulu: University of Hawaii Press).
Lester, A. (2001) *Imperial Networks: creating identities in nineteenth-century South Africa and Britain* (London: Routledge).

Levine, P. (2003) *Prostitution, Race, and Politics: policing venereal disease in the British Empire* (New York: Routledge).
Levine, P., ed. (2004) *Gender and Empire, the Oxford History of the British Empire Companion Series* (Oxford: Oxford University Press).
Logan, P. M. (1997) *Nerves and Narratives: a cultural history of hysteria in 19th-century British prose* (Berkeley: University of California Press).
Loomba, A. (1998, repr. 2005) *Colonialism/Postcolonialism*, 2nd edn (London: Routledge).
Lorimer, D. (1978) *Colour, Class and the Victorians: english attitudes to the Negro in the mid-nineteenth century* (Leicester: Leicester University Press).
MacKenzie, J. M. (1984) *Propaganda and Empire: the manipulation of British public opinion 1880–1960* (Manchester: Manchester University Press).
MacKenzie, J. M., ed. (1986) *Imperialism and Popular Culture* (Manchester: Manchester University Press).
MacKenzie, J. M., ed. (1992) *Popular Imperialism and the Military 1850–1950* (Manchester: Manchester University Press).
MacKenzie, J. M., ed. (2005) *Peoples, Nations and Cultures: an A-Z of the peoples of the world, past and present* (London: Weidenfeld and Nicholson).
MacKenzie, W. D. (1902) *John Mackenzie: South African missionary and statesman* (London: Hodder and Stroughton).
MacLeod, R. and Lewis, M., eds (1988) *Disease, Medicine, and Empire: perspectives on western medicine and the experience of European expansion* (London and New York: Routledge).
Magner, L. N. (1992) *A History of Medicine* (New York: Dekker).
Major, A. (2006) *Pious Flames: European encounters with sati 1500–1830* (Oxford: Oxford University Press).
Malik, K. (1996) *The Meaning of Race: race, history and culture in western society* (Basingstoke: Macmillan).
Mangan, J. A. and Walvin, J., eds (1987) *Manliness and Morality: middle-class masculinity in Britain and America 1800–1940* (Manchester: Manchester University).
Mani, L. (1998) *Contentious Traditions: the debate on sati in colonial India* (Berkeley: University of California Press).
Marshall, P. J., ed. (1998) *The Oxford History of the British Empire*, vol. 2, *the eighteenth century* (Oxford: Oxford University Press).
Maxwell, A. (1999) *Colonial Photography and Exhibitions: representations of the 'native' and the making of European identities* (London: Leicester University Press).
Mayhall, L., Levine, P. and Fletcher, I. C., eds (2000) *Women's Suffrage in the British Empire: citizenship, nation and race* (London: Routledge).
McCann, C., ed. (2003) *Feminist Theory Reader: local and global perspectives* (London: Routledge).
McClintock, A. (1995) *Imperial Leather: race, gender and sexuality in the colonial contest* (London: Routledge).
Metcalf, B. and Metcalf, T. (2006) *A Concise History of Modern India* (Cambridge: Cambridge University Press).
Metcalf, T. (1964) *The Aftermath of Revolt, India, 1857–1870* (London: Princeton University Press).
Middleton, K., ed. (1999) *Ancestors, Power and History in Madagascar* (Leiden: Brill).
Midgley, C., ed. (1998) *Gender and Imperialism* (Manchester: Manchester University Press).

Midgley, C. (2007) *Feminism and Empire: women activists in imperial Britain, 1790–1865* (London: Routledge).
Mitchell, D. T. and Snyder, S. L. (2000) *Narrative Prosthesis: disability and the dependencies of discourse* (Ann Arbor: University of Michigan Press).
Moffat, R. U. (1960) *John Smith Moffat C.M.G. Missionary: a memoir*, 1st published 1921 (New York: Negro Universities Press).
de Moor, J. and Wesseling, H. L., eds (1989) *Imperialism and War: essays on colonial wars in Asia and Africa* (Leiden: Universitaire pers Leiden).
Morgan, S., ed. (2002) *Women, Religion and Feminism in Britain 1750–1900* (Basingstoke: Palgrave).
Mukherjee, R. (2002) *Awadh in Revolt, 1857–1858: a study of popular resistance* (Delhi and London: Oxford University Press).
Nederveen P. J. (1992) *White on Black: images of Africa and Blacks in western popular culture* (London: Yale University Press).
Oliver, K. (2001) *Witnessing: beyond recognition* (Minneapolis: University of Minnesota Press).
Ottkenhaug, I. M. (2003) *Gender, Race and Religion: Nordic missions 1860–1940* (Oslo: Studia Missionalia Svecana XCI).
Paris, M. (2000) *Warrior Nation: images of war in British popular culture, 1850–2000* (London: Reaktion).
Pati, B. and Harrison, M., eds (2001) *Health, Medicine and Empire: perspectives on colonial India* (New Delhi: Orient Longman).
Paxton, N. L. (1999) *Writing Under the Raj: gender, race and rape in the British colonial imagination, 1830–1947* (New Brunswick: Rutgers University Press).
Paz, D. G. (1995) *Nineteenth Century Religious Traditions* (Connecticut: Greenwood).
Peires, J. B. (1981) *The House of Phalo: a history of the Xhosa people in the days of their independence* (Johannsberg: Raven Press).
Phillips, R. (2006) *Sex, Politics and Empire: a postcolonial geography* (Manchester: Manchester University Press).
Pierce, S. and Rao, A., eds (2002) *Discipline and the Other Body: correction, corporeality, colonialism* (London: Duke University Press).
Piggin, S. (1984) *Making Evangelical Missionaries, 1789–1858: the social background, motives and training of British Protestant missionaries to India, Evangelicals and society from 1750* (Oxfordshire: Adbingdon).
Poovey, M. (1995) *Making a Social Body: British cultural formation, 1830–1864* (Chicago: University of Chicago Press).
Porter, A., ed. (1999) *Oxford History of the British Empire*, vol. 3: *the nineteenth century* (Oxford: Oxford University Press).
Porter, A. (2004) *Religion versus Empire? British Protestant missionaries and overseas expansion, 1700–1914* (Manchester: Manchester University Press).
Porter, A., ed. (2003) *The Imperial Horizons of British Protestant Missions, 1880–1914* (Michigan: Grand Rapids).
Porter, B. (2004) *The Absent-Minded Imperialists: empire, society and culture in Britain* (Oxford: Oxford University Press).
Porter, R., ed. (2006) *The Cambridge History of Medicine* (Cambridge: Cambridge University Press).
Porterfield, A. (2005) *Healing in the History of Christianity* (Oxford: Oxford University Press).

Powell, A. A. (1993) *Muslims and Missionaries in Pre-Mutiny India* (Richmond: Curzon).
Pratt, M. L. (1992) *Imperial Eyes: travel writing and transculturation* (London: Routledge).
Price, R. (2008) *Making Empire: colonial encounters and the creation of imperial rule in nineteenth-century Africa* (Cambridge: Cambridge University Press).
Procida, M. (2002) *Married to the Empire: gender, politics and imperialism in India, 1883–1947* (Manchester: Manchester University Press).
Ranger, T. O. (1967) *Revolt in Southern Rhodesia, 1896–7: a study in African resistance* (London: Heinemann).
Ranger, T. O. (1985) *The Invention of Tribalism in Zimbabwe* (Gweru: Mambo Press).
Rasmussen, K. (1978) *Migrant Kingdom: Mzilikazi's Ndebele in South Africa* (London: Rex Collings).
Rattansi, A. (2007) *Racism: a very short introduction* (Oxford: Oxford University Press).
Richards, T. (1993) *The Imperial Archive: knowledge and the fantasy of empire* (London: Verso).
Robb, P. (2002) *A History of India* (Basingstoke: Palgrave).
Robinson, J. (1996) *Angels of Albion: women of the Indian Mutiny* (London: Viking).
Roper, M. and Tosh, J., eds (1991) *Manful Assertions: masculinities in Britain since 1800* (London: Routledge).
Ross, A. C. (2002) *David Livingstone: mission and empire* (London: Hambledon).
Ross, R. (1983) *Cape of Torments: slavery and resistance in South Africa* (London: Routledge and Kegan Paul).
Ross, R. (1999) *Status and Respectability in the Cape Colony, 1750–1870* (Cambridge: Cambridge University Press).
Ryan, J. (1997) *Picturing Empire: photography and the visualization of the British Empire* (London: Riktean).
Said, E. W. (1993) *Culture and Imperialism* (London: Knopf).
Said, E. W. (1995) *Orientalism: western conceptions of the Orient*, 1st published 1979 (London: Penguin).
Samkange, S. (1968) *Origins of Rhodesia* (London: Heinemann).
Samkange, S. (1985) *The Origin of African Nationalism in Zimbabwe* (Harare: Harare Pub. House).
Saunders, C., ed. (1998) *Black Leaders in Southern African History* (London: Heinemann).
Scarry, E. (1985) *The Body in Pain: the making and unmaking of the world* (Oxford: Oxford University Press).
Schwarz, B., ed. (1996) *The Expansion of England: race, ethnicity and cultural History* (London: Routledge).
Scott, J. S. and Griffiths, G., eds. (2005) *Mixed Messages: materiality, textuality, missions* (Basingstoke: Palgrave).
Scott, J. W. (1999) *Gender and the Politics of History* (New York: Columbia University Press).
Scully, P. (1997) *Liberating the Family?: gender and British slave emancipation in the rural Western Cape, South Africa, 1823–1853* (Oxford: James Currey).
Semple, R. A. (2003) *Missionary Women: gender, professionalism, and the Victorian idea of Christian mission* (Woodbridge: Boydell Press).
Shiels, W. J., ed. (1982) *The Church and Healing* (Oxford: Basil Blackwell).

Shillington, K. (1985) *The Colonisation of the Southern Tswana, 1870–1900* (Braamfontein: Ravan Press).

Shillito, E. (1923) *Khama: the great African chief* (London: LMS).

Shourie, A. (1994) *Missionaries in India: continuities, changes, dilemmas* (New Delhi: ASA Publications).

Sillery, A. (1971) *John Mackenzie of Bechuanalnd 1835–1899: a study in humanitarian imperialism* (Cape Town: Balkema).

Sinha, M. (1995) *Colonial Masculinity: the 'Manly Englishman' and the 'Effeminate Bengali' in the late nineteenth century* (Manchester: Manchester University Press).

Sontag, S. (1991) *Illness as Metaphor and AIDS and Its Metaphors* (London: Penguin).

Sontag, S. (2003) *Regarding the Pain of Others* (London: Hamish Hamilton).

Spiers, E. M. (1992) *The Late Victorian Army* (Manchester: Manchester University Press).

Spurr, D. (1993) *The Rhetoric of Empire: colonial discourse in journalism, travel writing and imperial administration* (Durham: Duke University Press).

Stanko, E. A., ed. (2003) *The Meanings of Violence* (London: Routledge).

Stanley, B. (1990) *The Bible and the Flag: Protestant missions and British imperialism in the nineteenth and twentieth centuries* (Leicester: Apollo).

Stanley, B., ed. (2001) *Christian Missions and the Enlightenment* (Richmond: Curzon).

Stepan, N. (1982) *The Idea of Race in Science* (London: MacMillan).

Stocking, G., Jnr. (1991) *Victorian Anthropology* (New York: Macmillan).

Stoler, A. L. (1995) *Race and the Education of Desire: Foucault's History of Sexuality and the colonial order of things* (London: Duke University Press).

Stoler, A. L. (2002) *Carnal Knowledge and Imperial Power: race and the intimate in colonial rule* (California: University of California Press).

Stoler, A. L., ed. (2006) *Haunted by Empire: geographies of intimacy in North American history* (Durham: Duke University Press).

Streak, M. (1974) *The Afrikaner as Viewed by the English, 1795–1854* (Cape Town: C. Struik).

Streets, H. (2004) *Martial Races, the military, race and masculinity in British imperial culture 1857–1914* (Manchester: Manchester University Press).

Sussman, H. (1995) *Victorian Masculinities: Victorian masculinities, manhood & masculine poetics in early Victorian literature and art* (Cambridge: Cambridge University Press).

Swenson, K. (2005) *Medical Women and Victorian Fiction* (Columbia and London: University of Missouri Press).

Temperley, H. (1991) *White Dreams, Black Africa: the anti-slavery expedition to the River Niger, 1841–1842* (London: Yale University Press).

Thomas, N. (1994) *Colonialism's Culture: anthropology, travel and government* (Cambridge: Polity Press).

Thompson, A. (2005) *The Empire Strikes Back? The impact of imperialism on Britain from the mid-nineteenth century* (Harlow: Pierson).

Thorne, S. (1999) *Congregational Missions, and the Making of an Imperial Culture in 19th-Century England* (California: California University Press).

Tosh, J. (1999) *A Man's Place: masculinity and the middle-class home in Victorian England* (New Haven and London: Yale University Press).

Tosh, J. (2005) *Manliness and Masculinities in Nineteenth-Century Britain: essays on gender, family, and empire* (Harlow: Longman).
Trentmann, F., ed. (2000) *Paradoxes of Civil Society: new perspectives on modern German and British history* (Oxford: Berghahn).
Twells, A. (2009) *The Heathen at Home and Overseas: the middle class and the civilising mission, Sheffield 1790–1843* (Basingstoke: Macmillan).
Vandervort, B. (1998) *Wars of Imperial Conquest in Africa, 1830–1914* (London: UCL).
Vaughan, M. (1991) *Curing Their Ills: colonial power and African illness* (Cambridge: Polity Press).
Walker, C., ed. (1990) *Women and Gender in Southern Africa to 1945* (London, Calremont).
Wallis, J. P. R., ed. (1945) *The Matabele Journals of Robert Moffat, 1829–1860* (London: Chatto and Windus).
Wallis, J. P. R. (1956) *The Zambezi Expedition of David Livingstone, 1858–1863* (London: Chatto & Windus).
Walls, A. F. (1996) *The Missionary Movement in Christian History: studies in the transmission of faith* (Edinburgh: T & T Clark).
Werbner, P. and Modood, T., eds (1997) *Debating Cultural Hybridity: multi-cultural identities and the politics of anti-racism* (London: Zed Books).
West, S., ed. (1996) *The Victorians and Race* (Aldershot: Scholar Press).
Whaley, J., ed. (1981) *Mirrors of Mortality: studies in the social history of death* (London: Europa).
Wheeler, M. (1990) *Death and the Future Life in Victorian Literature and Theology* (Cambridge: Cambridge University Press).
Wheeler, R. (2000) *The Complexion of Race: categories of difference in eighteenth-century British culture* (Pennsylvania: University of Pennsylvania Press).
Williams, S. C. (1999) *Religious Belief and Popular Culture in Southwark, c. 1880–1939* (Oxford: Oxford University Press).
Winther, P. C. (2003) *Anglo-European Science and the Rhetoric of Empire: malaria, opium, and British rule in India, 1756–1895* (Oxford: Lexington Books).
Wolffe, J. (1994) *God and Greater Britain: religion and national life in Britain and Ireland 1843–1945* (London: Routledge).
Woollacott, A. (2006) *Gender and Empire* (London: Palgrave).
Wray, M. (2006) *Not Quite White: white trash and the boundaries of whiteness* (Durham: Duke University Press).
Wright, P. and Treacher, A., eds (1982) *The Problem of Medical Knowledge: examining the social construction of medicine* (Edinburgh: Edinburgh University Press).
Youngs, T. (1994) *Travellers in Africa: British travelogues, 1850–1900* (Manchester: Manchester University Press).

Articles and chapters in edited collections

Abbink, J. (2000) 'Violation and Violence as a Cultural Phenomena' in J. Abbink and G. Aijmer (eds) *Meanings of Violence: a cross cultural perspective* (Oxford: Berg).
Ahmed, S. (2007) 'A Phenomenology of Whiteness', *Feminist Theory*, 8 (2), 149–68.

Anderson, W. (1990) 'Immunities of Empire: race, disease and the new tropical medicine 1900–1920', *Bulletin of the History of Medicine*, 70, 94–118.

Anderson, W. (1992) '"Where Every Prospect Pleases and Only Man Is Vile": laboratory medicine as colonial medicine', *Critical Enquiry*, 18 (3), 506–29.

Anderson, W. (1996) 'Race and Acclimatization in Colonial Medicine; disease, race, and empire', *Bulletin of the History of Medicine*, 70, 62–7.

Ashley, M. P. (2001) 'It's Only Teething... a report of the myths and modern approaches to teething', *British Dental Journal*, 191 (1), 4–8.

Bank, A. (1999) 'Losing Faith in the Civilizing Mission: the premature decline of humanitarian liberalism at the Cape, 1840–60' in M. Daunton and R. Halpern (eds) *Empire and Others: British encounters with indigenous peoples, 1600–1850* (London: UCL Press).

Bannerji, H. (1998) 'Age of Consent and Hegemonic Social Reform' in C. Midgley (ed.) *Gender and Imperialism* (Manchester: Manchester University Press).

Barringer, T. (2004) 'What Mrs Jellyby Might Have Read: missionary periodicals: a neglected source', *Victorian Periodical Review*, 37 (4), 46–72.

Beinart, W. (1992) 'Political and Collective Violence in Southern African Historiography', *Journal of Southern African Studies*, 18 (3), 455–86.

Bell, M. (1993) '"The Pestilence that Walketh in Darkness": imperial health, gender and images of South Africa c. 1880–1910', *Transactions of the Institute of British Geography*, 18, 327–41.

Bhabha, H. (1997) 'Of Mimicry and Man: the ambivalence of colonial discourse' in F. Cooper and A. L. Stoler (eds) *Tensions of Empire: colonial cultures in a bourgeois world* (London: California Press).

Bolt, C. (1984) 'Race and the Victorians' in C. C. Eldridge (ed.) *British Imperialism in the Nineteenth Century* (London: Macmillan).

Bradford, H. (1996) 'Women, Gender and Colonialism: rethinking the history of the British Cape Colony and its frontier zones, c. 1806–1970', *Journal of African History*, 37, 351–70.

Bradford, H. (2002) 'Gentlemen and Boers: Afrikaner nationalism, gender, and colonial warfare in the South African War' in G. Cuthbertson, A. Grundlingh, and M. Suttie (eds) *Writing a Wider War: rethinking gender, race and identity in the South African War 1899–1902* (Ohio: Ohio University Press).

Burton, A. (1996) 'Contesting the Zenana: the mission to make "Lady Doctors for India" 1874–1885', *The Journal of British Studies*, 35 (3), 368–97.

Burton, A. (2000) '"States of Injury", Josephine Butler on slavery, citizenship and the Boer War' in L. Mayhall, P. Levine, and I. C., Fletcher (eds) *Women's Suffrage in the British Empire: citizenship, nation and race* (London: Routledge).

Burton, A. (2000) 'Who Needs the Nation? Interrogating "British" history' in C. Hall (ed.) *Cultures of Empire: colonizers in Britain and the empire in the nineteenth and twentieth centuries* (Manchester: Manchester University Press).

Burton, A. (2000) 'Women and "Domestic" imperial culture, the case of Victorian Britain' in M. J. Boxer and J. H. Quataert (eds) *Connecting Spheres: European women in a globalizing world, 1500 to the present* (Oxford: Oxford University Press).

Cannadine, D. (1981) 'War and Death: grief and mourning in modern Britain' in J. Whaley (ed.) *Mirrors of Mortality: studies in the social history of death* (London: Europa).

Cleall, E. (2009) 'Missionary Masculinities and War: the LMS in Southern Africa, c. 1860–1899', *South African Historical Journal*, 61 (2), 232–52.

Cooper, F. and Stoler, A. L. (1997) 'Between Metropole and Colony: rethinking a research agenda' in F. Cooper and A. L. Stoler (eds) *Tensions of Empire: colonial cultures in a bourgeois world* (London: California Press).

Copland, I. (2006) 'Christianity as an Arm of Empire: the ambiguous case of India under the company, c. 1813–1858', *Historical Journal*, 49 (4), 1025–54.

Cox, J. (2004) 'Were Victorian Nonconformists the Worst Imperialists of them All?', *Victorian Studies*, 46 (2), 243–55.

Curtin, P. (1961) 'The White Man's Grave: image and reality, 1780–1850', *Journal of British Studies*, 1, 94–110.

Cuthbertson, G. (1987) 'Missionary Imperialism and Colonial Warfare: London Missionary Society attitudes to the South African War, 1899–1902', *South African Historian Journal*, 19, 93–114.

Dachs, A. (1972) 'Missionary Imperialism: the case of Bechuanaland', *Journal of African History*, 13 (2), 647–58.

D'Cruze, S. (2000) 'Unguarded Passions: violence and the every day' in S. D'Cruze (ed.) *Everyday Violence in Britain, 1850–1950: gender and class* (Essex: Pearson).

de Groot, J. (2000) '"Sex" and "Race"; the construction of language and image in the nineteenth century' in C. Hall (ed.) *Cultures of Empire Reader: colonizers in Britain and the Empire in the nineteenth and twentieth centuries* (Manchester: Manchester University Press).

Delius, P. and C. Glaser (2004) 'The Myths of Polygamy: a history of extra marital and multi-partnership sex in South Africa', *South African Historical Journal*, 50, 84–114.

Donald, J. and Rattansi, A. (1992) 'Introduction' in J. Donald and A. Rattansi (eds) *"Race", Culture and Difference* (London: Sage).

Endfield, G. H. and Nash, D. J. (2005) '"Happy is the Bride the Rain Falls On": climate, health and "the woman question" in nineteenth-century missionary documentation', *Transactions of the Institute of British Geographers*, 30, 368–86.

Erlank, N. (2003) 'Sexual Misconduct and Church Power on Scottish Mission Stations in Xhosaland, South Africa, in the 1840s', *Gender and History*, 15, 69–84.

Etherington, N. (1987) 'Missionary Doctors and African Healers in Mid Victorian South Africa', *Suid-Afrikaanse Historiese Journal/ South African Historical Journal*, 19, 77–93.

Fitzgerald, R. (1996) 'A "Peculiar and Exceptional Measure": the call for women medical missionaries for India in the later nineteenth century' in R. A. Bickers and R. Seton (eds) *Missionary Encounters: sources and issues* (Surrey: Curzon Press).

Fitzgerald, R. (2001) '"Clinical Christianity": The Emergence of Medical Work as a missionary strategy in colonial India, 1800–1914' in B. Pati and M. Harrison (eds) *Health, Medicine and Empire: perspectives on colonial India* (New Delhi: Orient Longman).

Francis-Dehqani, G. (2002) 'Medical Missions and the History of Feminism: Emmeline Stuart of the CMS Persia Mission' in S. Morgan (ed.) *Women Religion and Feminism in Britain, 1750–1900* (Basingstoke: Palgrave).

Gaitskell, D. (2003) 'Rethinking Gender Roles: the field experience of women missionaries in South Africa' in A. Porter (ed.) *The Imperial Horizons of British Protestant Missions, 1880–1914* (Michigan: Grand Rapids).

Grimshaw, P. (1999) 'Colonising Motherhood: evangelical social reformers and Koorie women in Victoria, Australia, 1880s to the early 1900s', *Women's History Review*, 8, 329–46.

Grimshaw, P. (2004) 'Faith, Missionary Life, and the Family' in P. Levine (ed.) *Gender and Empire: the Oxford History of the British Empire Companion Series* (Oxford: Oxford University Press).

Guy, J. (1996) 'Shaka KaSenzargakhona – a reassessment', *Journal of Natal and Zulu History*, 16, 1–29.

Haggis, J. (1998) '"A Heart that Has Felt the Love of God and Longs for Others to Know It": conventions of gender, tensions of self and constructions of difference in offering to be a lady missionary', *Women's History Review*, 7, 171–92.

Hall, C. (2004) 'Of Gender and Empire: reflections on the nineteenth century' in P. Levine (ed.) *Gender and Empire: the Oxford History of the British Empire Companion Series* (Oxford: Oxford University Press).

Hall, C. (2006) 'Commentary' in A. L. Stoler (ed.) *Haunted by Empire: geographies of intimacy in North American history* (Durham: Duke University Press).

Hall, S. (1992) 'The West and the Rest' in S. Hall and B. Gieben (eds) *Formations of Modernity* (Cambridge: Polity Press).

Hall, S. (1997) 'The Spectacle of the Other' in S. Hall (ed.) *Representation: cultural representations and signifying practices* (London: Sage).

Hall, S. (2000) 'Conclusion: the multi-cultural question' in B. Hesse (ed.) *Un/settled Multiculturalisms: diasporas, entanglements, transruptions* (London: Zed).

Hall, S. (2007) 'Discourse and Power: the west and the rest' in T. D. Gupta (ed.) *Race and Racialization: essential readings* (Toronto: Canadian Scholars' Press).

Hardiman, D. (2006) 'Introduction' in D. Hardiman (ed.) *Healing Bodies, Saving Souls: medical missions in Asia and Africa* (Amsterdam: Rodopi).

Harries, P. (2005) 'Anthropology' in Norman Etherington (ed.) *Missions and Empire: the Oxford history of the British Empire companion series* (Oxford: Oxford University Press).

Harrison, M. (1996) '"The Tender Frame of Man": disease, climate, and racial difference in India and the West Indies, 1760–1860', *Bulletin of the History of Medicine*, 70, 68–93.

Heasman, K. (1964) 'The Medical Mission and the Care of the Sick Poor in Nineteenth-Century England', *The Historical Journal*, 7, 230–45.

Hinchliffe, P. (1984) 'The Blantyre Scandal: Scottish missionaries and colonialism', *Journal of Theology for Southern Africa*, 46, 29–38

Holmes, M. S. (2007) 'Victorian Fictions of Interdependency: Gaskell, Craik, and Yonge', *Journal of Literary Disability*, 2 (1), 29–41.

Hunt, T. (2002) 'Introduction: the colonial gaze' in T. L. Hunt and M. R. Lessard (eds) *Women and the Colonial Gaze* (Basingstoke: Palgrave).

Iwakuma, M. (2002) 'The Body as Embodiment: an investigation of the body by Merleu-Ponty' in M. Corker and T. Shakespeare (eds) *Disability/Postmodernity: embodying disability theory* (London: Continuum).

Inden, R. (1986) 'Orientalist Constructions of India', *Modern Asian Studies*, 20 (3), 401–46.

JanMohamed, A. R. (2006) 'The Economy of Manchean Allegory' in B. Ashcroft, G. Griffiths, and H. Tiffin (eds) *The Postcolonial Studies Reader*, 2nd edn (London: Routledge).

Jones, A. (2003) 'Welsh Missionary Journalism in India, 1880–1947' in J. F. Codell (ed.) *Imperial Co-Histories: national identities and the British and colonial press* (Madison: Fairleigh Dickinson University Press).

Kakar, S. (1996) 'Leprosy in British India, 1860–1940: colonial politics and missionary medicine', *Medical History*, 40, 215–30.

Kilshaw, S. (2004) '"004. Friendly Fire": the construction of Gulf War Syndrome narratives', *Anthropology and Medicine*, 11 (2), 149–60.

Kiple, K. F. and Kriemhild, C. O. (1996) 'Race, War and Tropical Medicine in the Eighteenth-Century Caribbean' in D. Arnold (ed.) *Warm Climates and Western Medicines* (Amsterdam: Rodopi).

Kolsky, E. (2005) 'Codification and the Rule of Colonial Difference: criminal procedure in British India', *Law and History Review*, 25, 631–85.

Kolsky, E. (2007) 'Crime and Punishment on the Tea Plantations of Colonial India' in M. D. Dubber and L. Farmer (eds) in *Modern Histories of Crime and Punishment* (Stanford: Stanford University Press).

Kripal, J. J. and McDermott, R. F. (2003) 'Introducing Kālī Studies' in J. J. Kripal and R. F. McDermott (eds) *Encountering Kālī: in the margins, at the center, in the west* (Berkeley: University of California Press).

Kupperman, K. O (1984) 'Fear of Hot Climates in the Anglo-American Colonial Experience', *The William and Mary Quarterly*, 3rd Ser., 42 (2), 213–40.

Laidlaw, Z. (2007) 'Heathens, Slaves and Aborigines: Thomas Hodgkin's critique of missions and anti-slavery', *History Workshop Journal*, 64, 133–62.

Lambert, D. and Lester, A. (2006) 'Politics and the Captive Audience: William Shrewsbury in the Caribbean and the Cape Colony' in D. Lambert and A. Lester (eds) *Colonial Lives Across the British Empire: imperial careering in the long nineteenth century* (Cambridge: Cambridge University Press).

Langmore, D. (1989) 'The Object Lesson of a Civilised, Christian Home' in M. Jolly and M. Macintyre (eds) *Family and Gender in the Pacific: domestic contradictions and the colonial impact* (Cambridge: Cambridge University Press).

Laqueur, T. W. (1989) 'Bodies, Details, and the Humanitarian Narrative' in L. Hunt (ed.) *The New Cultural History* (Berkeley: University of California Press).

Lester, A. (2006) 'Imperial Circuits and Networks: geographies of the British Empire', *History Compass*, 4 (1), 124–41.

Levine, P. (2004) 'Sexuality, Gender, and Empire' in P. Levine (ed.) *Gender and Empire: the Oxford history of the British Empire companion series* (Oxford: Oxford University Press).

Leys, C. (1965) 'Violence in Africa', *Transition*, 21, 17–20.

Long, U. (1950) 'Introduction' in E. L. Price (ed.) *The Journals of Elizabeth Lees Price. Written in Bechuanaland, Southern Africa, 1854–1883 with an epilogue 1889–1900*, with an introduction and annotations by U. Long (London: Edward Arnold).

Lorimer, D. A. (1988) 'Theoretical Racism in Late-Victorian Anthropology', *Victorian Studies*, 25, 405–30.

MacKenzie, J. M. (1992) 'Introduction: popular imperialism and the military' in J. M. MacKenzie (ed.) *Popular Imperialism and the Military 1850–1950* (Manchester: Manchester University Press).
Mandler, P. (2000) '"Race" and "Nation" in Mid-Victorian Thought' in S. Collini, R. Whatmore, and B. Young (eds) *History, Religion and Culture: British intellectual history 1750–1850* (Cambridge: Cambridge University Press).
Mani, L. (2003) 'Multiple Mediations: feminist scholarship in the age of multinational reception' in C. McCann (ed.) *Feminist Theory Reader: local and global perspectives* (London: Routledge).
Maughan, S. S. (2000) 'Civic Culture, Women's Foreign Missions, and the British Imperial Imagination, 1860–1914' in F. Trentmann (ed.) *Paradoxes of Civil Society: new perspectives on modern German and British history* (Oxford: Berghahn).
McCulloch, J. (2004) 'Empire and Violence, 1900–1939' in P. Levine (ed.) *Gender and Empire, the Oxford History of the British Empire Companion Series* (Oxford: Oxford University Press).
Midgley, C. (2000) 'From Supporting Missions to Petitioning Parliament: British women and the evangelical campaign against sati in India, 1813–30' in K. Gleadle (ed.) *Women in British Politics, 1780–1860: the power of the petticoat* (Basingstoke: Macmillan).
Midgley, C. (2006) 'Can Women Be Missionaries? Envisioning female agency in the early nineteenth-century British Empire', *Journal of British Studies*, 45, 335–58.
Moore, R. J. (1999) 'Imperial India, 1858–1914' in Andrew Porter (ed.) *The Oxford History of the British Empire*, vol. 3: *the Nineteenth Century* (Oxford: Oxford University Press).
Morgan, J. L. (2005) 'Male Travellers, Female Bodies, and the Gendering of Racial Ideology, 1500–1770' in T. Ballantyne and A. M. Burton (eds) *Bodies in Contact: rethinking colonial encounters in world history* (Durham: Duke University Press).
Mukherjee, R. (1990) '"Satan Let Loose Upon the Earth": the Kanpur massacres in India in the Revolt of 1857', *Past and Present*, 92–116.
Nair, J. (2000) 'Uncovering the *Zenana*: visions of Indian womanhood in Englishwomen's writings, 1813–1940' in C. Hall (ed.) *Cultures of Empire: A Reader: colonizers in Britain and the Empire in the nineteenth and twentieth centuries* (Manchester: Manchester University Press).
Oddie, G. O. (1986) 'Hook-Swinging and Popular Religion in South India during the Nineteenth Century', *Indian Economic Social History Review*, 23, 93–106.
Palmegiano, E. M. (1991) 'The Indian Mutiny in the Mid-Victorian Press', *Journal of Newspaper and Periodical History*, 7, 3–11.
Parker, K. (1996) 'Fertile Land, Romantic Spaces, Uncivilized Peoples: English travel writing about the Cape of Good Hope, 1800–1850' in B. Schwarz (ed.) *The Expansion of England: race, ethnicity and cultural history* (London: Routledge).
Paul, J. (1977) 'Medicine and Imperialism in Morocco', *MERIP* [Middle East Research Information Project] *Reports*, 60, 3–12.
Paxton, N. L. (1992) 'Mobilising Chivalry: rape in British Novels about the Indian Uprising of 1857', *Victorian Studies*, 36, 5–30.
Pelling, M. (2001) 'The Meaning of Contagion: reproduction, medicine and metaphor' in A. Bashford and C. Hooker (eds) *Contagion: historical and cultural studies* (London: Routledge).

Pierce, S. and Rao, A. (2002) 'Discipline and the Other Body: humanitarianism, violence and the colonial exception' in A. Rao and S. Pierce (eds) *Discipline and the Other Body: correction, corporeality, colonialism* (London: Duke University Press).

Porter, A. (2005) 'An Overview, 1700–1914' in N. Etherington (ed.) *Missions and Empire: the Oxford History of the British Empire Companion Series* (Oxford: Oxford University Press).

Porter, B. (2004) ' "Empire, What Empire?" Or Why 80% of early and mid-Victorians were deliberately kept in ignorance of it', *Victorian Studies*, 46 (2), 254–63.

Porter, R. (2006) 'Medical Science' in R. Porter (ed.) *The Cambridge History of Medicine* (Cambridge: Cambridge University Press).

Prochaska, F. K. (1978) 'Little Vessels: children in the nineteenth-century English missionary movement', *The Journal of Imperial and Commonwealth History*, 6 (2), 103–19.

Quayson, A. (2002) 'Looking Awry: tropes of disability in postcolonial writing' in D. T. Goldberg and A. Quayson (eds) *Relocating Postcolonialism* (Oxford: Blackwell).

Ranger, T. O. (1982) 'Medical Science and Pentecost: the dilemma of Anglicanism in Africa' in W. J. Shiels (ed.) *The Church and Healing* (Oxford: Basil Blackwell).

Rao, A. (2006) 'Problems of Violence, States of Terror: torture in colonial India' in S. Pierce and A. Rao (eds) *Discipline and the Other Body: correction, corporeality, colonialism* (London: Duke University Press).

Render, M. A. (2001) ' "Sentiments of a Private Nature": a comment on Ann Laura Stoler's "Tense and Tender Ties" ', *Journal of American History*, 88, 882–7.

Ross, R. (1995) 'The Social and Political Theology of Western Cape Missions' in H. Bredekamp and R. Ross (eds) *Missions and Christianity in South African History* (Johannesburg: Witwatersrand University Press).

Rowbotham, J. (2000) ' "Soldiers of Christ?" Images of female missionaries in late nineteenth-century Britain', *Gender and History*, 12, 82–106.

Savage, D. W. (1997) 'Missionaries and the Development of a Colonial Ideology of Female Education in India', *Gender and History*, 9 (2), 201–21.

Scott, J. W. (1986) 'Gender: a useful category of historical analysis', *The American Historical Review*, 91 (5), 1053–73.

Semple, R. A. (2008) 'Missionary Manhood: professionalism, belief and masculinity in the nineteenth-century British imperial field', *The Journal of Imperial and Commonwealth History*, 36 (3), 397–415.

Setel, P. (1991) ' "A Good Moral Tone": Victorian ideals of health and the judgements of persons in nineteenth-century travel and mission accounts from East Africa', *Working Papers in African Studies, African Studies Center, Boston University*.

Seton, R. (1996) ' "Open Doors for Female Labourers": women candidates of the London Missionary Society, 1875–1914' in R. Bickers and R. Seton (eds) *Missionary Encounters: sources and issues* (Surrey: Curzon).

Shephard, B. (1986) 'Showbiz Imperialism: the case of Peter Lobengula' in J. MacKenzie (ed.) *Imperialism and Popular Culture* (Manchester: Manchester University Press).

Sherry, M. (2007) 'Postcolonizing Disability', *Wagadu*, 4, 10–22.

Skeie, K. H. (1999) 'Building God's Kingdom: the importance of the house to nineteenth-century Norwegian missionaries in Madagascar' in K. Middleton (ed.) *Ancestors, Power and History in Madagascar* (Leiden: Brill).
Spivak, G. (1985) 'Can the Subaltern Speak? Speculations on widow sacrifice', *Wedge*, 7–8, 120–30.
Stanfield, R. (2009) 'Violence and the Intimacy of Imperial Ethnography: the endeavour in the Pacific' in T. Ballantyne and A. Burton (eds) *Moving Subjects: gender, mobility, and intimacy in an age of global Empire* (Urbana: University of Illionois Press).
Stanko, E. A. (2003) 'Introduction: conceptualising the meanings of violence' in E. Stanko (ed.) *The Meanings of Violence* (London: Routledge).
Stoler, A. L. (1989) 'Making Empire Respectable: the politics of race and sexual morality in 20th-century colonial cultures', *American Ethnologist*, 16 (4), 634–60.
Stoler, A. L. (1989) 'Rethinking Colonial Categories: European communities and the boundaries of rule', *Comparative Studies in Society and History*, 31 (1), 134–61.
Stoler, A. L. (1997) 'On Political and Psychological Essentialisms', *Ethos*, 25 (1), 101–06.
Stoler, A. L. (1997) 'Racial Histories and Their Regimes of Truth', *Political Power and Social Theory*, 5 (11), 183–206.
Stoler, A. L. (2001) ' "Tense and Tender Ties": the politics of comparison in North American history and (post) colonial studies', *The Journal of American History*, 88, 829–65.
Stoler, A. L. (2006) 'Intimidations of Empire: predicaments of the tactile and unseen' in A. L. Stoler (ed.) *Haunted by Empire: geographies of intimacy in North American history* (Durham and London: Duke University Press).
Strange, C. (2006) 'The "Shock" of Torture: a historiographical challenge', *History Workshop Journal*, 6, 135–53.
Stuart, J. (2007) 'Beyond Sovereignty?: British missionaries and transnationalism, 1890–1950' in K. Grant, P. Levine, and F. Trentmann (eds) *Beyond Sovereignty: Britain, Empire and transnationalism, c.1880–1950* (Basingstoke: Palgrave).
Summers, C. (1999) 'Mission Boys, Civilized Men and Marriage: educated African men in the missions of Southern Rhodesia 1920–1945', *Journal of Religious History*, 23, 1, 75–91.
Thorne, S. (2006) 'Religion and Empire at Home' in C. Hall and S. O. Rose (eds) *At Home with the Empire: metropolitan culture and the imperial world* (Cambridge: Cambridge University Press).
Urban, H. B. (2003) ' "India's Darkest Heart", Kālī in the colonial imagination' in J. J. Kripal and R. F. McDermott (eds) *Encountering Kālī: in the margins, at the center, in the west* (Berkeley: University of California Press).
Van der Geest, S. (1990) 'Missionaries and Anthropologists: brothers under the skin', *Man*, New Series 25 (4), 588–601.
Walls, A. C. (1982) ' "The Heavy Artillery of the Missionary Army": the domestic importance of the nineteenth-century medical missionary' in W. J. Shiels (ed.) *The Church and Healing* (Oxford: Basil Blackwell).
Washbrook, D. A. (1990) 'India, 1818–1860: the two faces of colonialism' in A. Porter (ed.) *The Oxford History of the British Empire*, vol. 3, *the nineteenth century* (Oxford: Oxford University Press).

Werbner, P. (1997) 'Essentialising Essentialism, Essentialising Science: ambivalence and multiplicity in the constructions of racism and ethnicity' in P. Werbner and T. Modood (eds) *Debating Cultural Hybridity: multi-cultural identities and the politics of anti-racism* (London: Zed Books).

Williams, P. C. (1982) 'Healing and Evangelism: the place of medicine in later Victorian Protestant missionary thinking' in W. J. Shiels (ed.) *The Church and Healing* (Oxford: Basil Blackwell).

Unpublished sources

Brewis, G. (2009) 'The Making of an Imperial Ideal of Service: Britain and India before 1914' (University of East London: unpublished PhD thesis).

Cleall, E. (2004) 'The Heathen at Home and Overseas. India and Britain in the 1850s' (University of Sheffield: unpublished BA thesis).

Cleall, E. (2005) 'The Missionary Contribution to Imperial Display: missionary exhibitions 1869–1939' (University of Sheffield: unpublished MA thesis).

Cleall, E. (2009) 'Thinking with Missionaries: Discourses of Difference in India and Southern Africa' (University College London: unpublished PhD thesis).

Dussart, F. (2005) 'The Servant/Employer Relationship in Nineteenth Century England and India' (University of London: unpublished PhD thesis).

Grey, D. (2008) 'Discourses of Infanticide in England, 1880–1822' (University of Roehampton: unpublished PhD thesis).

Haggis, J. (1991) 'Professional Ladies and Working Wives: female missionaries in the London Missionary Society and its South Travancore District, South India in the 19th century' (Manchester University: unpublished PhD thesis).

Manktelow, E. J. (2010) 'Missionary Families and the Formation of the Missionary Enterprise: the London Missionary Society and the Family 1795–1875' (Kings College London: unpublished PhD thesis).

Stuart, D. I. (1994) '"Of Savages and Heroes"; discourses of race, nation and gender in the evangelical missions to Southern Africa in the early nineteenth century' (Institute of Commonwealth Studies: unpublished PhD thesis).

Online resources

Yale Online Database of Missionary Periodicals. http://research.yale.edu:8084/missionperiodicals/ (Accessed May 2009).

Index

Note: locators with letters 'f' and 'n' refer to figures and notes in the text.